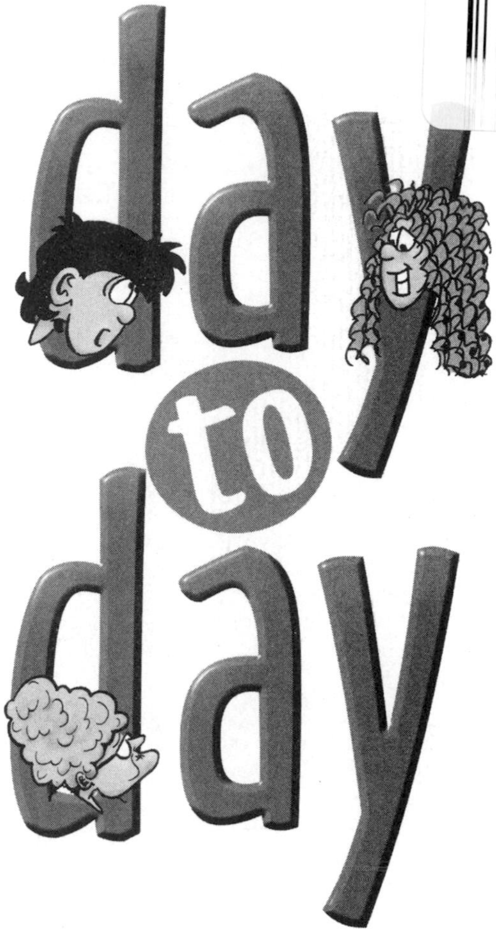
day
to
day

A "Day To Day" Collection by Deborah Peyton

To my daughters, Jaime-Lynn and Krista,
for living with my crazy deadlines.
To my husband and best friend, Derrick,
who with unfailing grace bears
this addictive habit of mine.
To the three of you, I owe everything.

For information write to
Fine-Tooning, P.O. Box 1449 Station A,
Fredericton, New Brunswick, E3A 5E3

Day to Day may be viewed at:
http://www.fine-tooning.com

2nd edition

Canadian Cataloguing in Publication Data

Peyton, Deborah, 1963-

    Day to day

    2nd ed.

    ISBN 0-9682807-2-2

I. Title. II. Title: Day to day collection.

NC1449.P49A4 1999   741.5'971   C99-950170-4

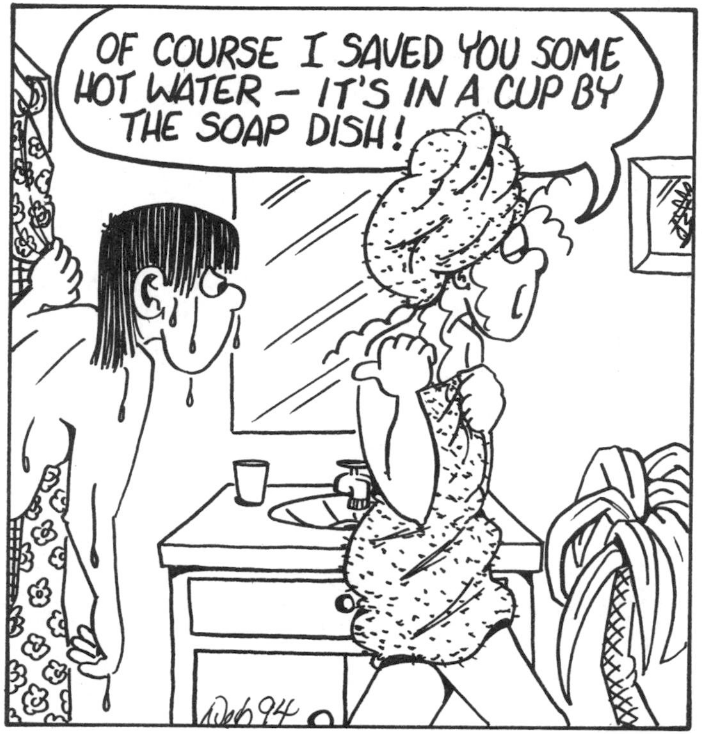
OF COURSE I SAVED YOU SOME HOT WATER – IT'S IN A CUP BY THE SOAP DISH!
Deb 94

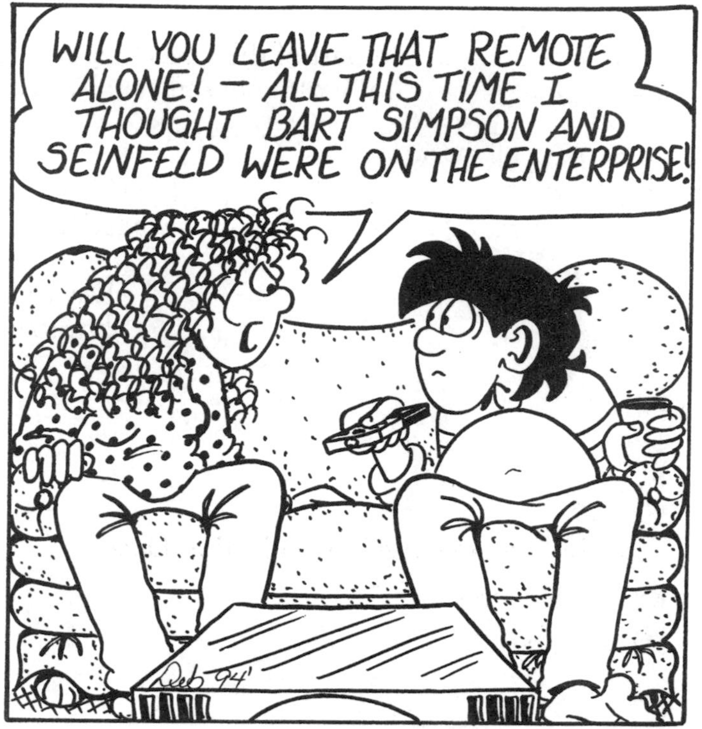
WILL YOU LEAVE THAT REMOTE ALONE! – ALL THIS TIME I THOUGHT BART SIMPSON AND SEINFELD WERE ON THE ENTERPRISE!
Deb 94'

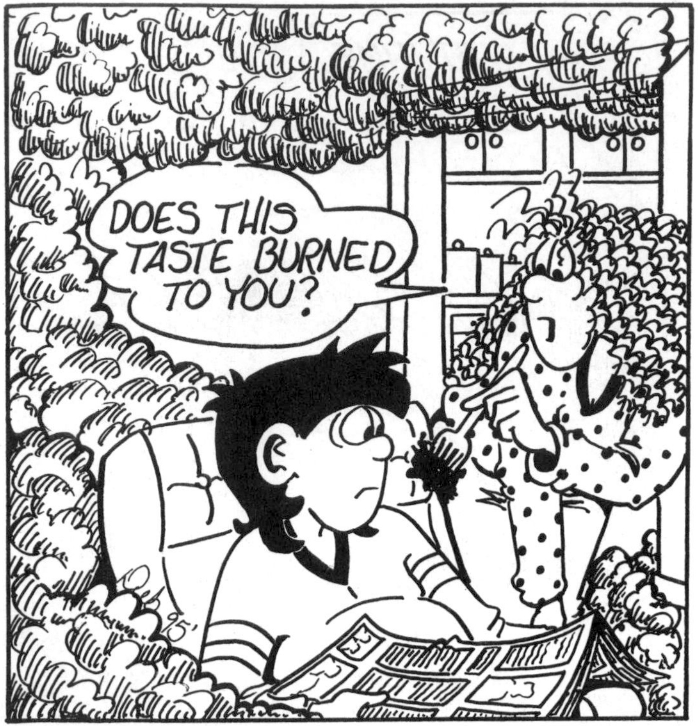
DOES THIS TASTE BURNED TO YOU?
Deb 95'

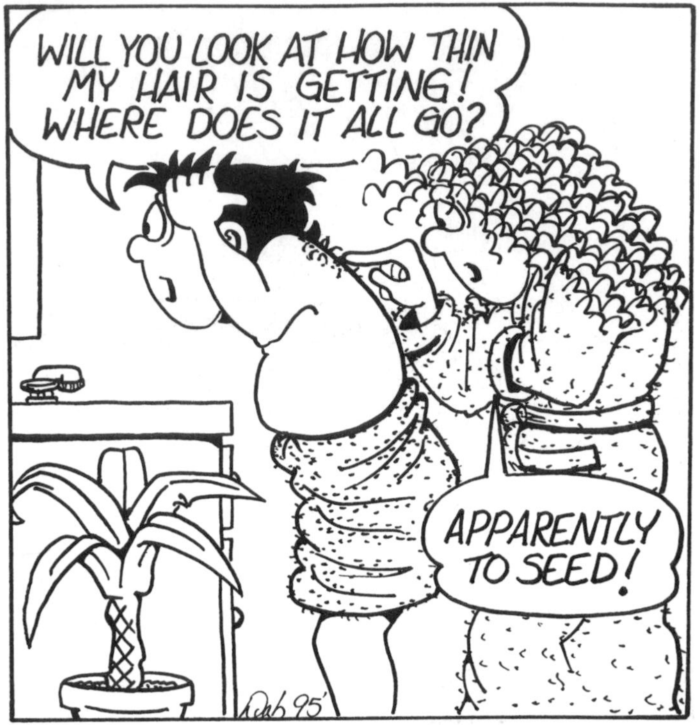
WILL YOU LOOK AT HOW THIN MY HAIR IS GETTING! WHERE DOES IT ALL GO?
APPARENTLY TO SEED!
Deb 95'

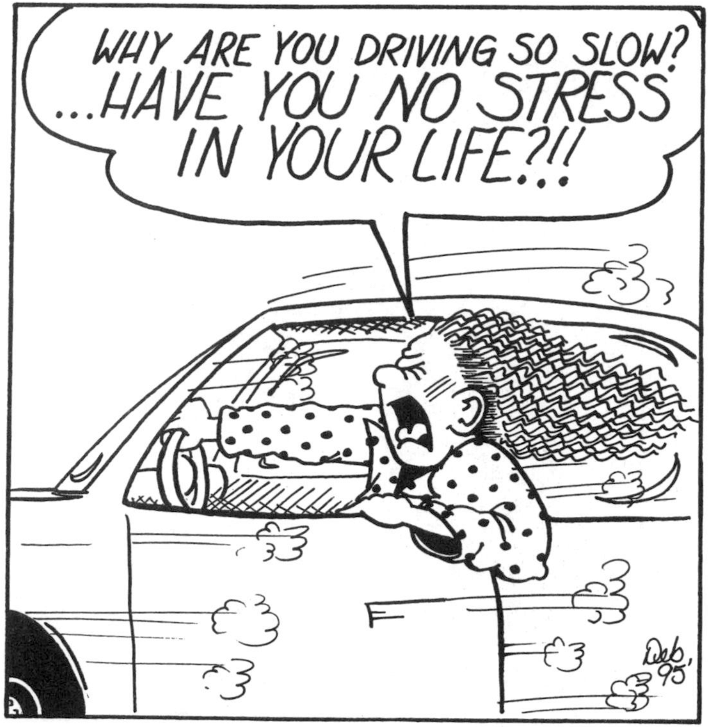
WHY ARE YOU DRIVING SO SLOW? ...HAVE YOU NO STRESS IN YOUR LIFE?!!
Deb 95'

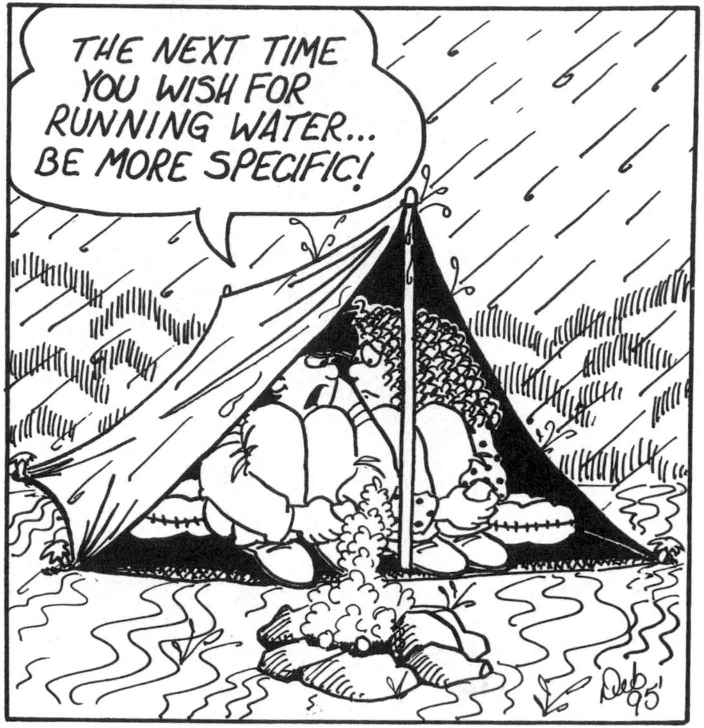
THE NEXT TIME YOU WISH FOR RUNNING WATER... BE MORE SPECIFIC!
Deb 95'

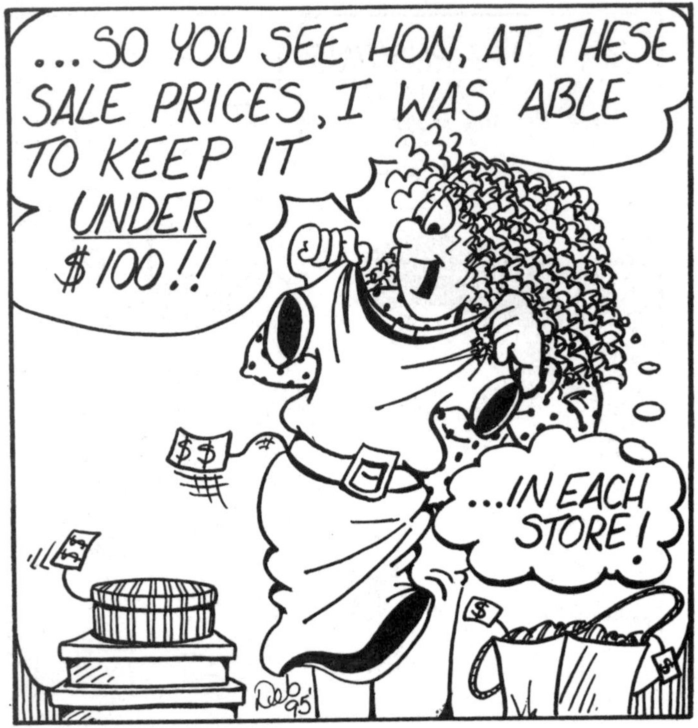
...SO YOU SEE HON, AT THESE SALE PRICES, I WAS ABLE TO KEEP IT UNDER $100!!
...IN EACH STORE!
Deb 95'

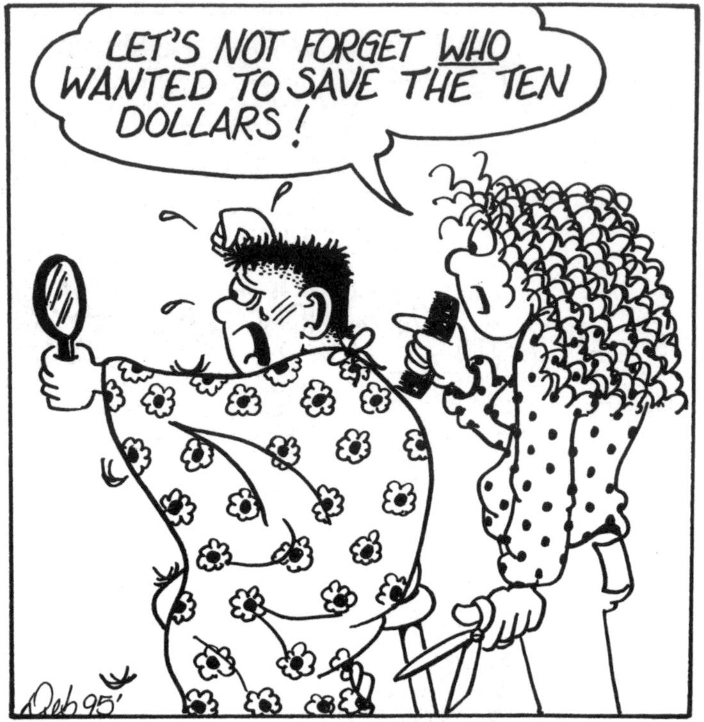
LET'S NOT FORGET WHO WANTED TO SAVE THE TEN DOLLARS!
Deb 95'

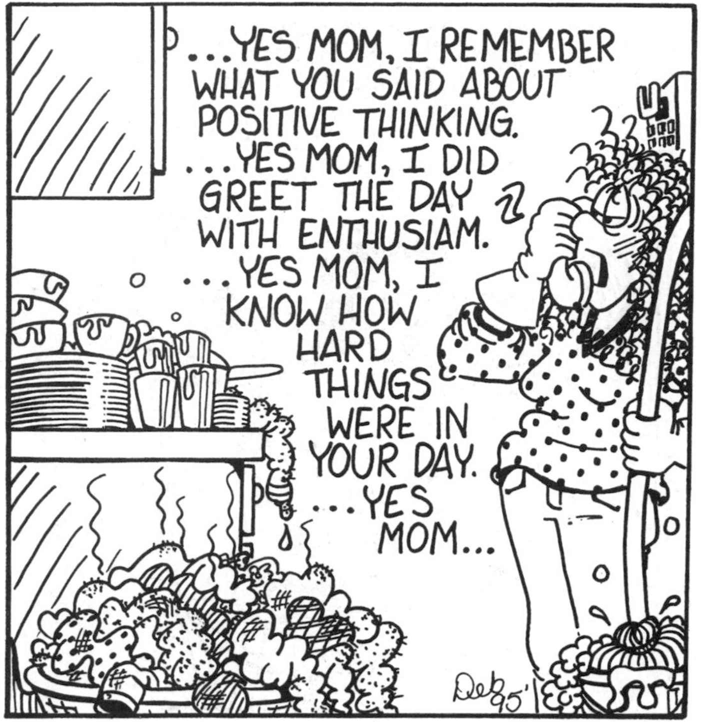
...YES MOM, I REMEMBER WHAT YOU SAID ABOUT POSITIVE THINKING.
...YES MOM, I DID GREET THE DAY WITH ENTHUSIAM.
...YES MOM, I KNOW HOW HARD THINGS WERE IN YOUR DAY.
...YES MOM...
Deb 95'

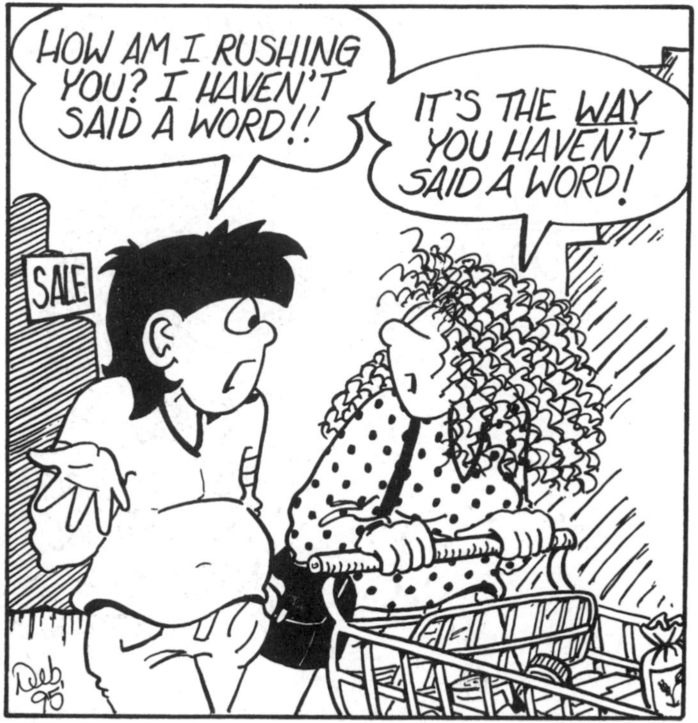
SALE
HOW AM I RUSHING YOU? I HAVEN'T SAID A WORD!!
IT'S THE WAY YOU HAVEN'T SAID A WORD!
Deb 95'

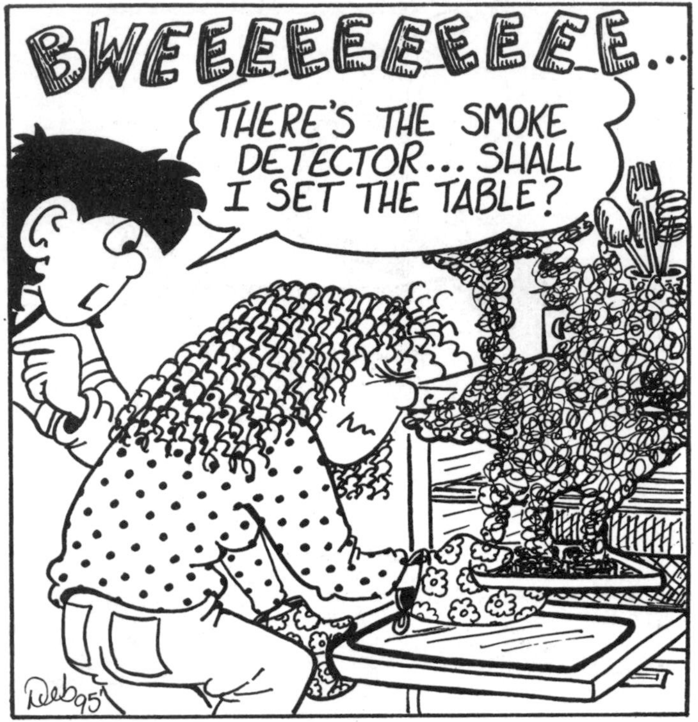
BWEEEEEEEEEE...
THERE'S THE SMOKE DETECTOR... SHALL I SET THE TABLE?
Deb 95'

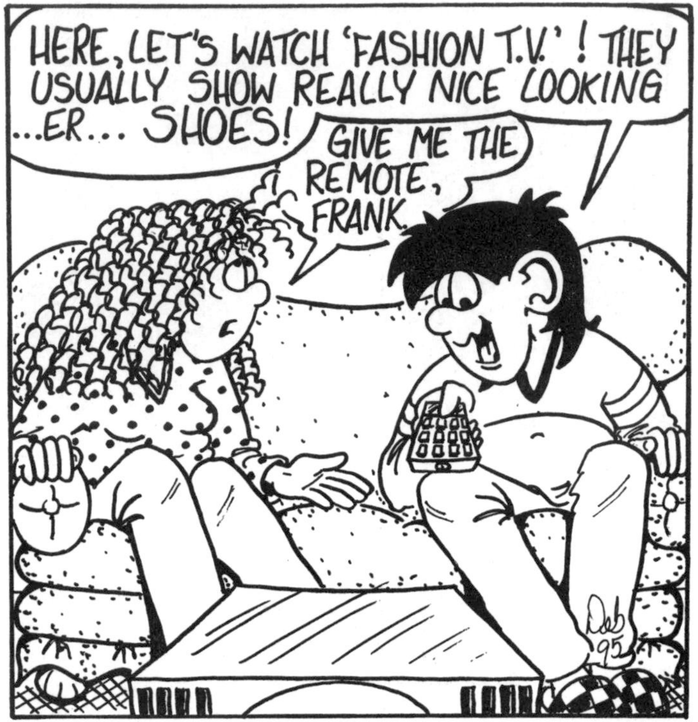
HERE, LET'S WATCH 'FASHION T.V.'! THEY USUALLY SHOW REALLY NICE LOOKING ...ER... SHOES!
GIVE ME THE REMOTE, FRANK.
Deb 95

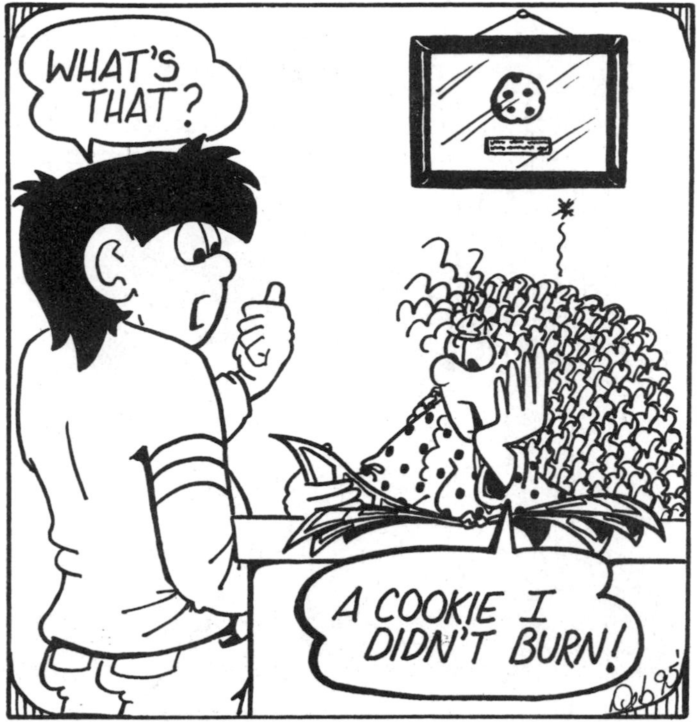
WHAT'S THAT?
A COOKIE I DIDN'T BURN!

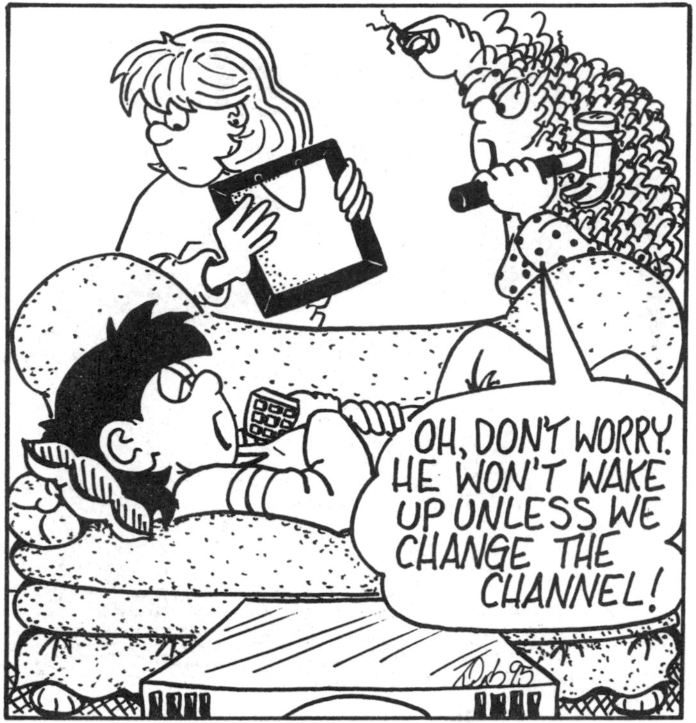
OH, DON'T WORRY. HE WON'T WAKE UP UNLESS WE CHANGE THE CHANNEL!

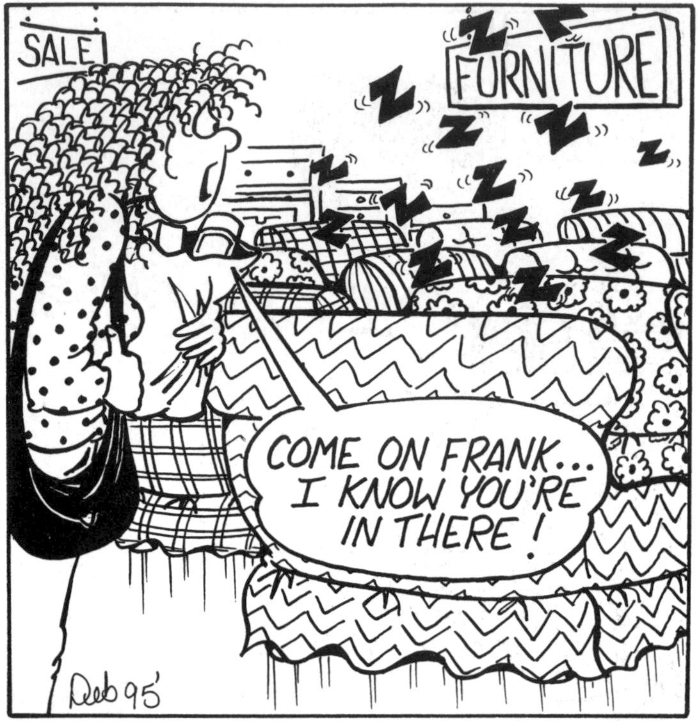
SALE
FURNITURE
COME ON FRANK... I KNOW YOU'RE IN THERE!
Deb 95'

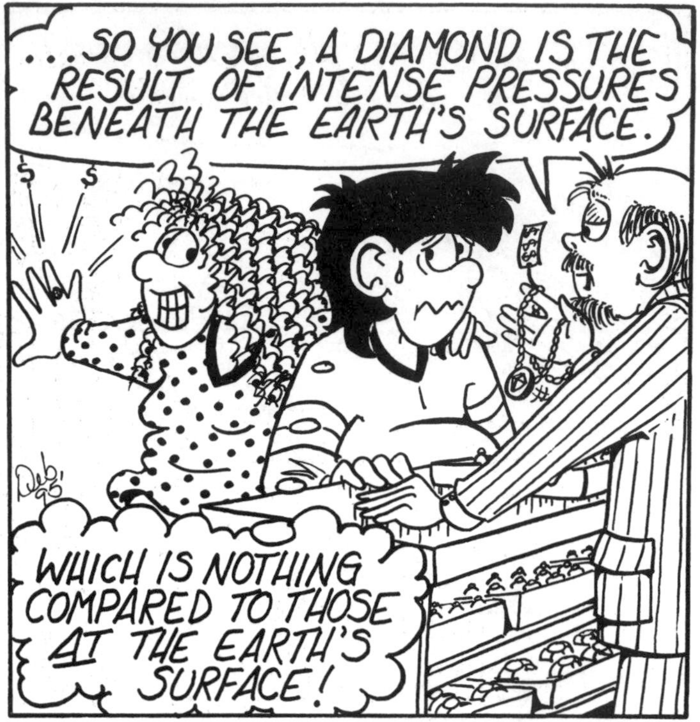
...SO YOU SEE, A DIAMOND IS THE RESULT OF INTENSE PRESSURES BENEATH THE EARTH'S SURFACE.
WHICH IS NOTHING COMPARED TO THOSE AT THE EARTH'S SURFACE!

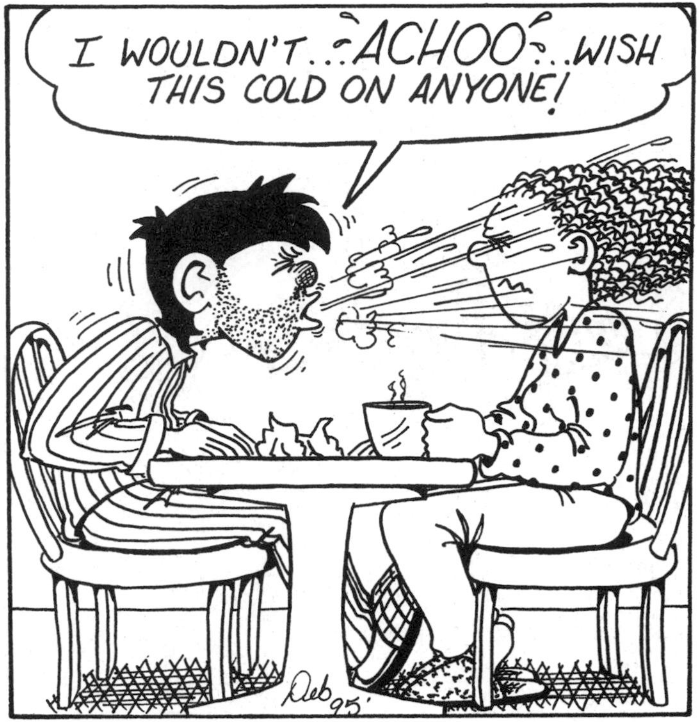
I WOULDN'T...ACHOO...WISH THIS COLD ON ANYONE!
Deb 95'

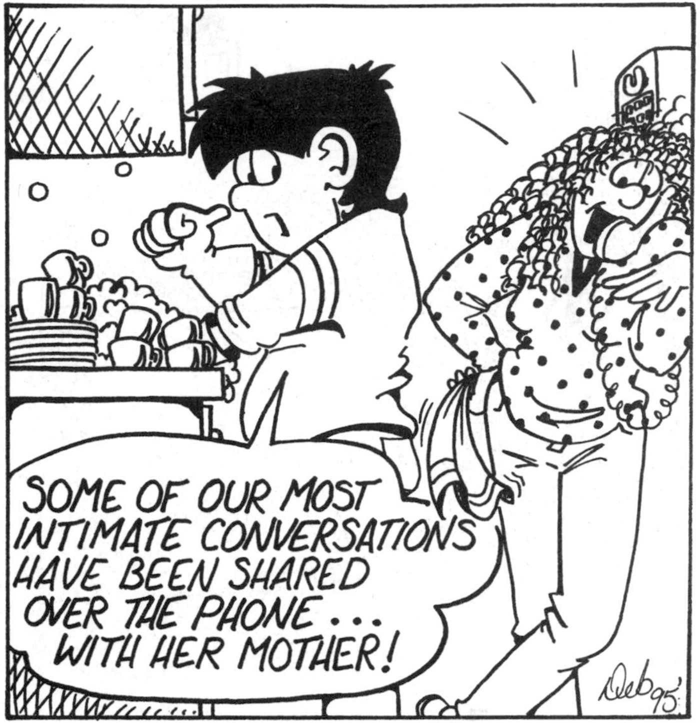
SOME OF OUR MOST INTIMATE CONVERSATIONS HAVE BEEN SHARED OVER THE PHONE... WITH HER MOTHER!
Deb 95'

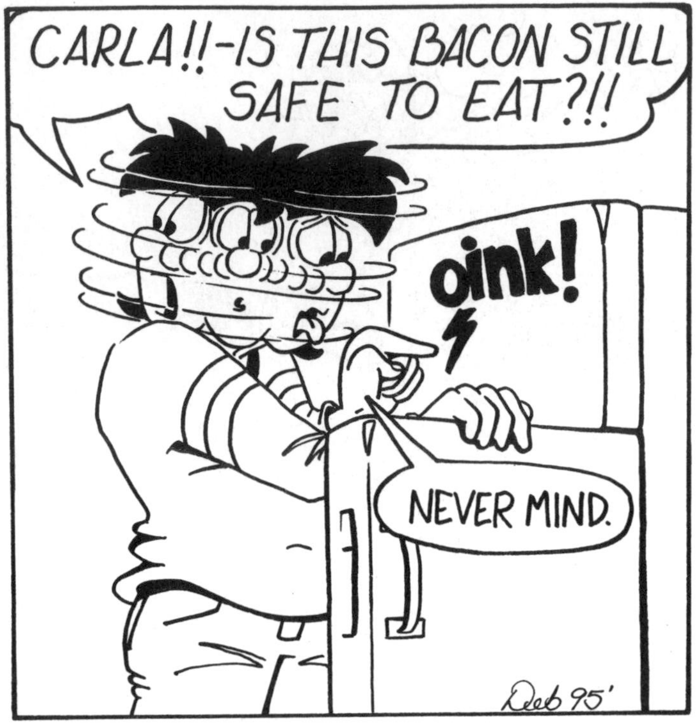
CARLA!!-IS THIS BACON STILL SAFE TO EAT?!!
oink!
NEVER MIND.
Deb 95'

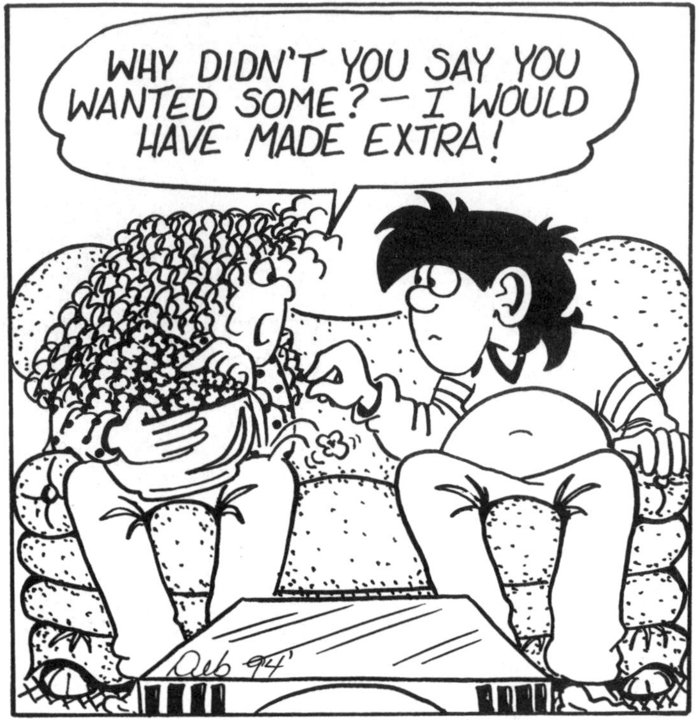
WHY DIDN'T YOU SAY YOU WANTED SOME? — I WOULD HAVE MADE EXTRA!
Deb 94'

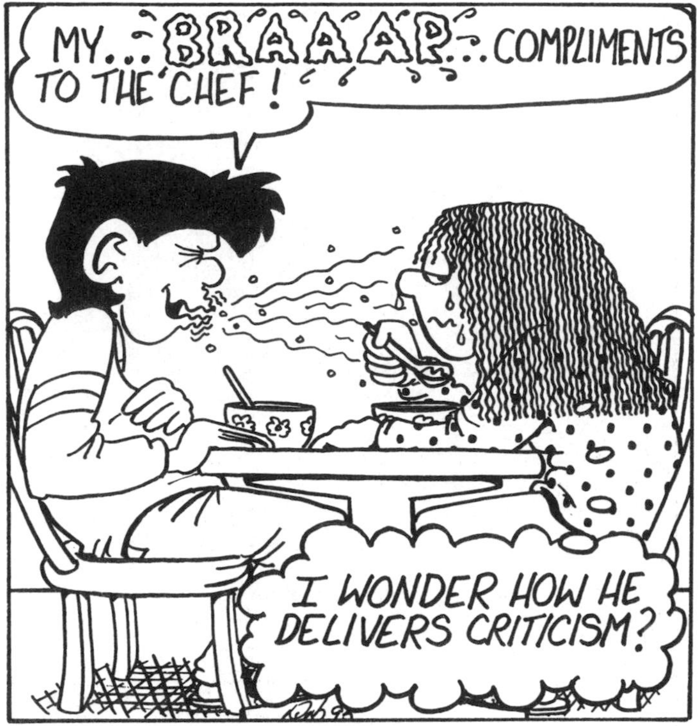
MY... BRAAAP... COMPLIMENTS TO THE 'CHEF!
I WONDER HOW HE DELIVERS CRITICISM?

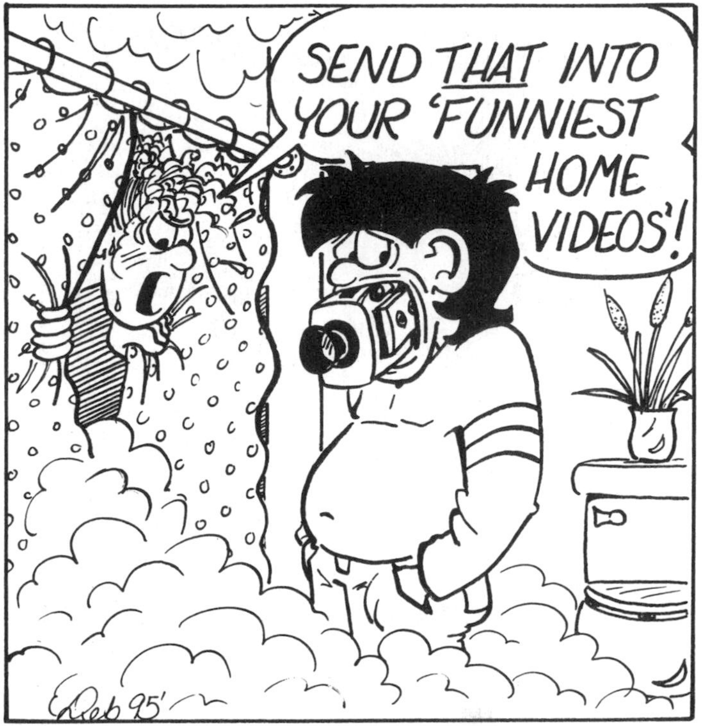
SEND THAT INTO YOUR 'FUNNIEST HOME VIDEOS'!

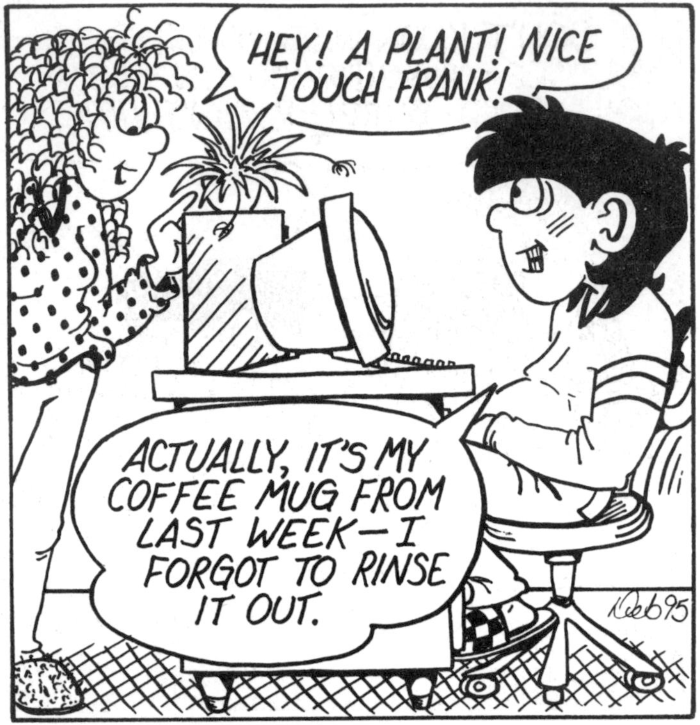
HEY! A PLANT! NICE TOUCH FRANK!
ACTUALLY, IT'S MY COFFEE MUG FROM LAST WEEK—I FORGOT TO RINSE IT OUT.
Deb 95

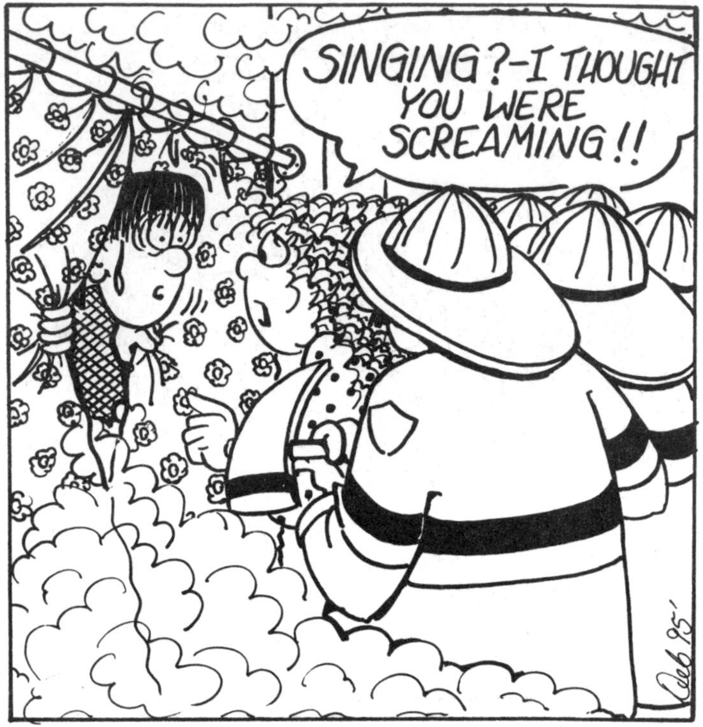
SINGING?-I THOUGHT YOU WERE SCREAMING!!
Deb 95'

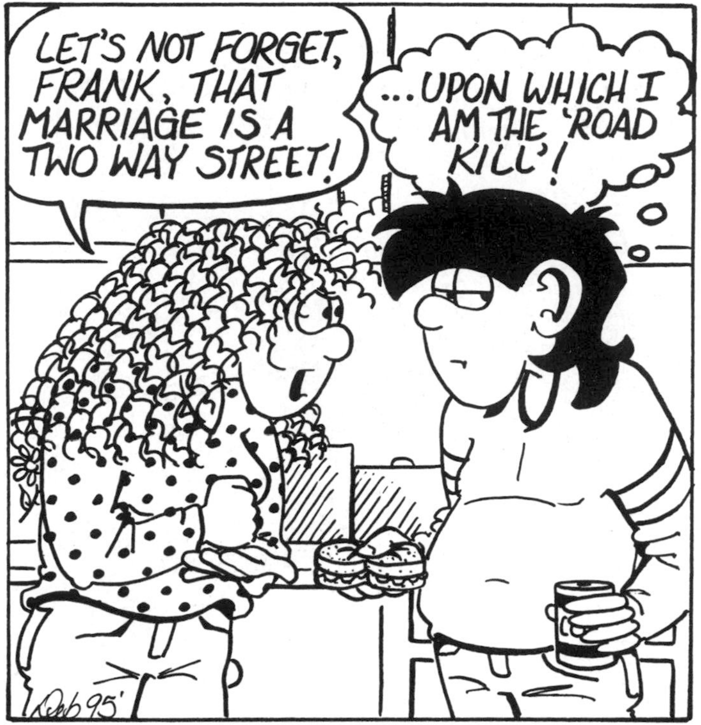
LET'S NOT FORGET, FRANK, THAT MARRIAGE IS A TWO WAY STREET!
...UPON WHICH I AM THE 'ROAD KILL'!
Deb 95'

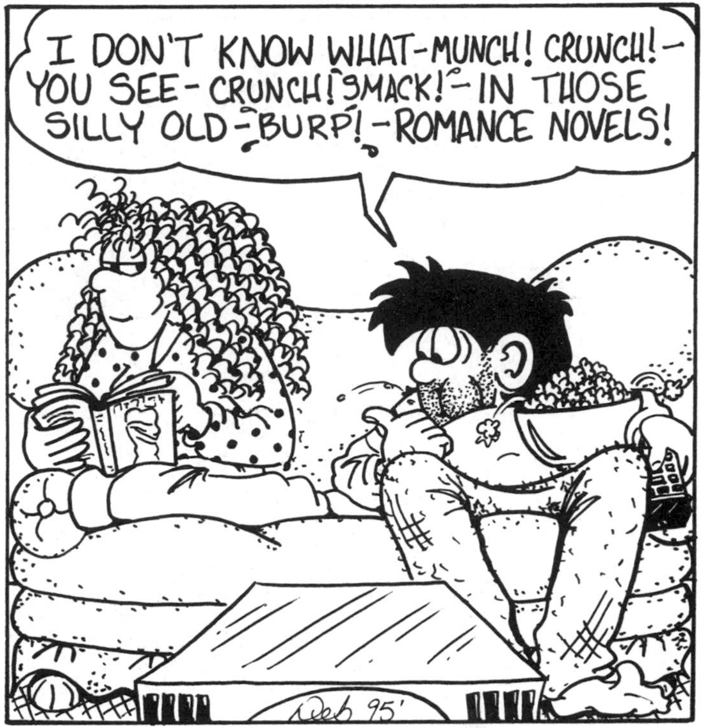
I DON'T KNOW WHAT-MUNCH! CRUNCH!- YOU SEE- CRUNCH! SMACK!- IN THOSE SILLY OLD-BURP!-ROMANCE NOVELS!
Deb 95'

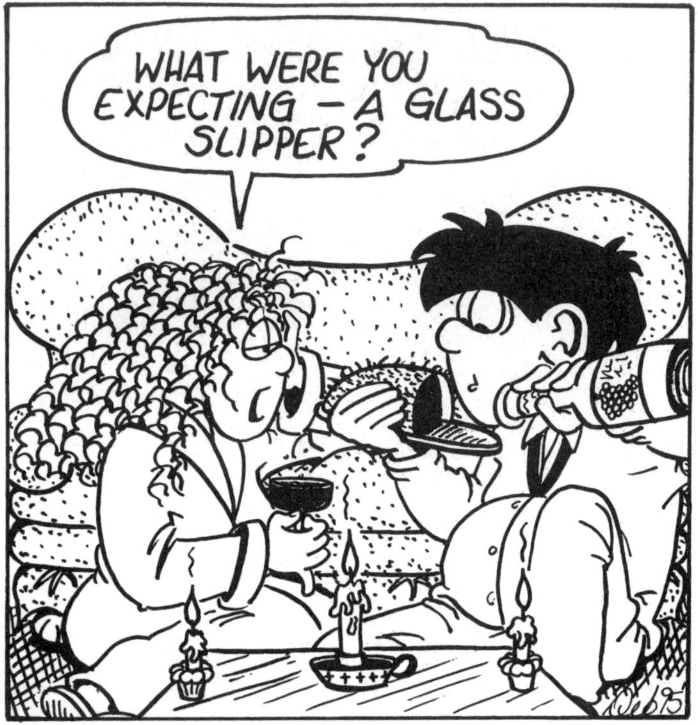
WHAT WERE YOU EXPECTING — A GLASS SLIPPER?
Deb 95

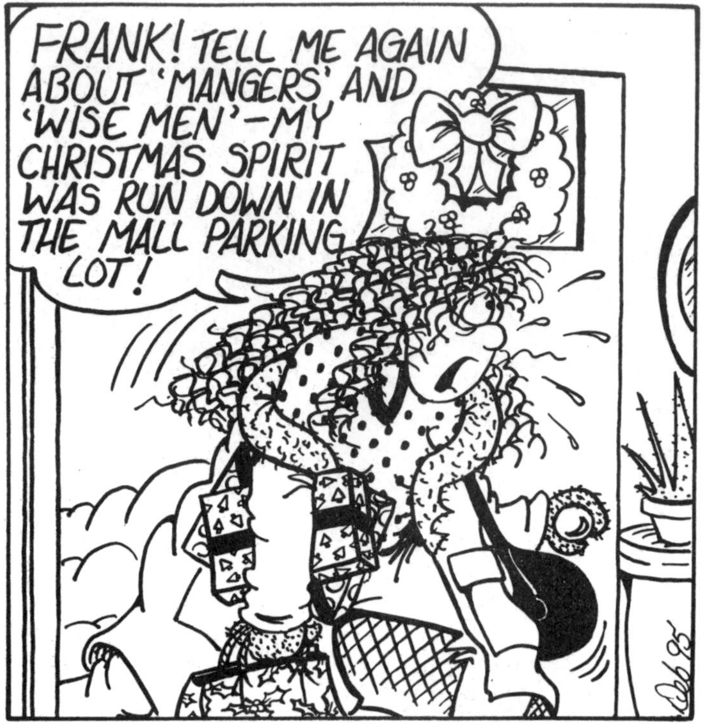
FRANK! TELL ME AGAIN ABOUT 'MANGERS' AND 'WISE MEN'—MY CHRISTMAS SPIRIT WAS RUN DOWN IN THE MALL PARKING LOT!
Deb 95

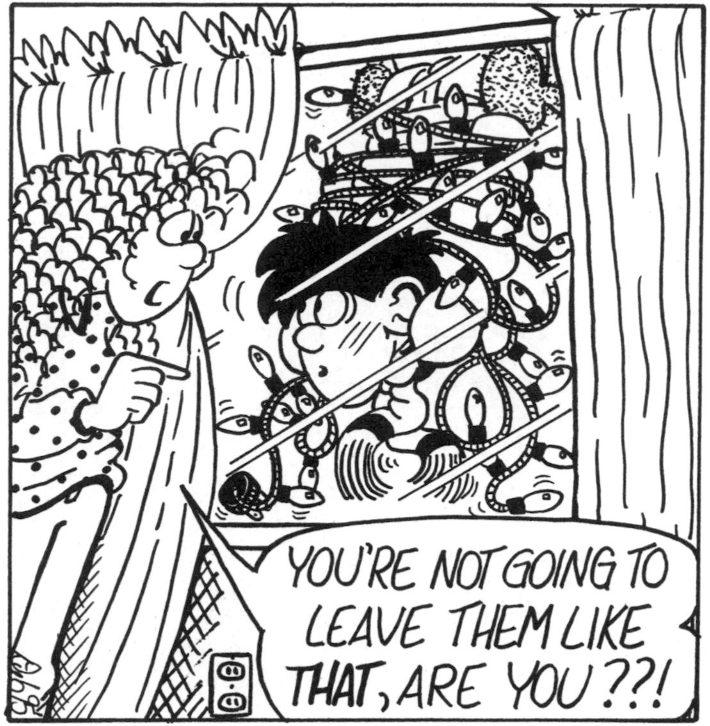
YOU'RE NOT GOING TO LEAVE THEM LIKE **THAT**, ARE YOU??!
Deb95

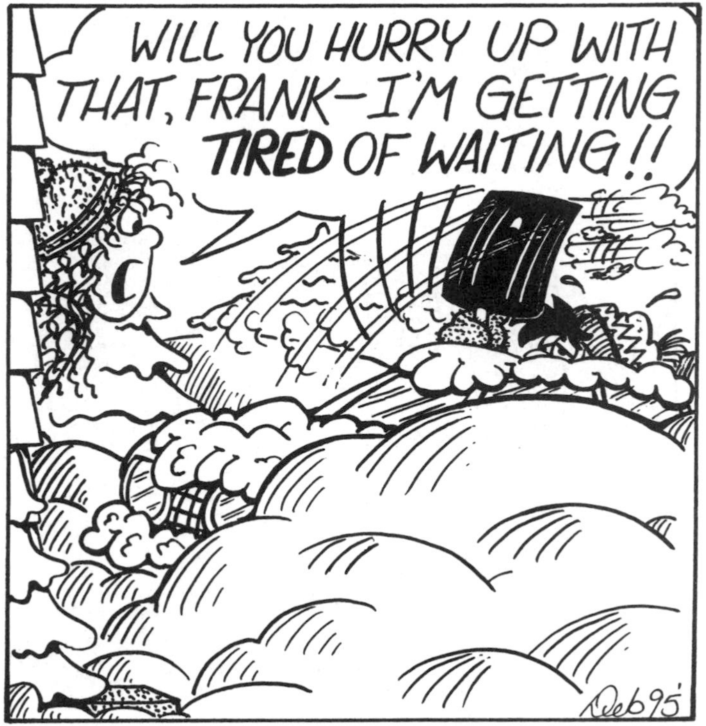
WILL YOU HURRY UP WITH THAT, FRANK—I'M GETTING **TIRED** OF WAITING!!
Deb95'

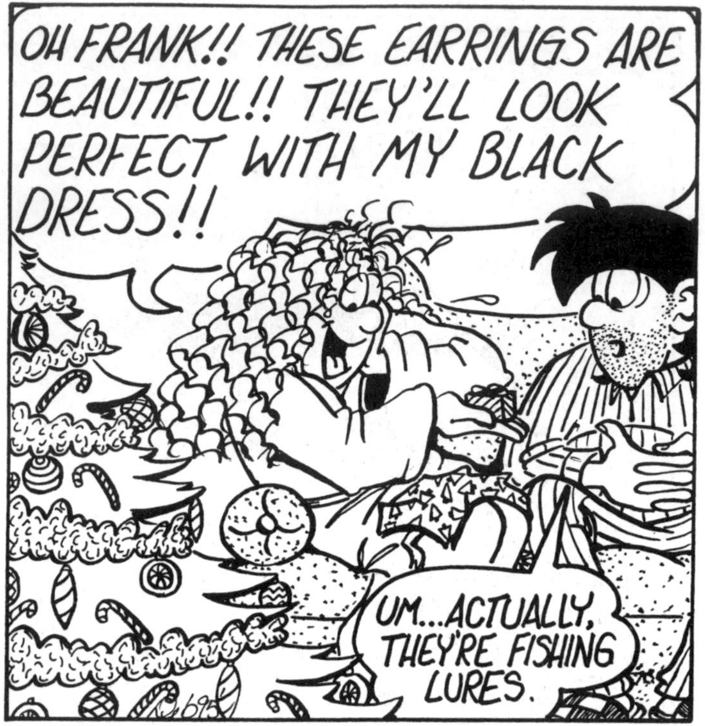
OH FRANK!! THESE EARRINGS ARE BEAUTIFUL!! THEY'LL LOOK PERFECT WITH MY BLACK DRESS!!
UM...ACTUALLY, THEY'RE FISHING LURES.

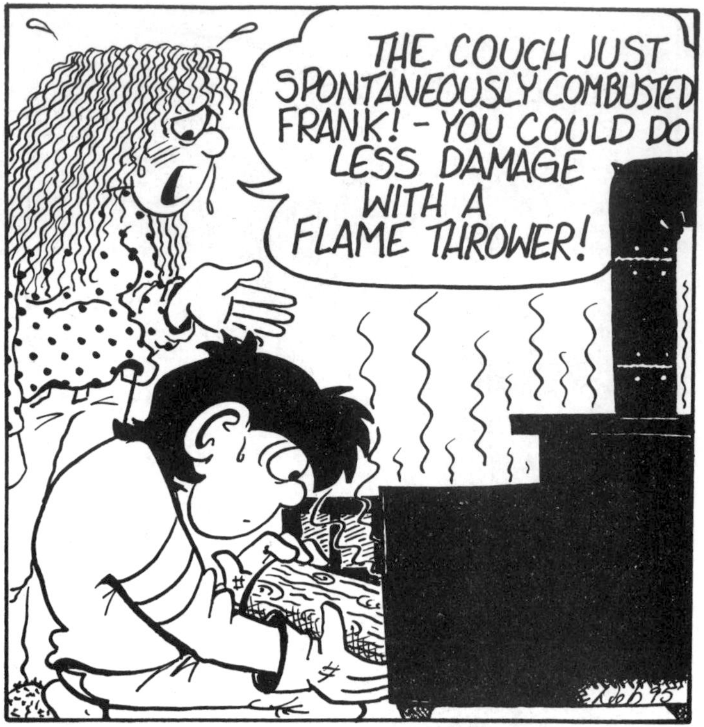
THE COUCH JUST SPONTANEOUSLY COMBUSTED FRANK! - YOU COULD DO LESS DAMAGE WITH A FLAME THROWER!

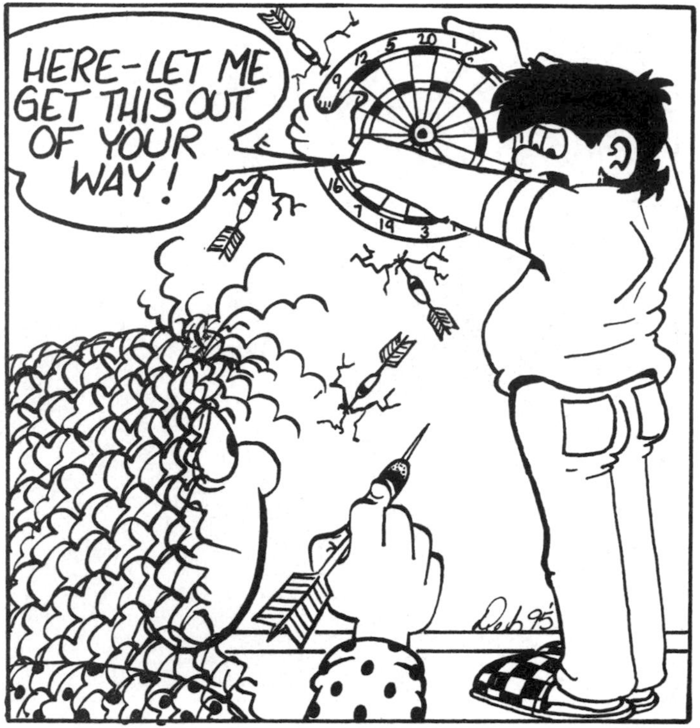
HERE-LET ME GET THIS OUT OF YOUR WAY!
Deb 95'

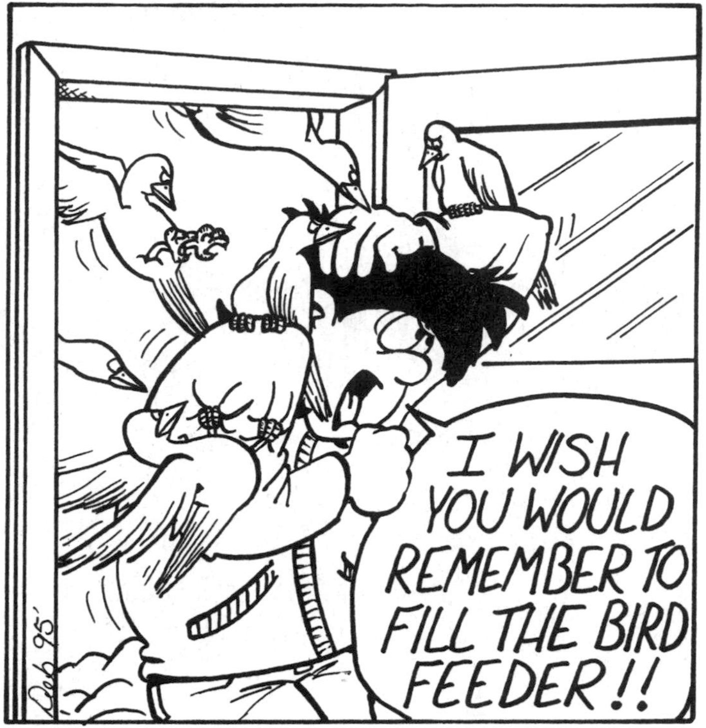
I WISH YOU WOULD REMEMBER TO FILL THE BIRD FEEDER!!
Deb 95'

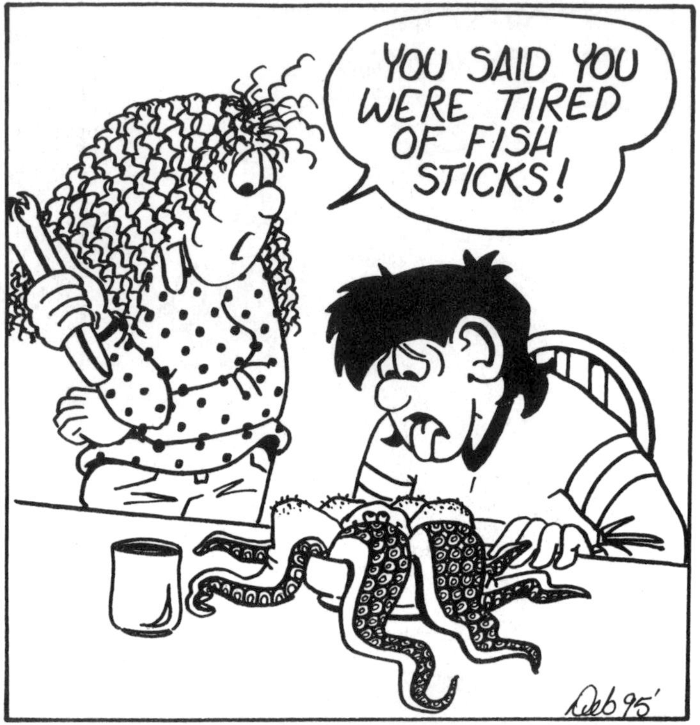
YOU SAID YOU WERE TIRED OF FISH STICKS!
Deb 95'

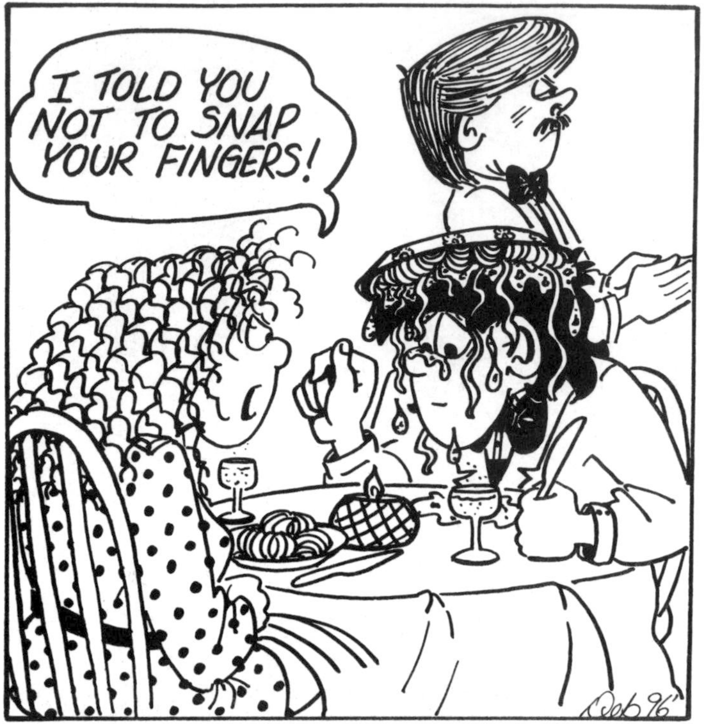
I TOLD YOU NOT TO SNAP YOUR FINGERS!
Deb 96'

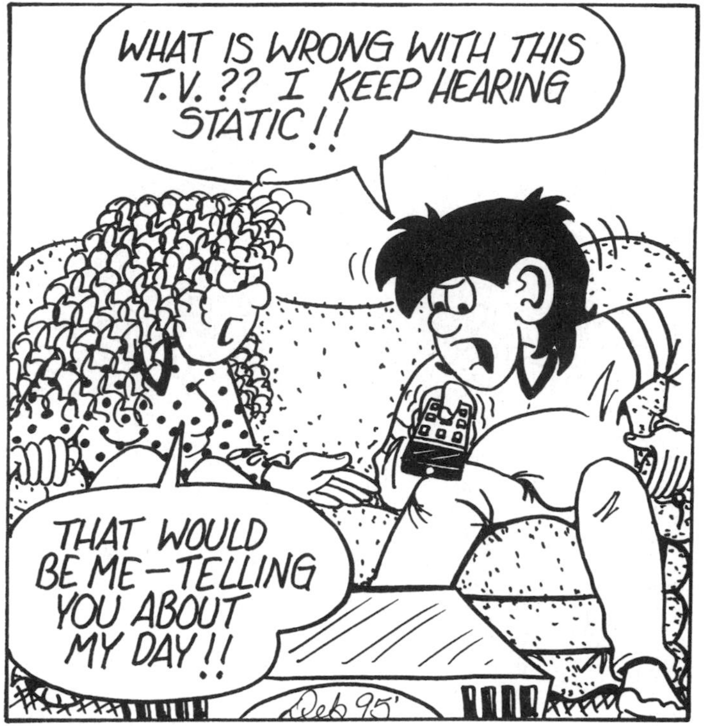
WHAT IS WRONG WITH THIS T.V. ?? I KEEP HEARING STATIC !!
THAT WOULD BE ME—TELLING YOU ABOUT MY DAY !!
Deb 95'

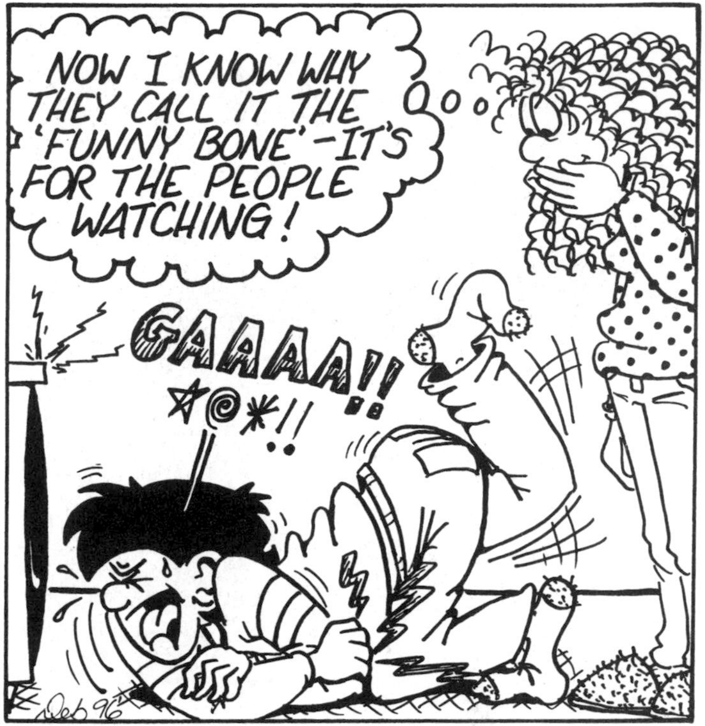
NOW I KNOW WHY THEY CALL IT THE 'FUNNY BONE'—IT'S FOR THE PEOPLE WATCHING !
GAAAAA!!
☆@✱!!
Deb 96'

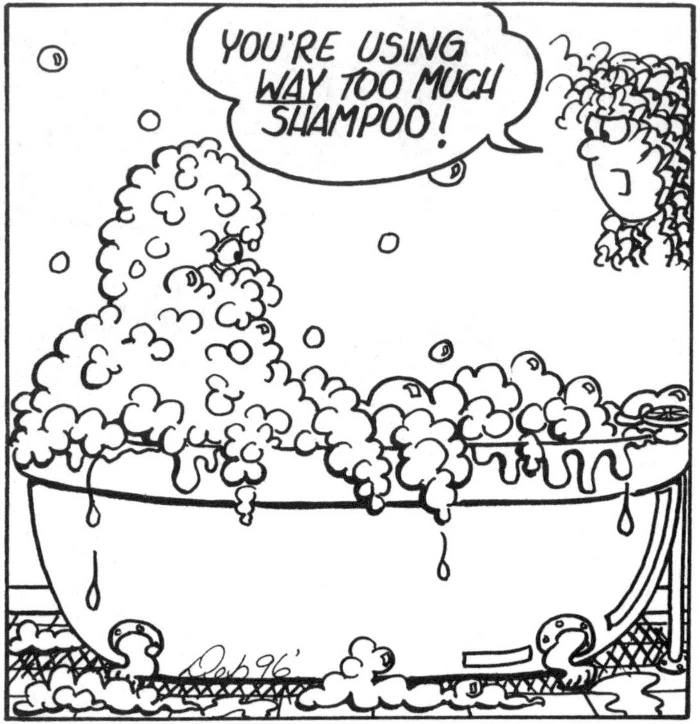
YOU'RE USING WAY TOO MUCH SHAMPOO!

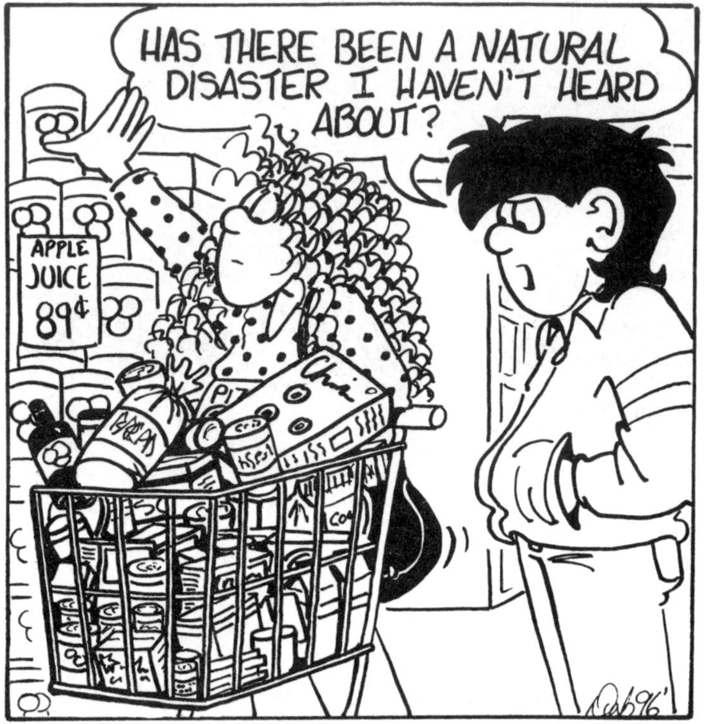
HAS THERE BEEN A NATURAL DISASTER I HAVEN'T HEARD ABOUT?
APPLE JUICE 89¢

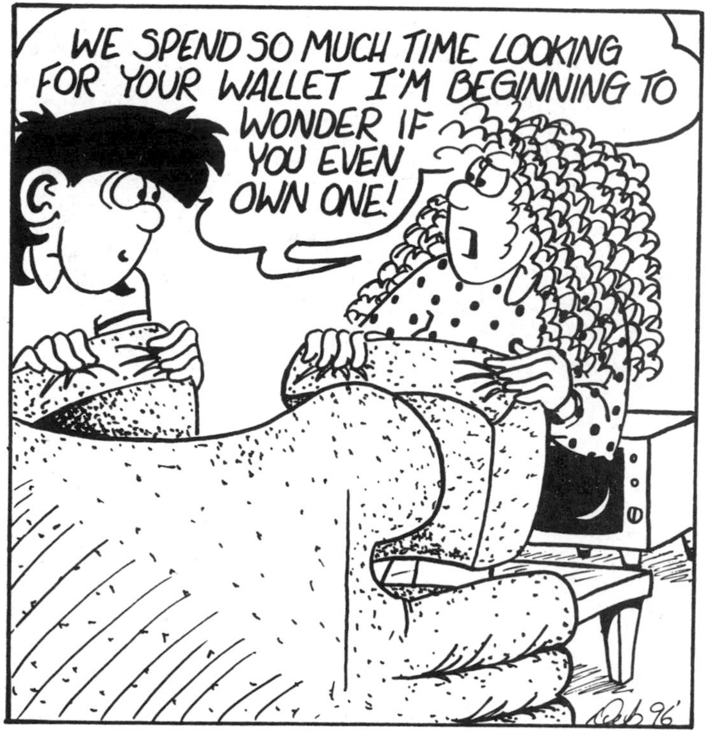
WE SPEND SO MUCH TIME LOOKING FOR YOUR WALLET I'M BEGINNING TO WONDER IF YOU EVEN OWN ONE!
Deb 96'

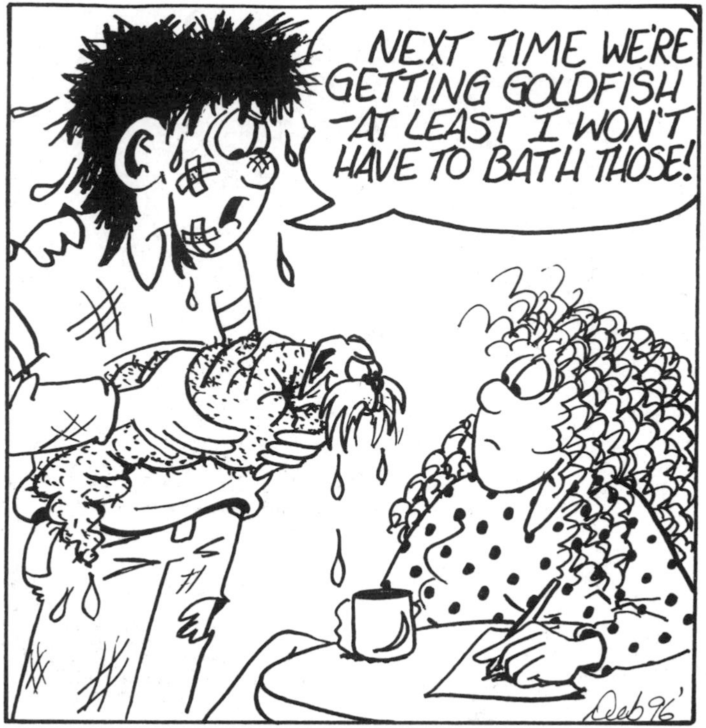
NEXT TIME WE'RE GETTING GOLDFISH —AT LEAST I WON'T HAVE TO BATH THOSE!
Deb 96'

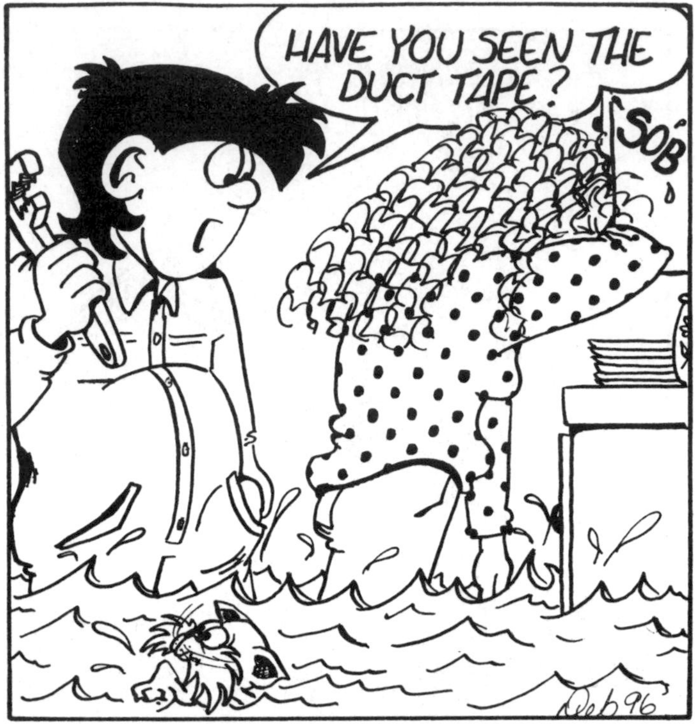
HAVE YOU SEEN THE DUCT TAPE?
SOB
Deb 96

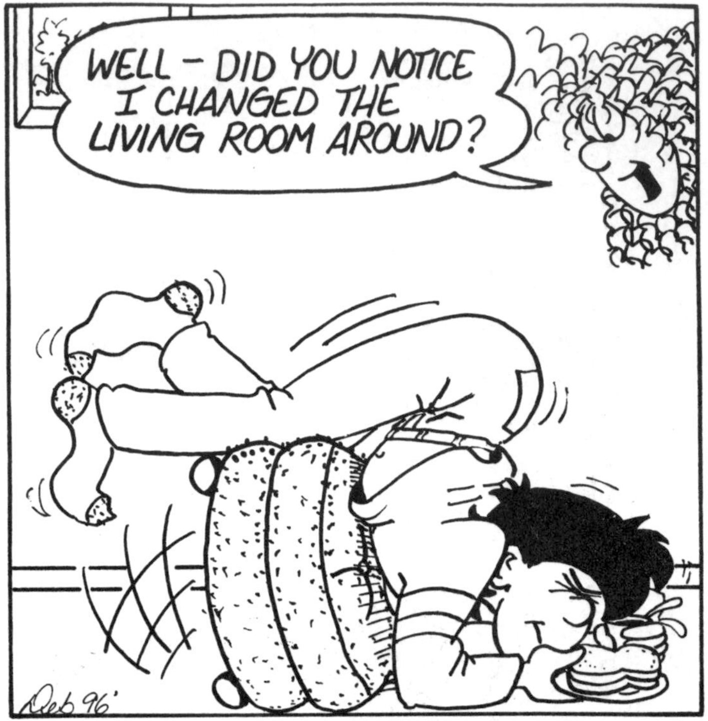
WELL - DID YOU NOTICE I CHANGED THE LIVING ROOM AROUND?
Deb 96'

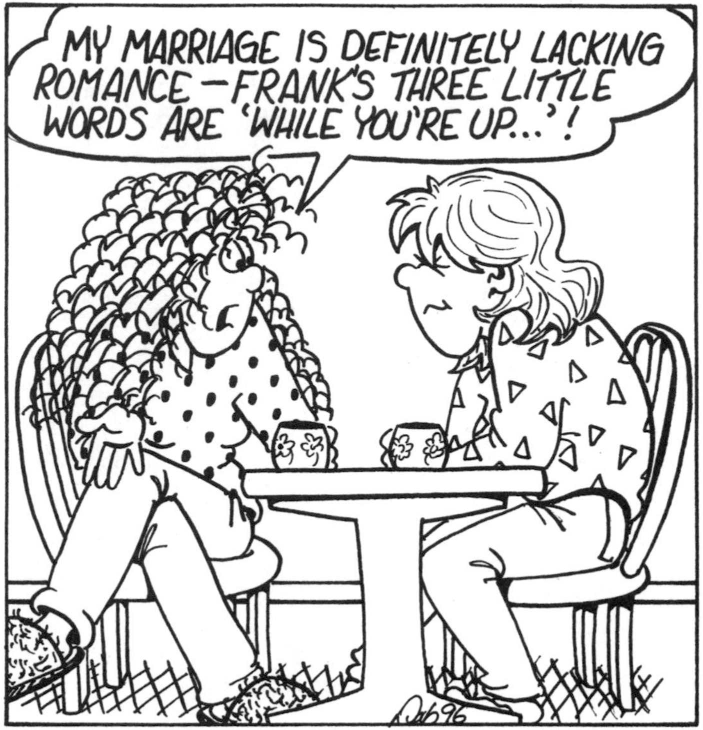
MY MARRIAGE IS DEFINITELY LACKING ROMANCE—FRANK'S THREE LITTLE WORDS ARE 'WHILE YOU'RE UP...'!

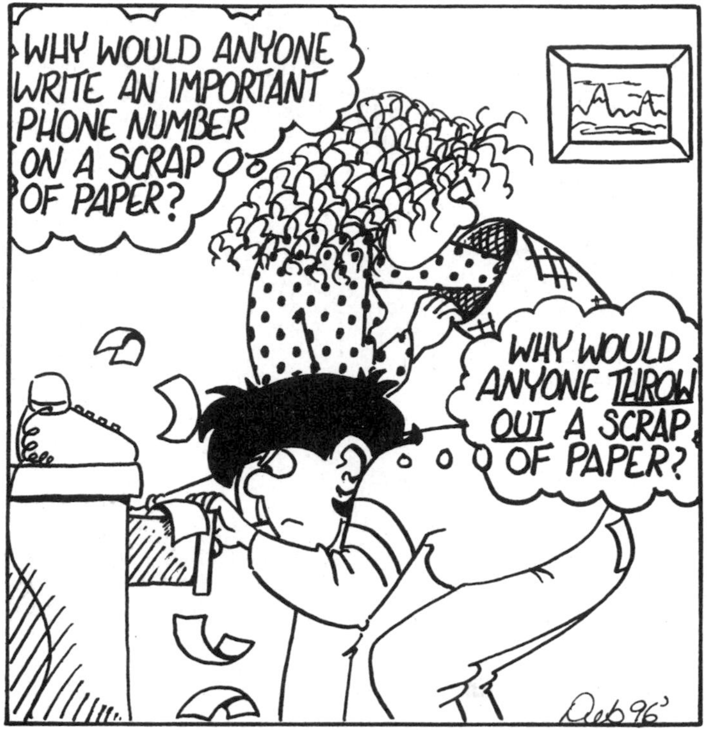
WHY WOULD ANYONE WRITE AN IMPORTANT PHONE NUMBER ON A SCRAP OF PAPER?
WHY WOULD ANYONE THROW OUT A SCRAP OF PAPER?

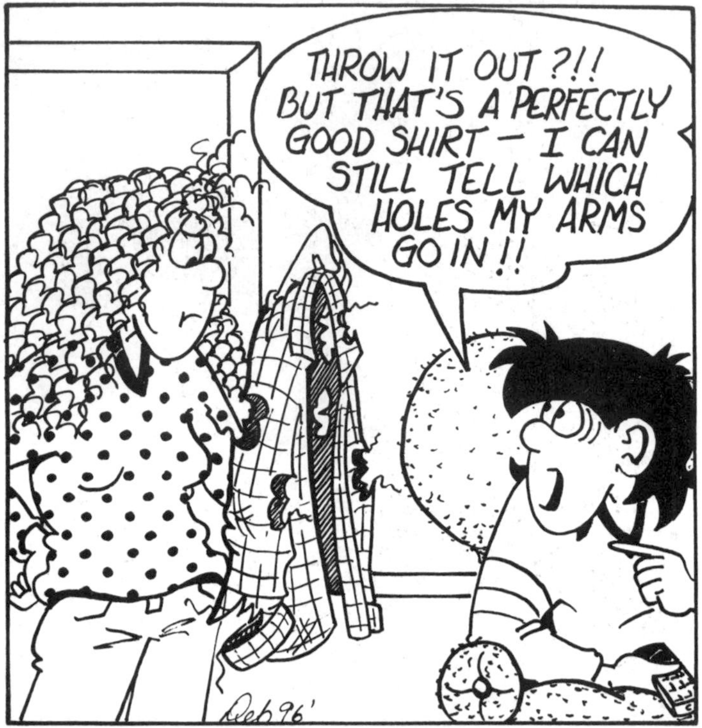
THROW IT OUT ?!! BUT THAT'S A PERFECTLY GOOD SHIRT — I CAN STILL TELL WHICH HOLES MY ARMS GO IN !!
Deb 96'

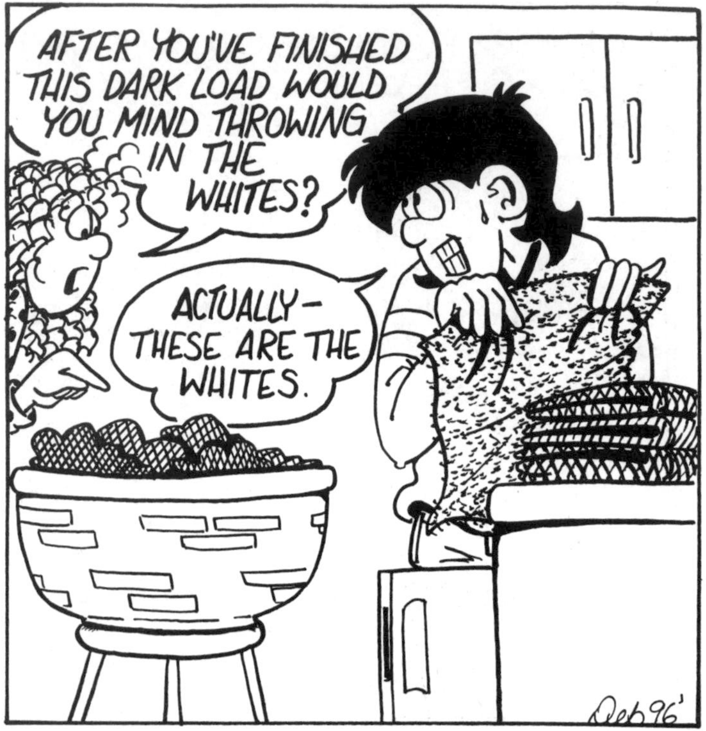
AFTER YOU'VE FINISHED THIS DARK LOAD WOULD YOU MIND THROWING IN THE WHITES?
ACTUALLY — THESE ARE THE WHITES.
Deb 96'

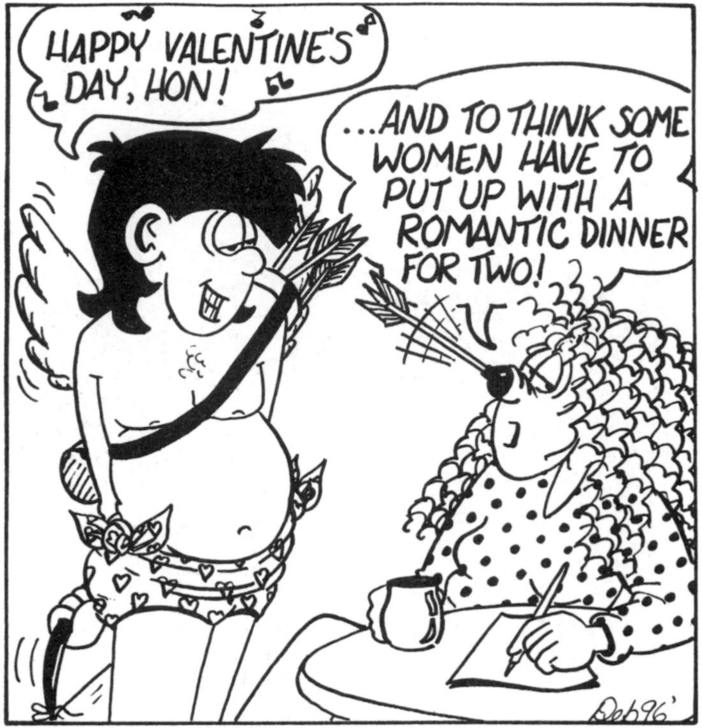
HAPPY VALENTINE'S DAY, HON!
...AND TO THINK SOME WOMEN HAVE TO PUT UP WITH A ROMANTIC DINNER FOR TWO!
Deb96'

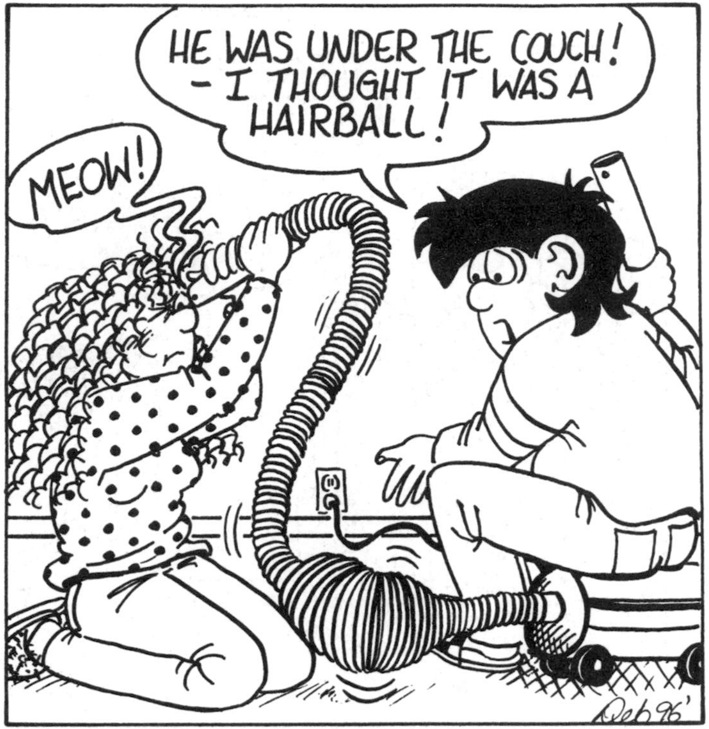
HE WAS UNDER THE COUCH! - I THOUGHT IT WAS A HAIRBALL!
MEOW!
Deb96'

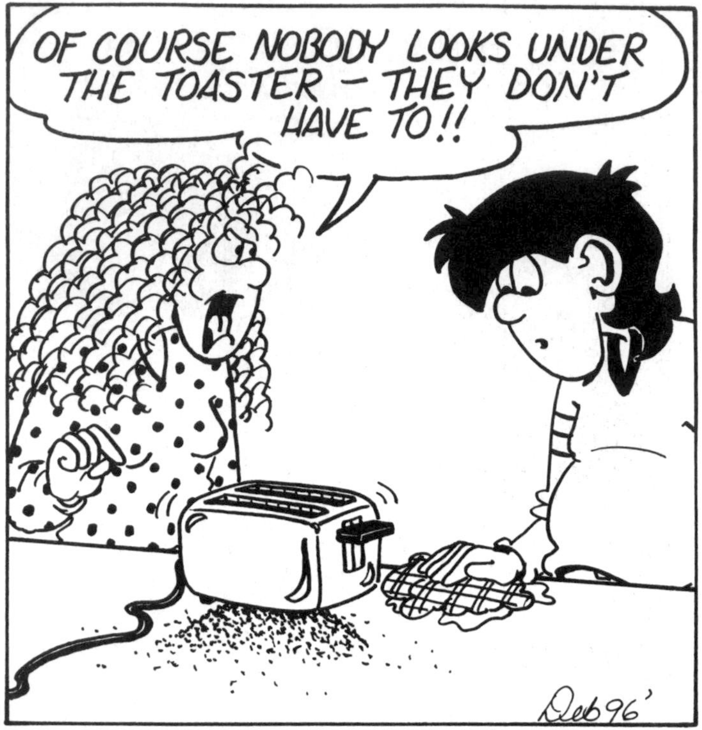
OF COURSE NOBODY LOOKS UNDER THE TOASTER - THEY DON'T HAVE TO!!
Deb 96'

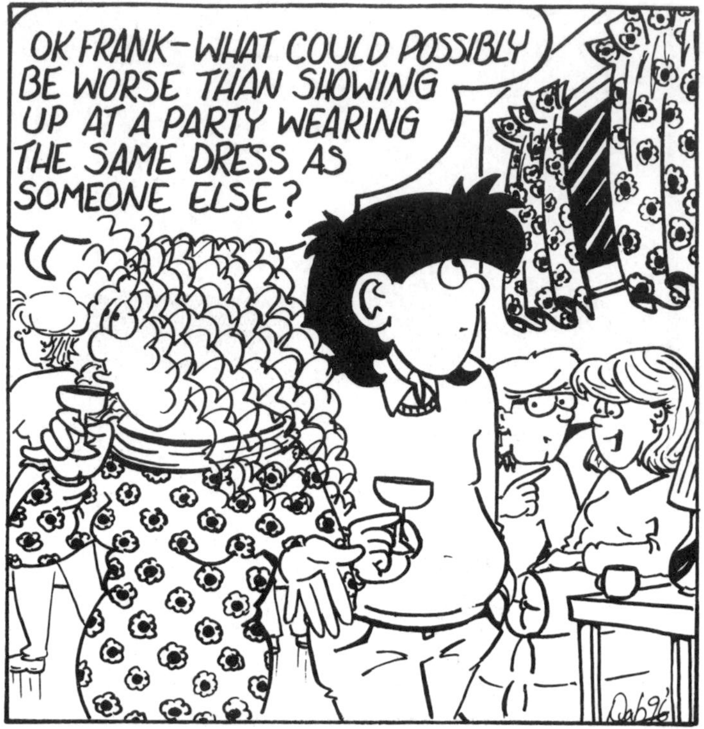
OK FRANK-WHAT COULD POSSIBLY BE WORSE THAN SHOWING UP AT A PARTY WEARING THE SAME DRESS AS SOMEONE ELSE?
Deb 96'

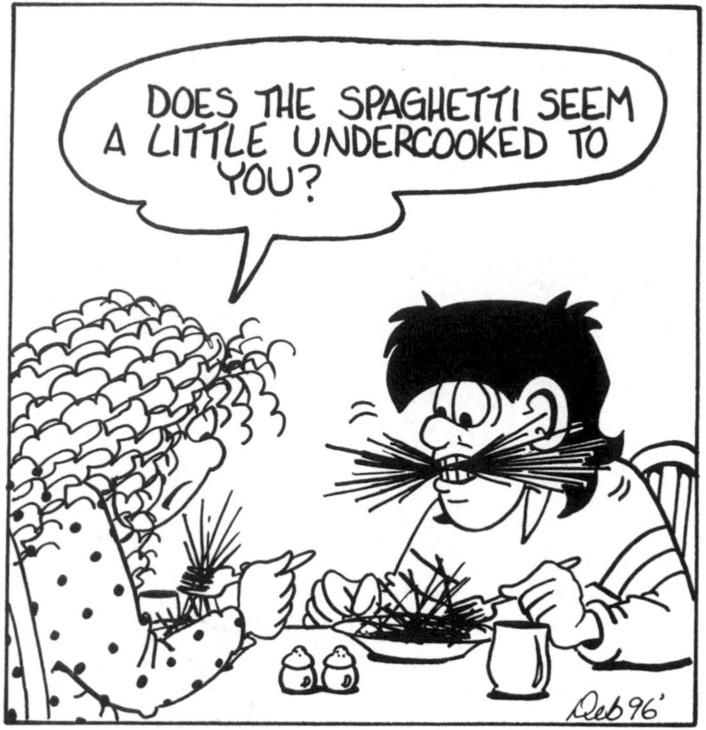
DOES THE SPAGHETTI SEEM A LITTLE UNDERCOOKED TO YOU?
Deb 96'

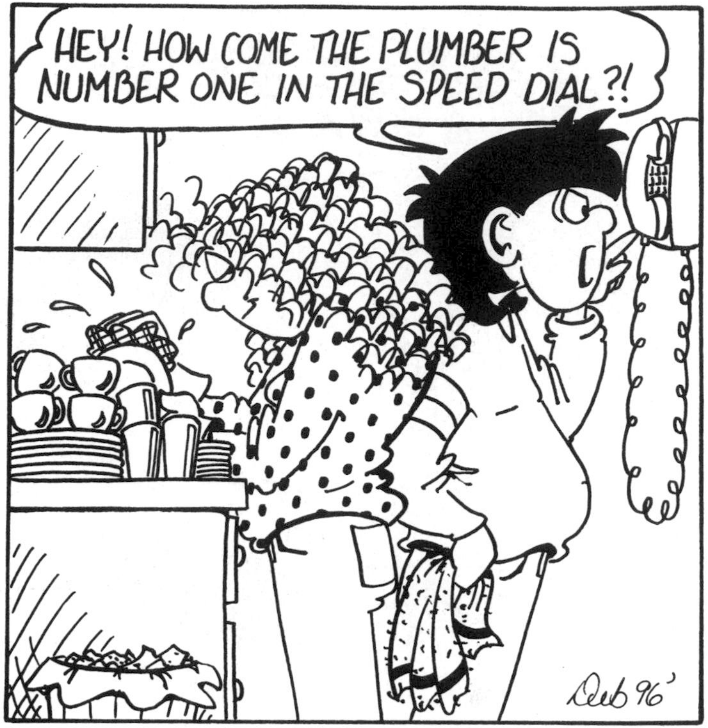
HEY! HOW COME THE PLUMBER IS NUMBER ONE IN THE SPEED DIAL?!
Deb 96'

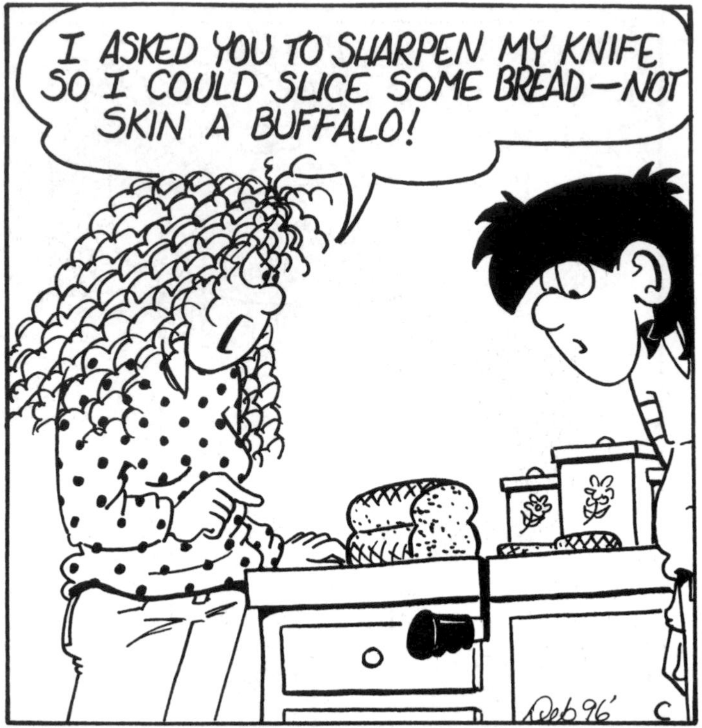
I ASKED YOU TO SHARPEN MY KNIFE SO I COULD SLICE SOME BREAD—NOT SKIN A BUFFALO!
Deb 96'

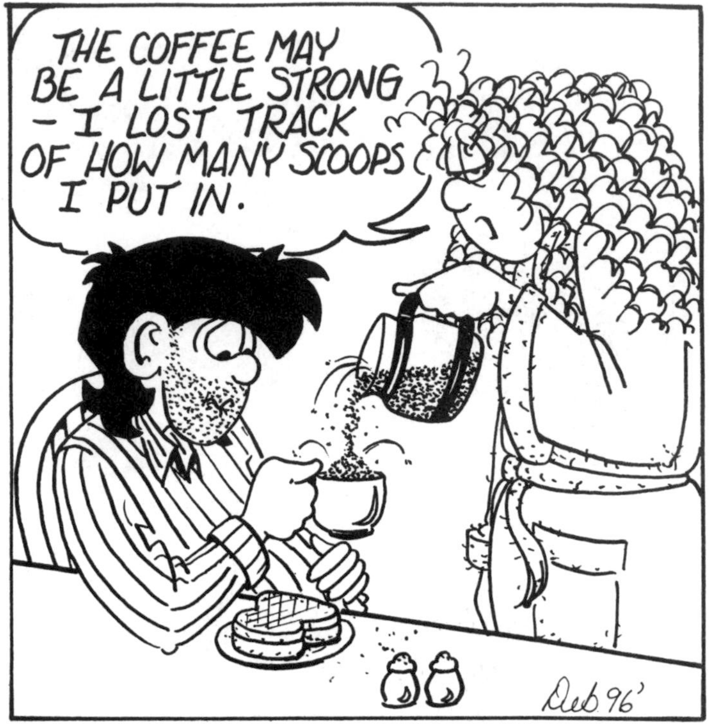
THE COFFEE MAY BE A LITTLE STRONG – I LOST TRACK OF HOW MANY SCOOPS I PUT IN.
Deb 96'

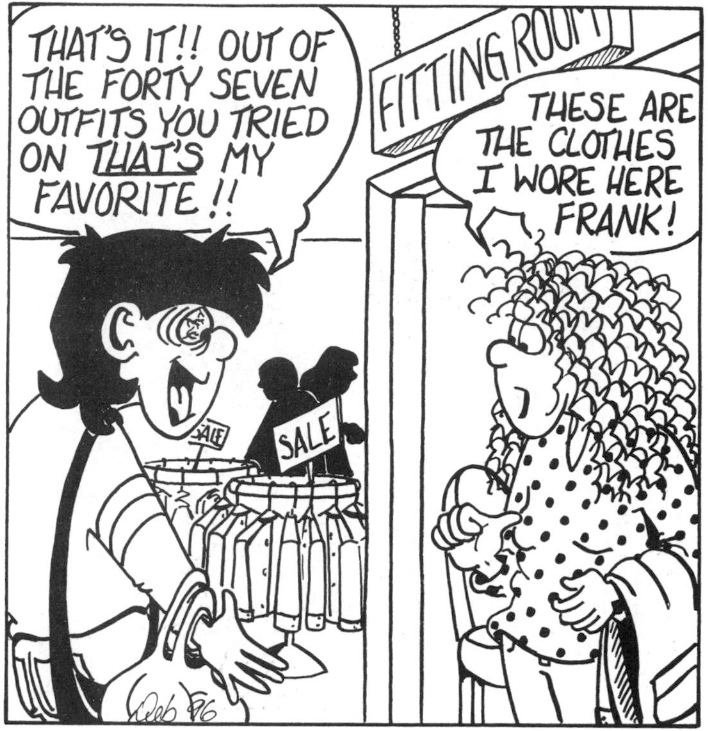
THAT'S IT!! OUT OF THE FORTY SEVEN OUTFITS YOU TRIED ON THAT'S MY FAVORITE!!
FITTING ROOM
THESE ARE THE CLOTHES I WORE HERE FRANK!
SALE
SALE
Deb 96

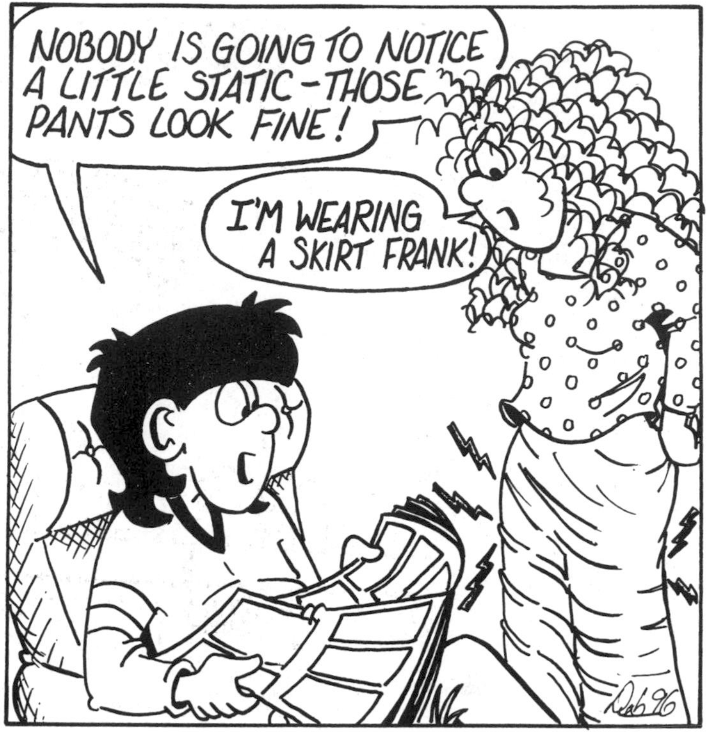
NOBODY IS GOING TO NOTICE A LITTLE STATIC - THOSE PANTS LOOK FINE!
I'M WEARING A SKIRT FRANK!
Deb 96

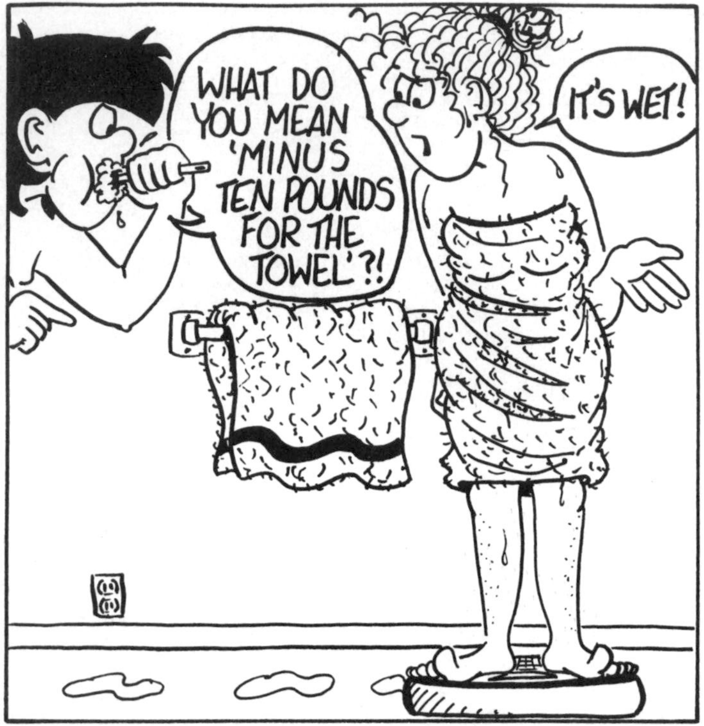
WHAT DO YOU MEAN 'MINUS TEN POUNDS FOR THE TOWEL'?!
IT'S WET!

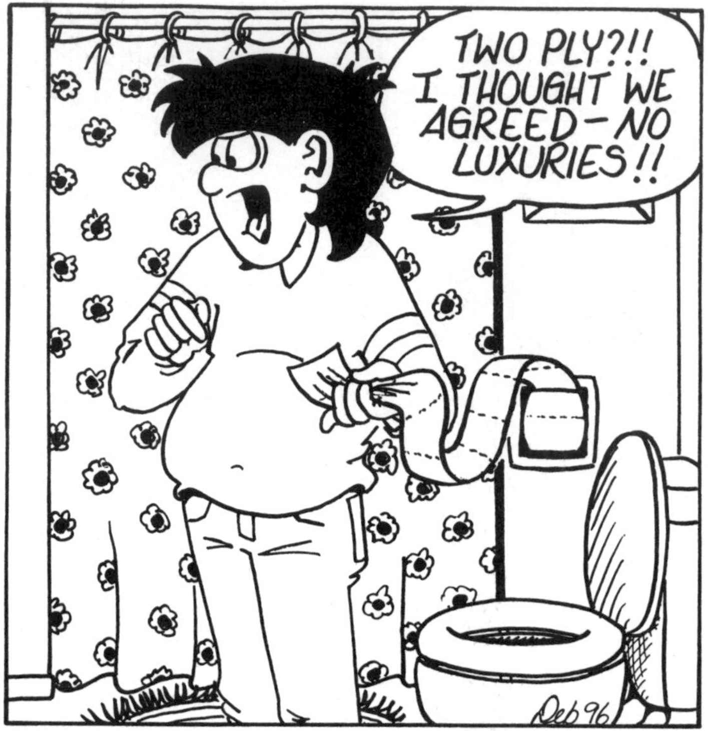
TWO PLY?!! I THOUGHT WE AGREED—NO LUXURIES!!
Deb 96

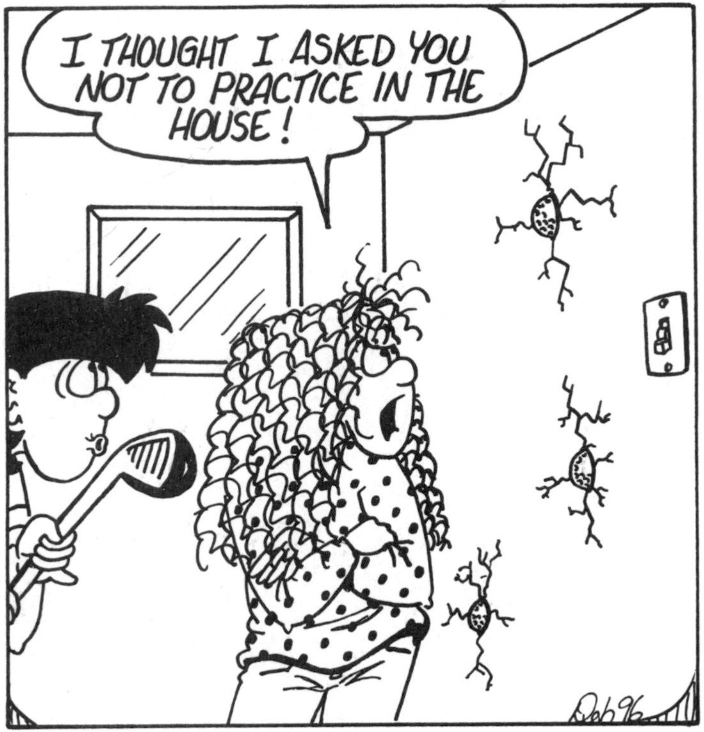
I THOUGHT I ASKED YOU NOT TO PRACTICE IN THE HOUSE!
Deb96

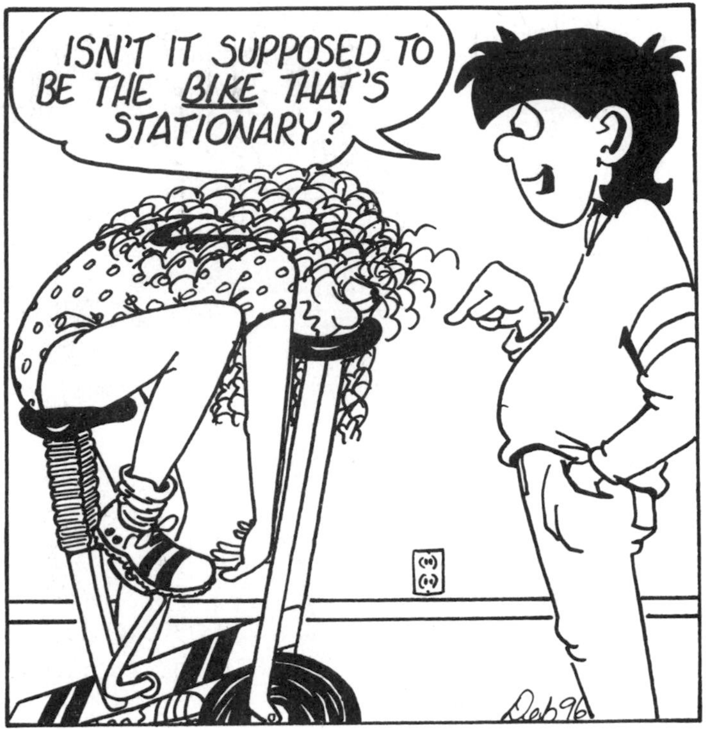
ISN'T IT SUPPOSED TO BE THE BIKE THAT'S STATIONARY?
Deb96

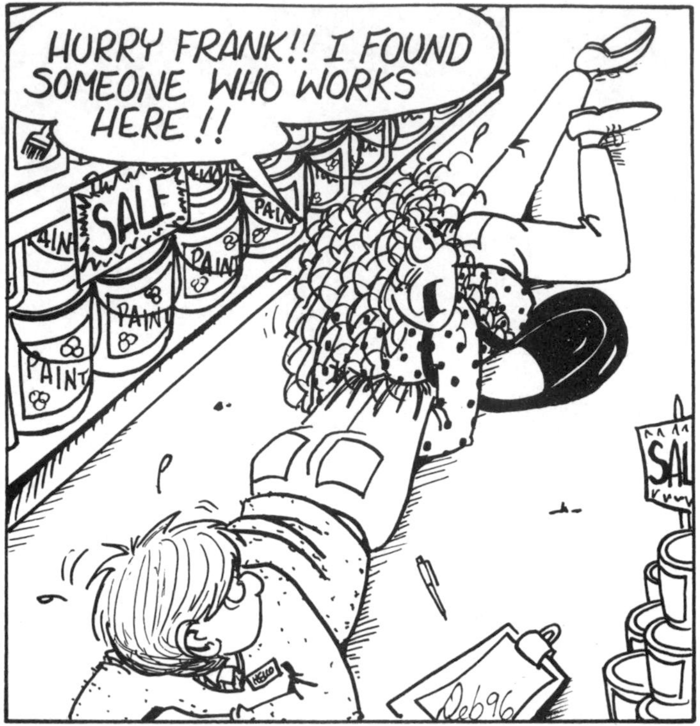
HURRY FRANK!! I FOUND SOMEONE WHO WORKS HERE!!
SALE
PAINT
Deb96

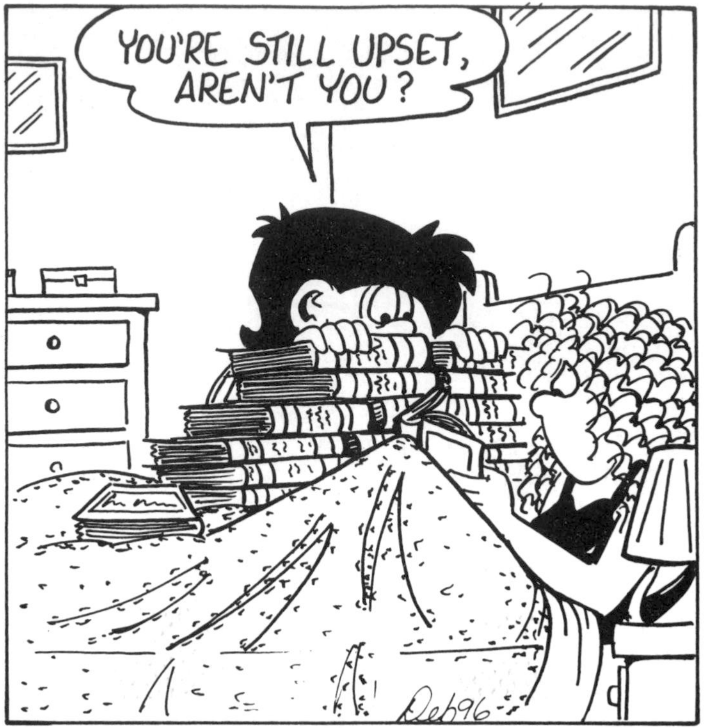
YOU'RE STILL UPSET, AREN'T YOU?
Deb96

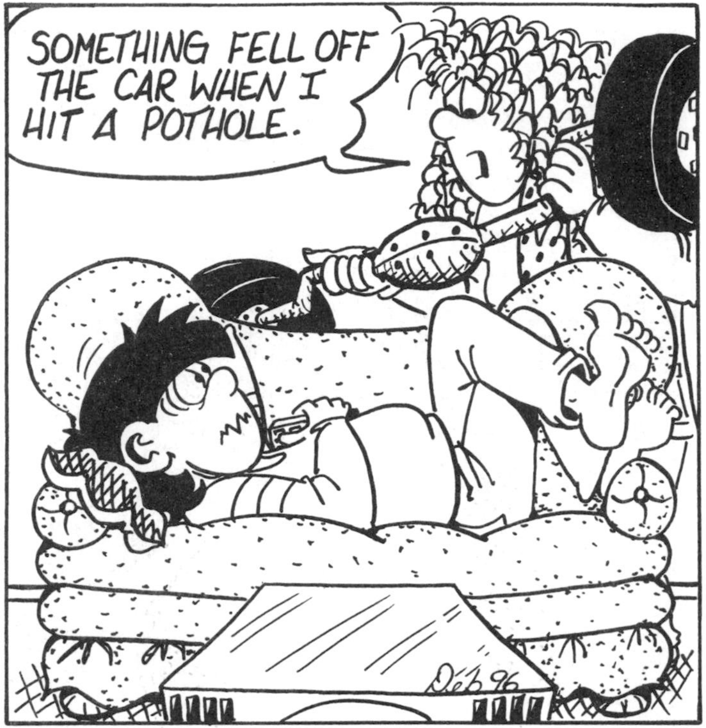
SOMETHING FELL OFF THE CAR WHEN I HIT A POTHOLE.
Deb96

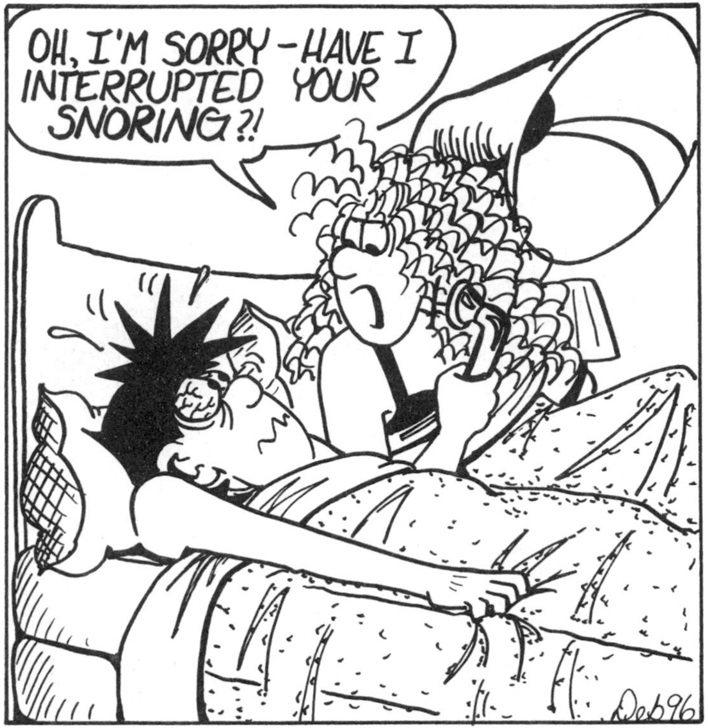
OH, I'M SORRY - HAVE I INTERRUPTED YOUR SNORING?!
Deb96

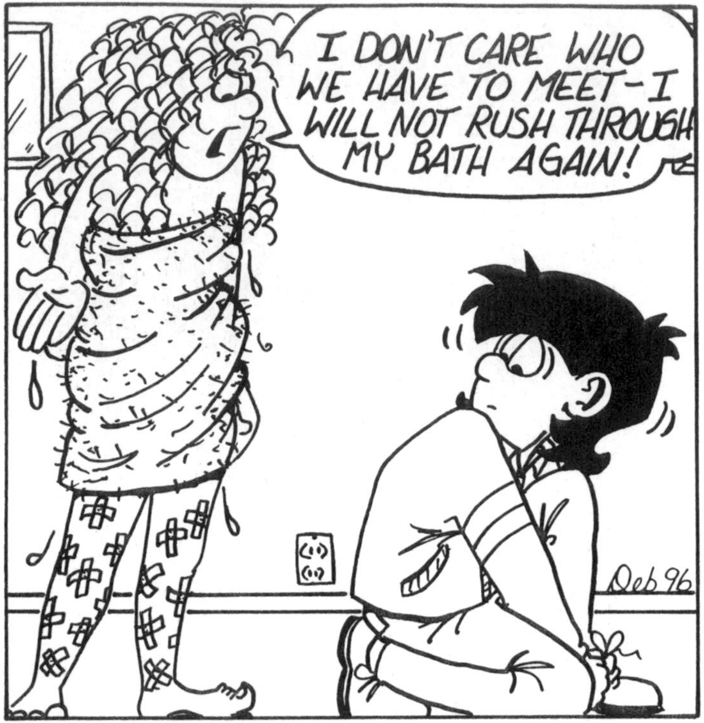
I DON'T CARE WHO WE HAVE TO MEET-I WILL NOT RUSH THROUGH MY BATH AGAIN!
Deb 96

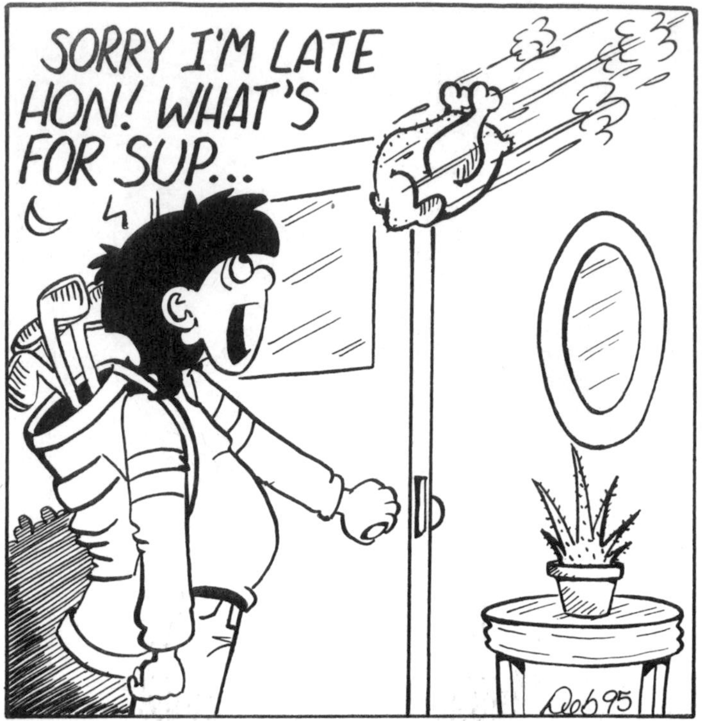
SORRY I'M LATE HON! WHAT'S FOR SUP...
Deb 95

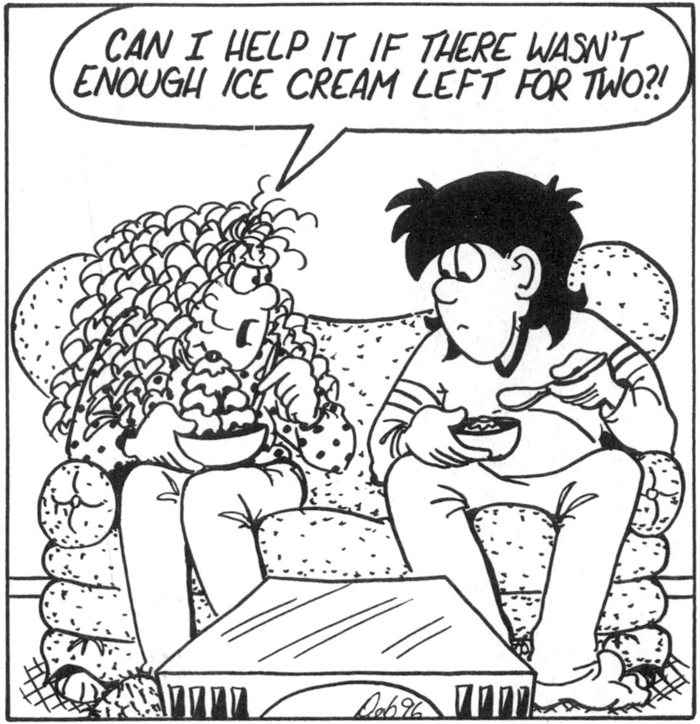
CAN I HELP IT IF THERE WASN'T ENOUGH ICE CREAM LEFT FOR TWO?!

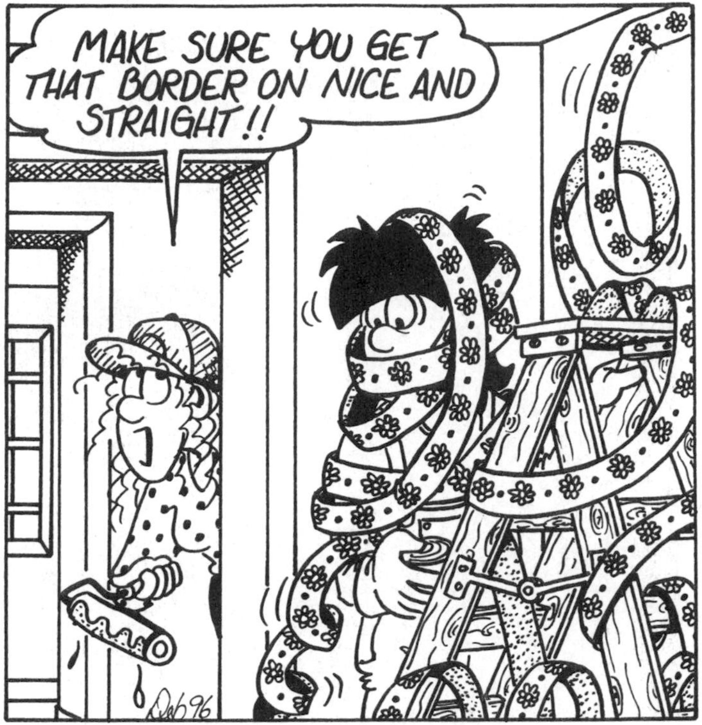
MAKE SURE YOU GET THAT BORDER ON NICE AND STRAIGHT!!

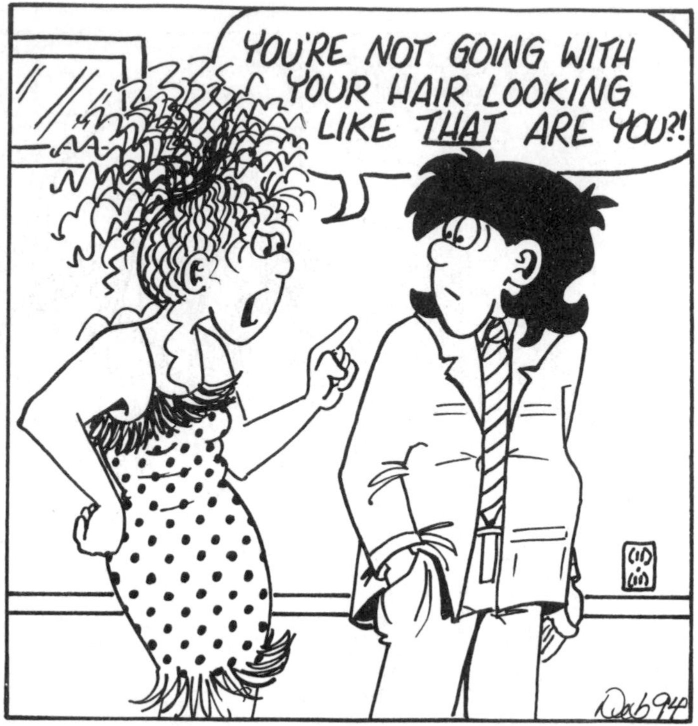
YOU'RE NOT GOING WITH YOUR HAIR LOOKING LIKE THAT ARE YOU?!
Dab94

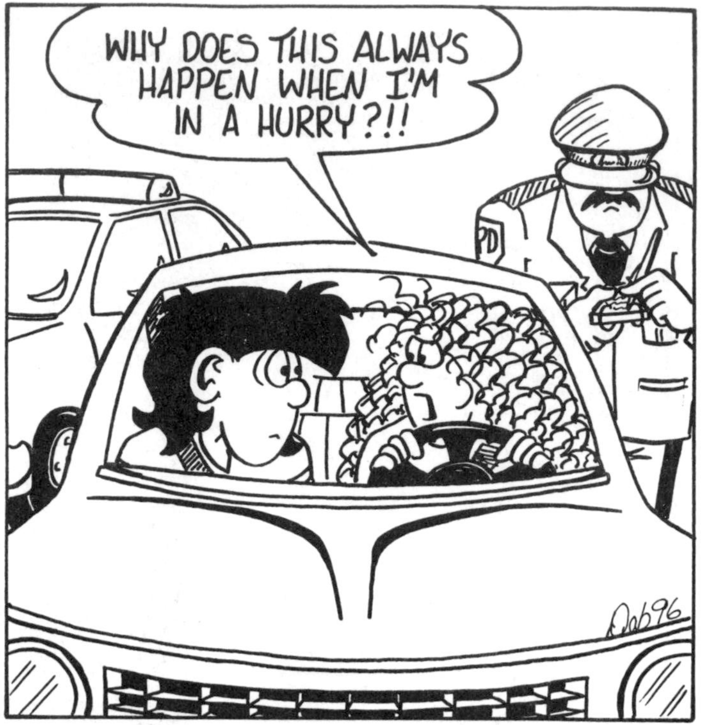
WHY DOES THIS ALWAYS HAPPEN WHEN I'M IN A HURRY?!!
PD
Dab96

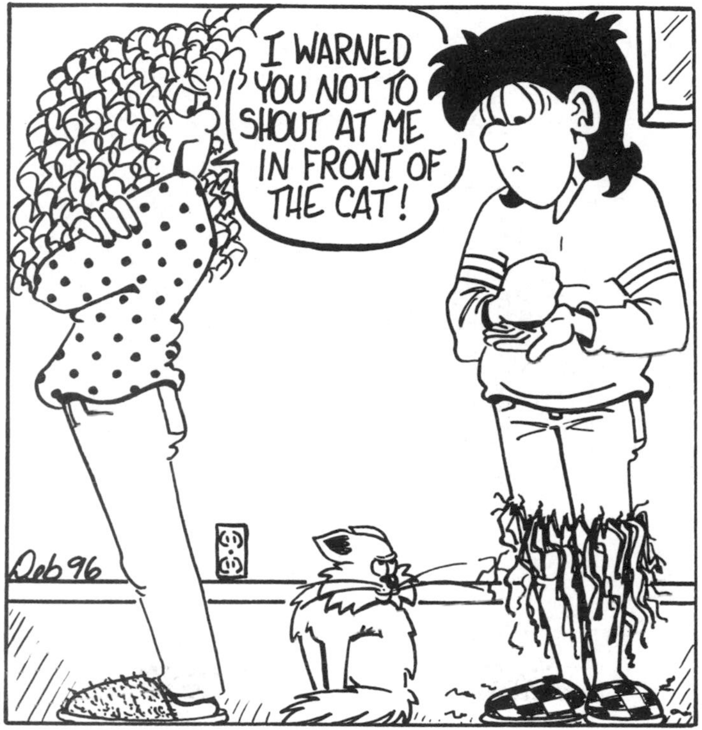
I WARNED YOU NOT TO SHOUT AT ME IN FRONT OF THE CAT!
Deb 96

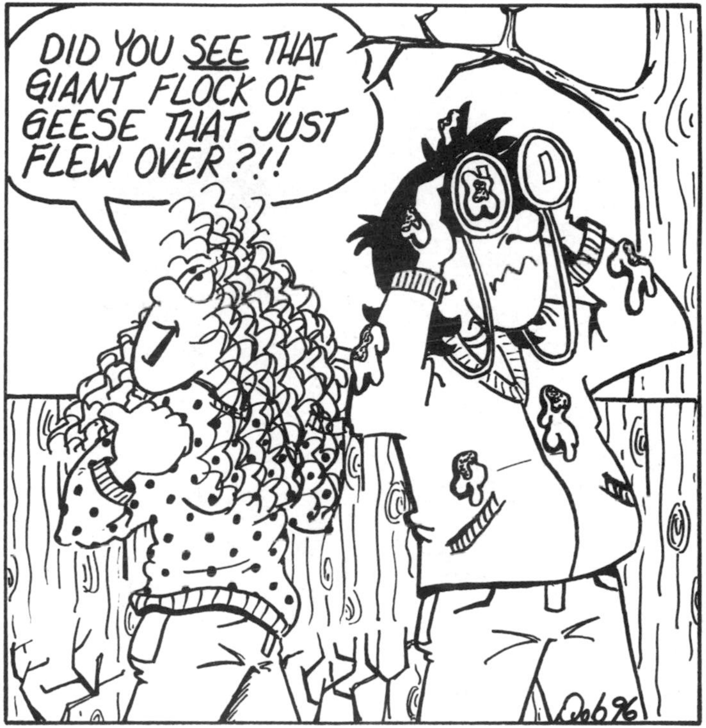
DID YOU SEE THAT GIANT FLOCK OF GEESE THAT JUST FLEW OVER?!!
Deb 96

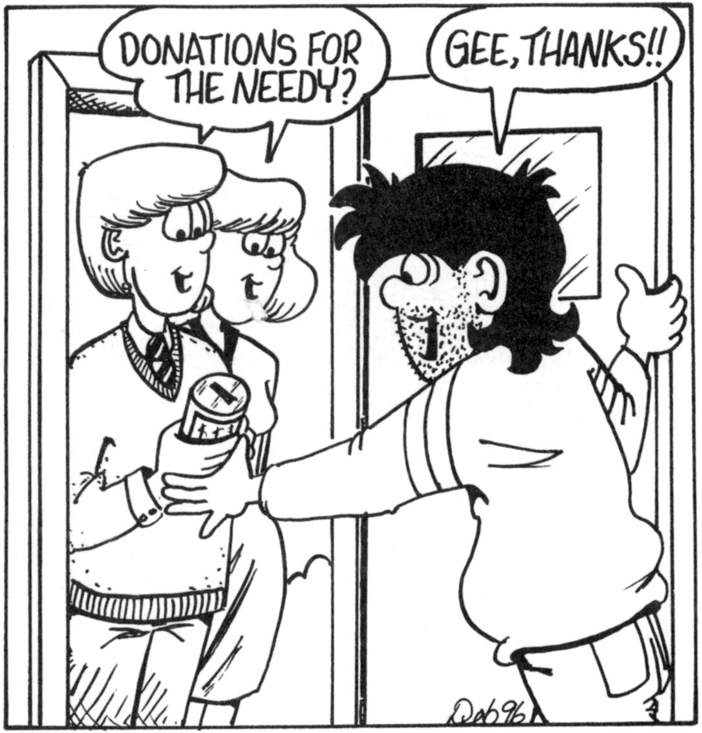
DONATIONS FOR THE NEEDY?
GEE, THANKS!!

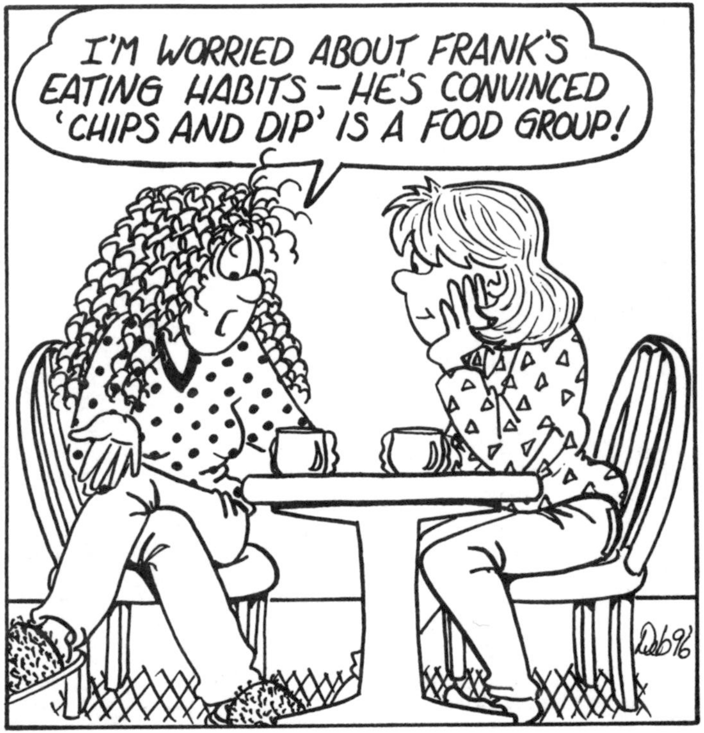
I'M WORRIED ABOUT FRANK'S EATING HABITS – HE'S CONVINCED 'CHIPS AND DIP' IS A FOOD GROUP!

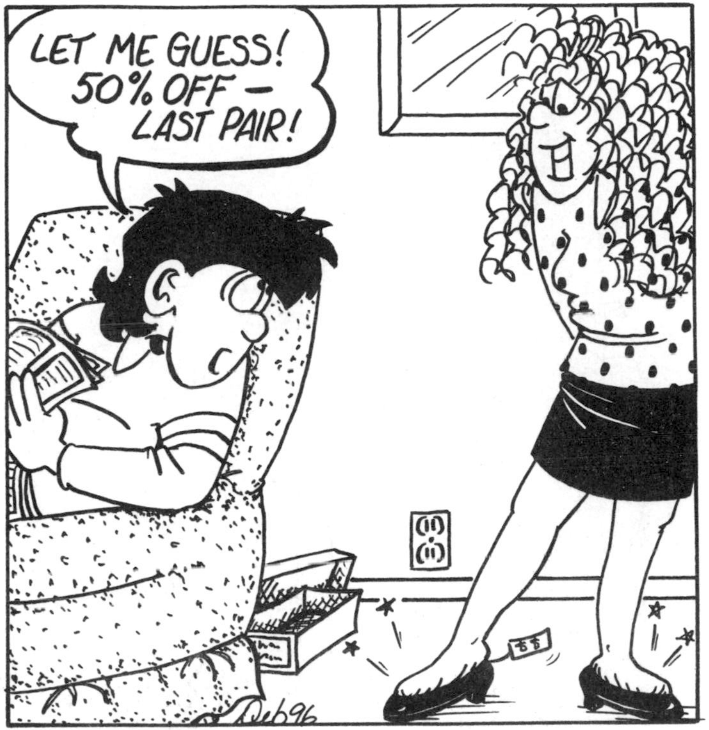
LET ME GUESS! 50% OFF — LAST PAIR!
Deb96

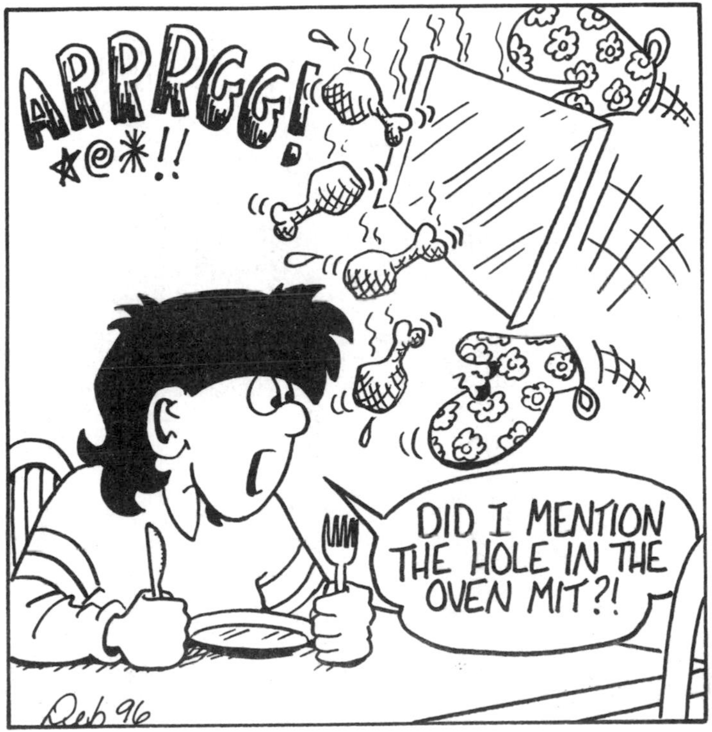
ARRRGG!
☆@✱!!
DID I MENTION THE HOLE IN THE OVEN MIT?!
Deb 96

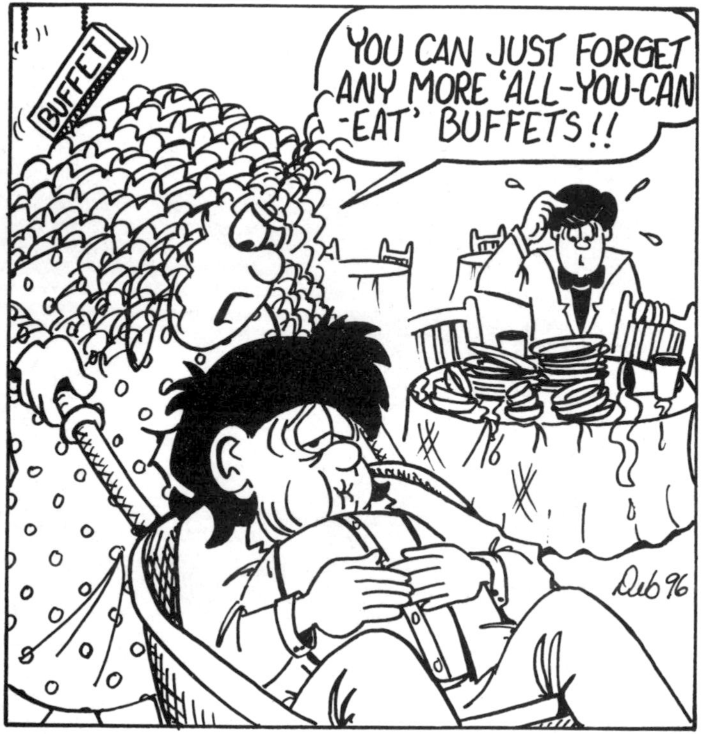
BUFFET
YOU CAN JUST FORGET ANY MORE 'ALL-YOU-CAN-EAT' BUFFETS!!
Deb 96

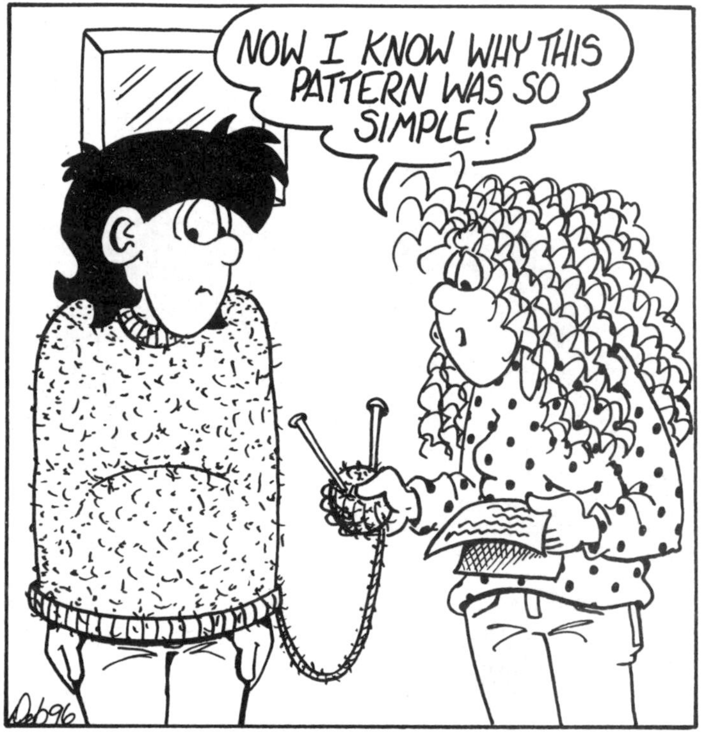
NOW I KNOW WHY THIS PATTERN WAS SO SIMPLE!
Deb 96

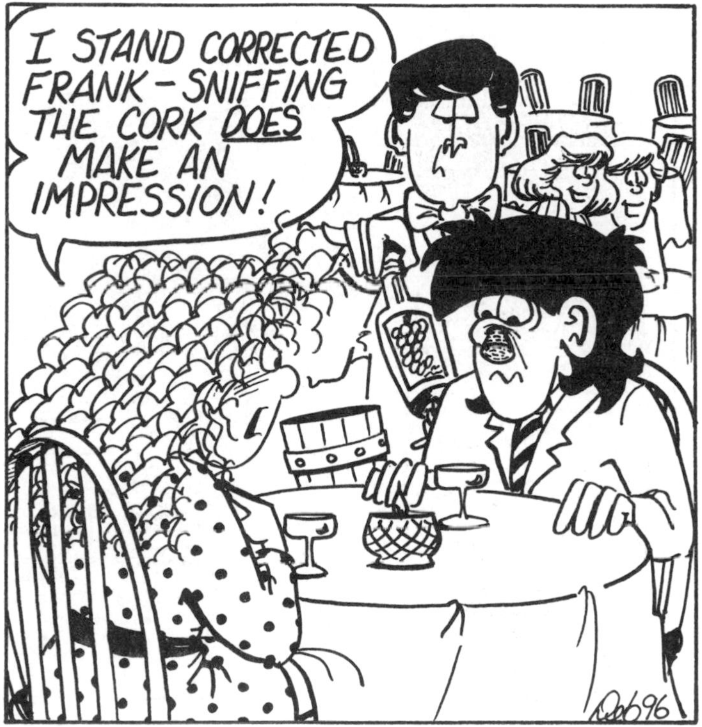
I STAND CORRECTED FRANK - SNIFFING THE CORK DOES MAKE AN IMPRESSION!
Deb96

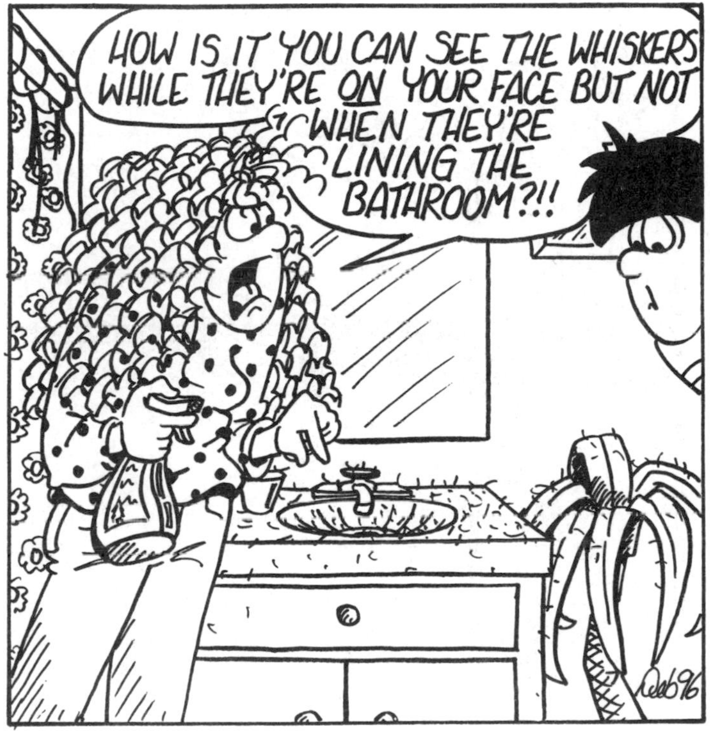
HOW IS IT YOU CAN SEE THE WHISKERS WHILE THEY'RE ON YOUR FACE BUT NOT WHEN THEY'RE LINING THE BATHROOM?!!
Deb96

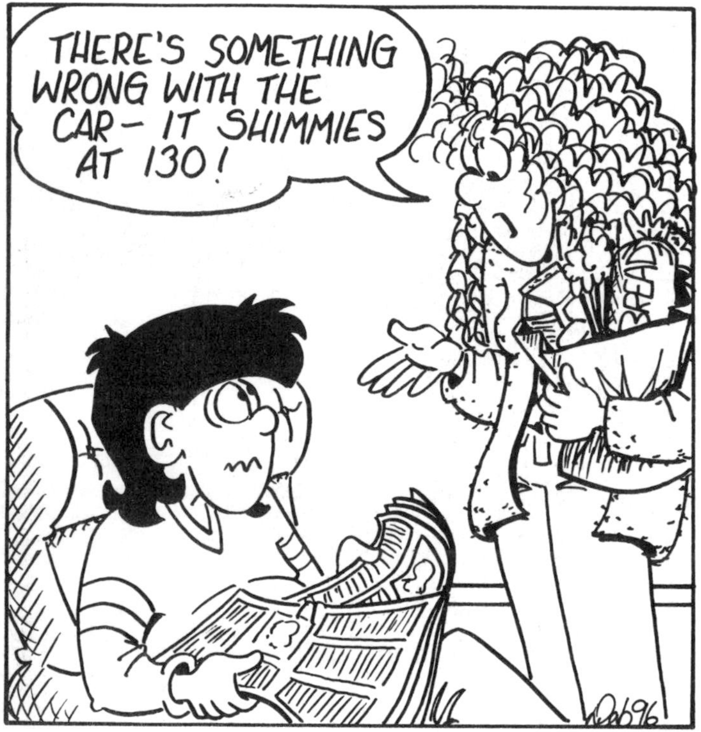
THERE'S SOMETHING WRONG WITH THE CAR– IT SHIMMIES AT 130!
BREAD
Dab96

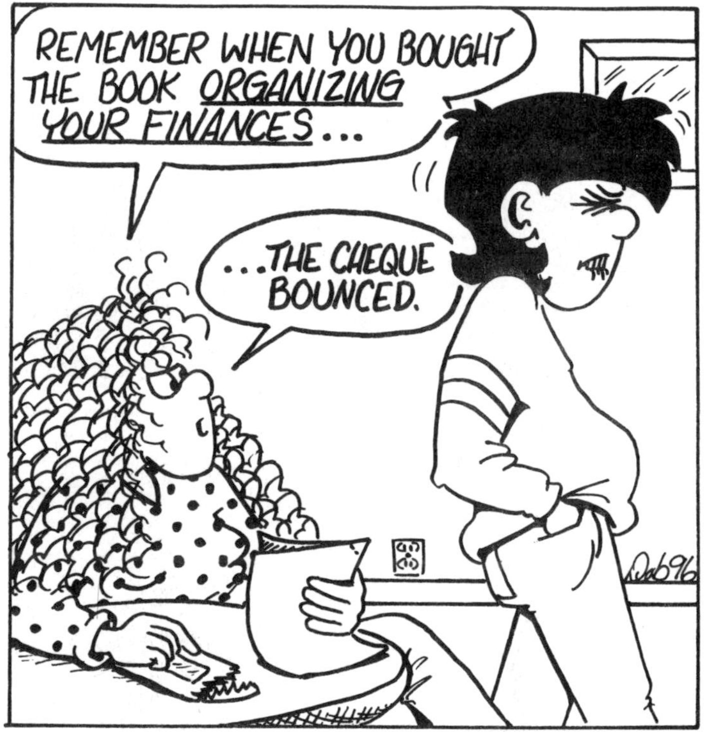
REMEMBER WHEN YOU BOUGHT THE BOOK ORGANIZING YOUR FINANCES...
...THE CHEQUE BOUNCED.
Dab96

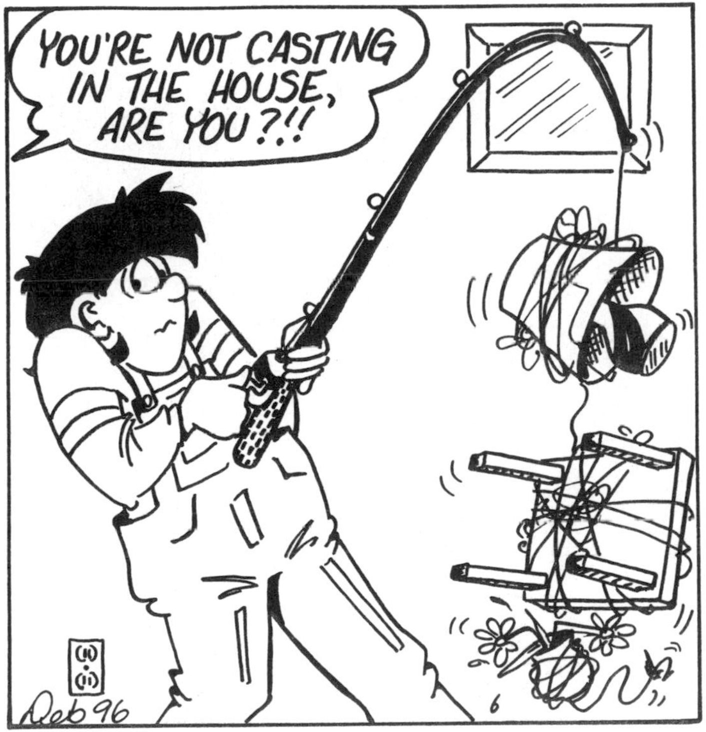
YOU'RE NOT CASTING IN THE HOUSE, ARE YOU?!!
Deb 96

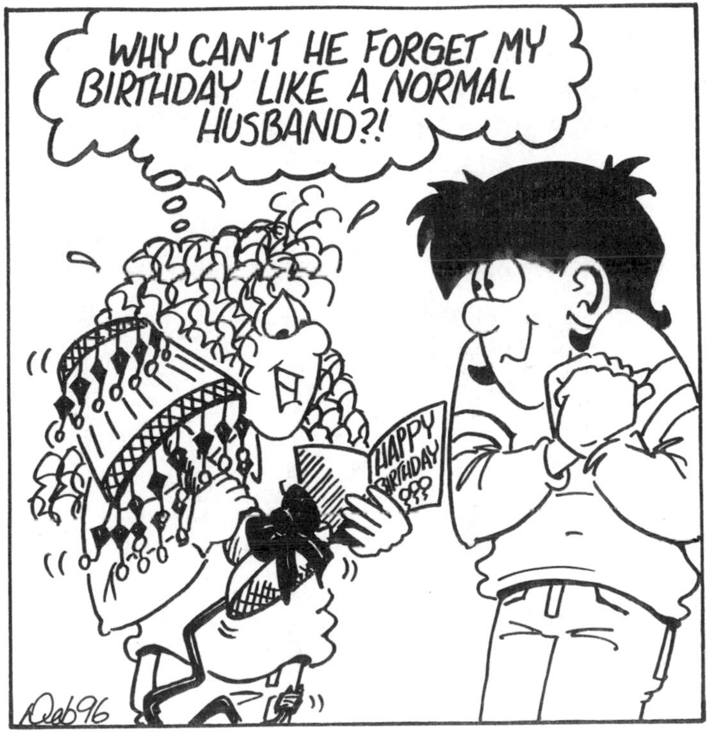
WHY CAN'T HE FORGET MY BIRTHDAY LIKE A NORMAL HUSBAND?!
HAPPY BIRTHDAY
Deb 96

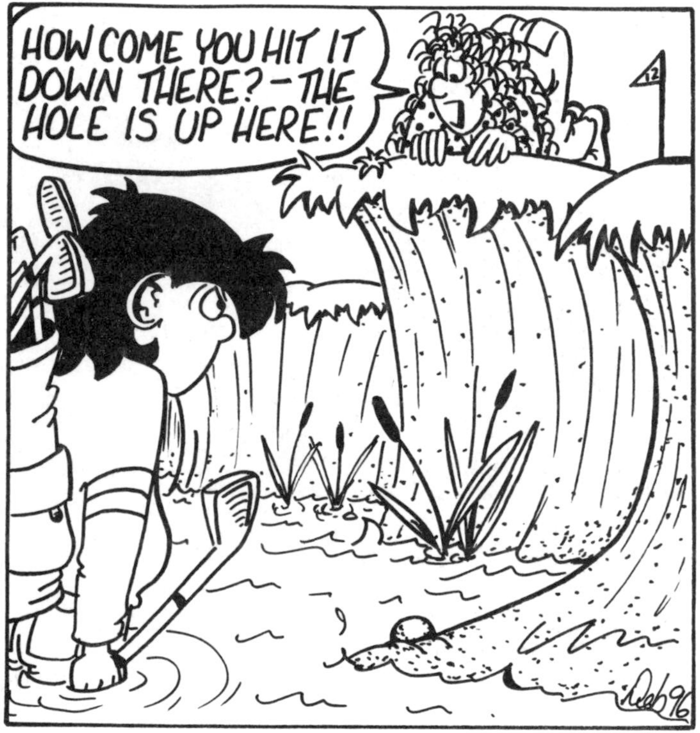
HOW COME YOU HIT IT DOWN THERE? - THE HOLE IS UP HERE!!
12
Deb 96

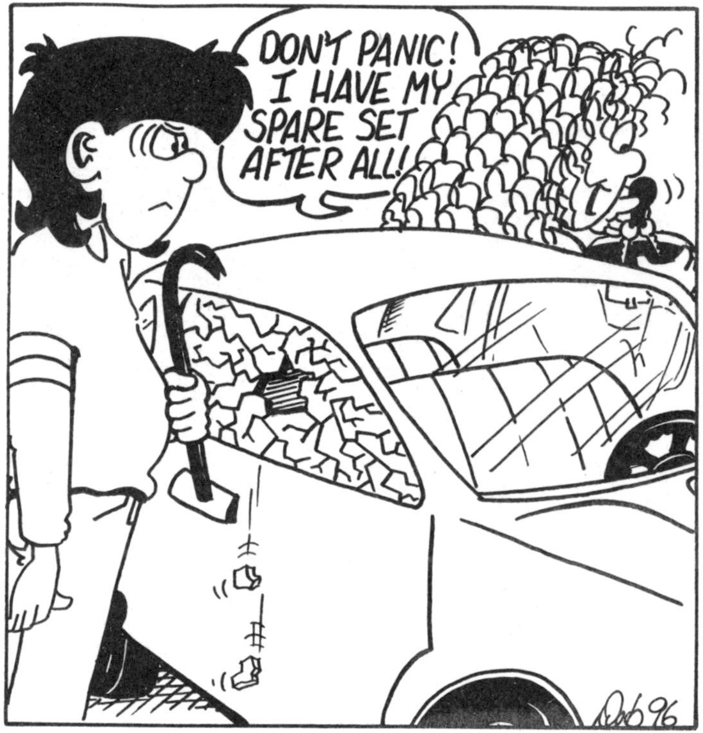
DON'T PANIC! I HAVE MY SPARE SET AFTER ALL!
Deb 96

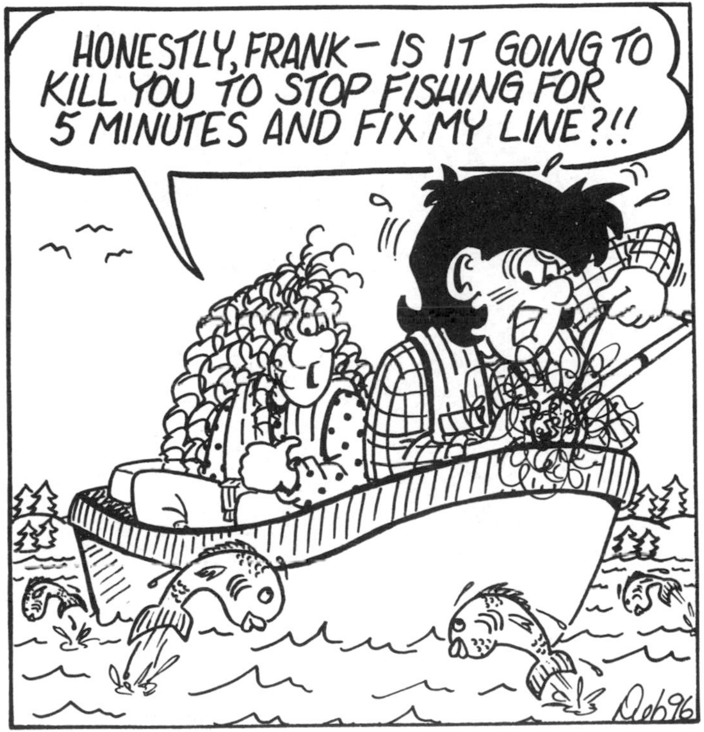
HONESTLY, FRANK— IS IT GOING TO KILL YOU TO STOP FISHING FOR 5 MINUTES AND FIX MY LINE?!!
Deb96

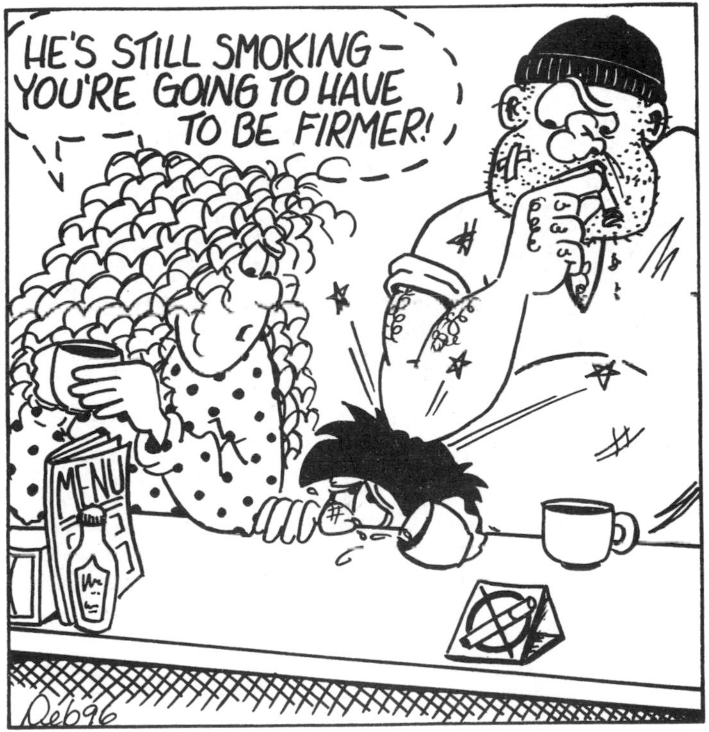
HE'S STILL SMOKING— YOU'RE GOING TO HAVE TO BE FIRMER!
MENU
Deb96

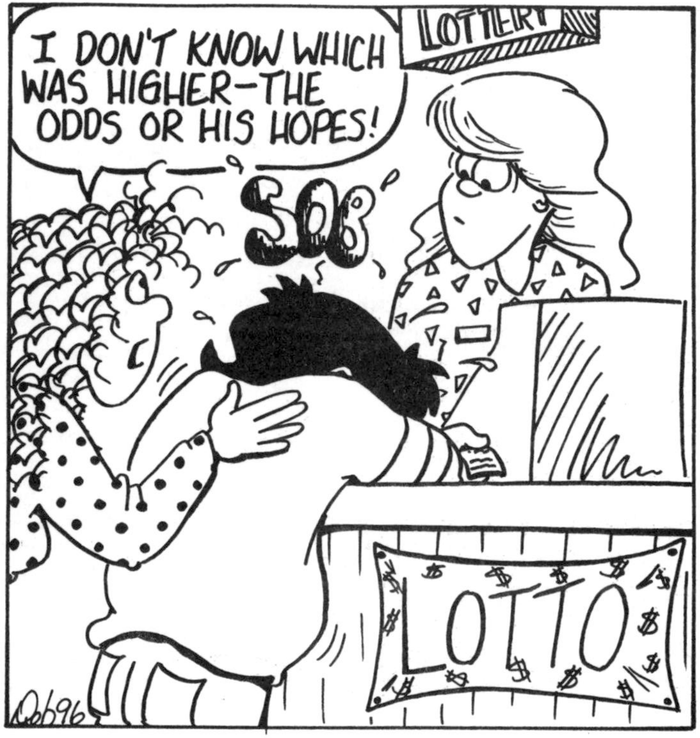
LOTTERY
I DON'T KNOW WHICH WAS HIGHER—THE ODDS OR HIS HOPES!
SOB
LOTTO
Deb96

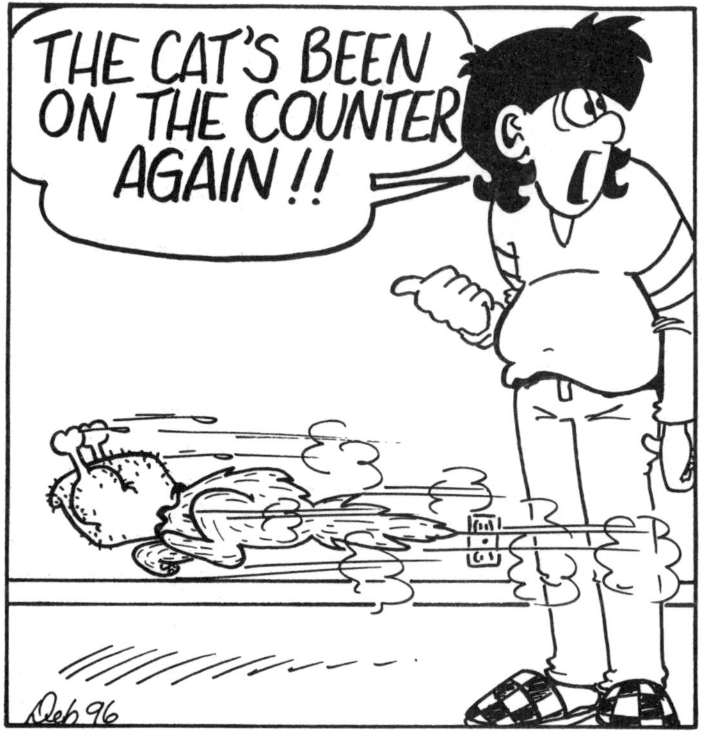
THE CAT'S BEEN ON THE COUNTER AGAIN!!
Deb 96

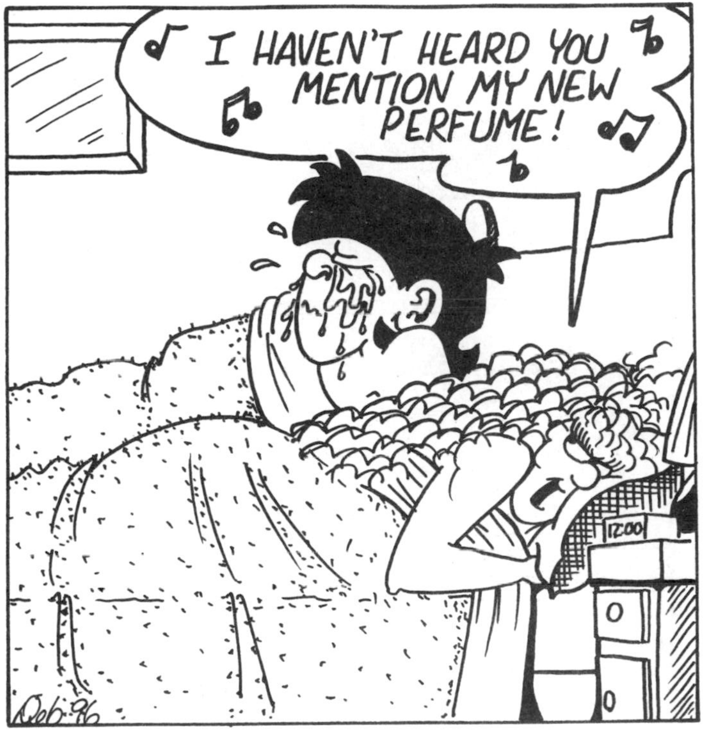
I HAVEN'T HEARD YOU MENTION MY NEW PERFUME!
Deb 96

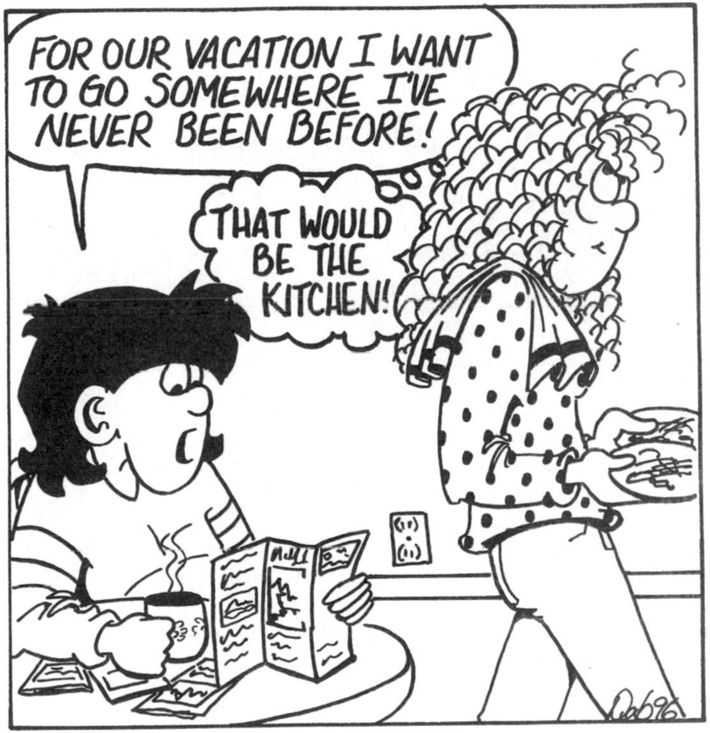
FOR OUR VACATION I WANT TO GO SOMEWHERE I'VE NEVER BEEN BEFORE!
THAT WOULD BE THE KITCHEN!
Deb96

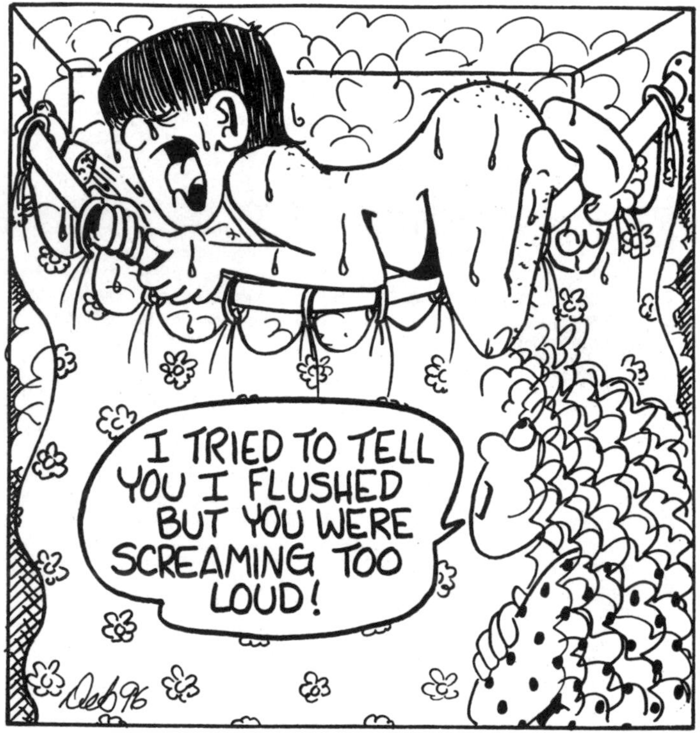
I TRIED TO TELL YOU I FLUSHED BUT YOU WERE SCREAMING TOO LOUD!
Deb 96

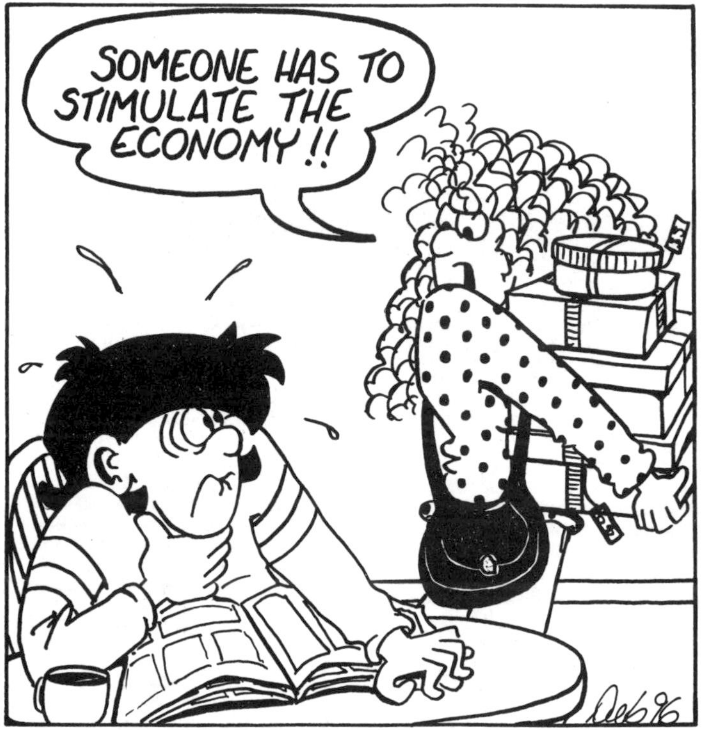
SOMEONE HAS TO STIMULATE THE ECONOMY!!
Deb 96

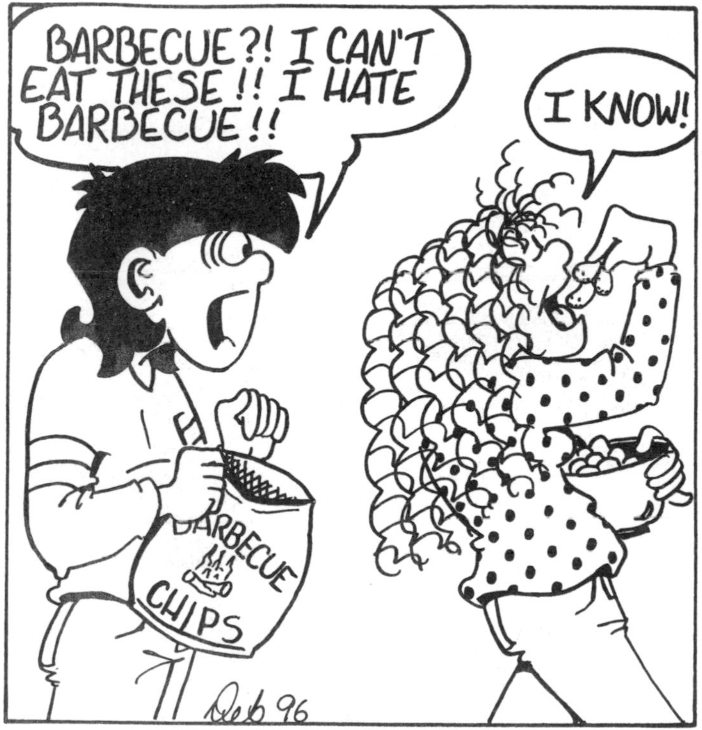
BARBECUE?! I CAN'T EAT THESE!! I HATE BARBECUE!!
I KNOW!
BARBECUE CHIPS
Deb 96

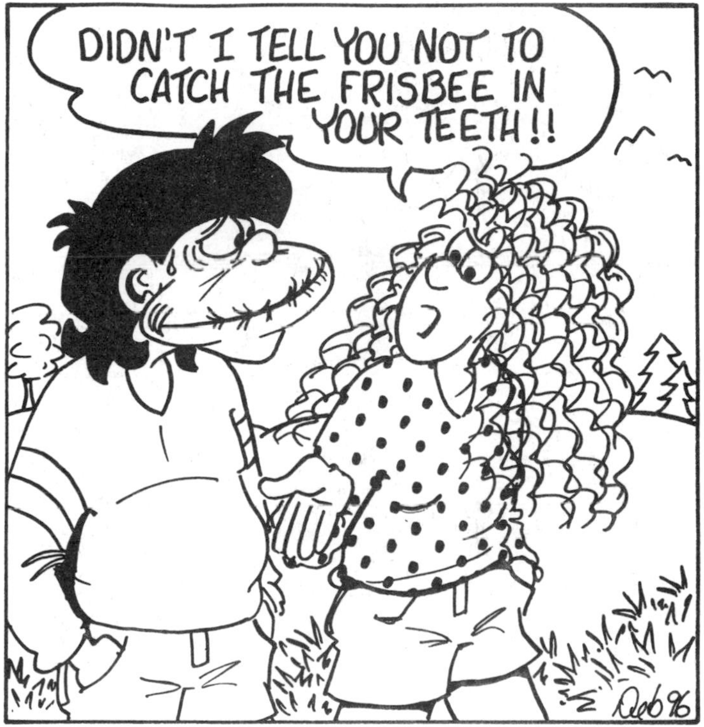
DIDN'T I TELL YOU NOT TO CATCH THE FRISBEE IN YOUR TEETH!!
Deb 96

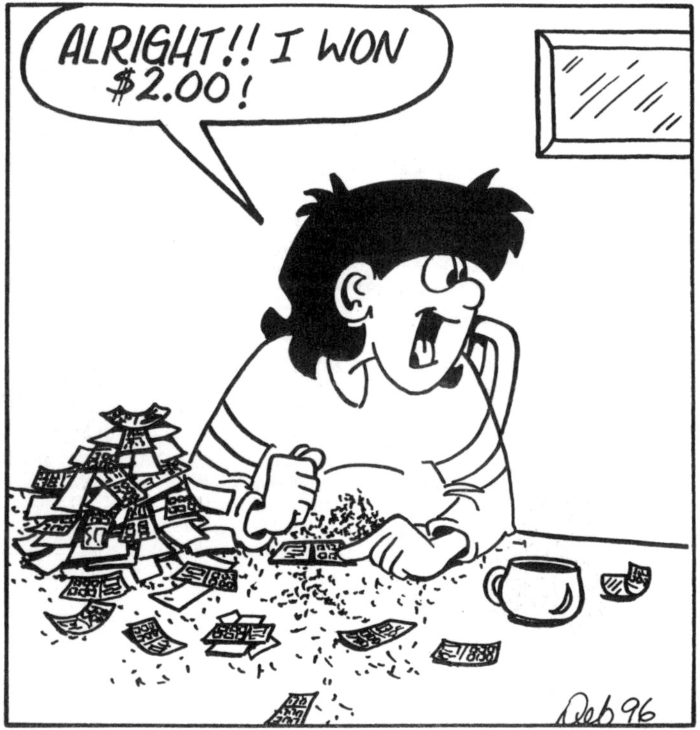
ALRIGHT!! I WON $2.00!
Deb 96

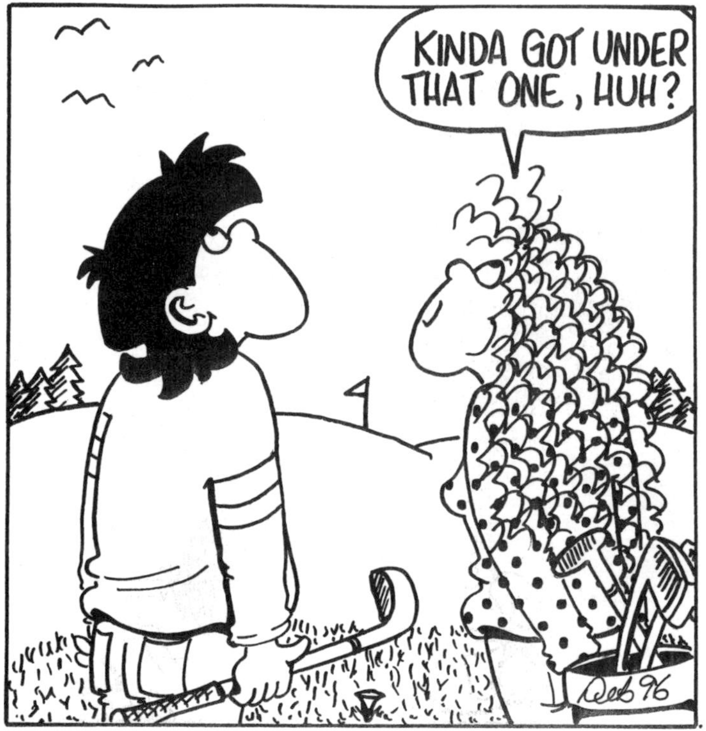
KINDA GOT UNDER THAT ONE, HUH?
Deb 96

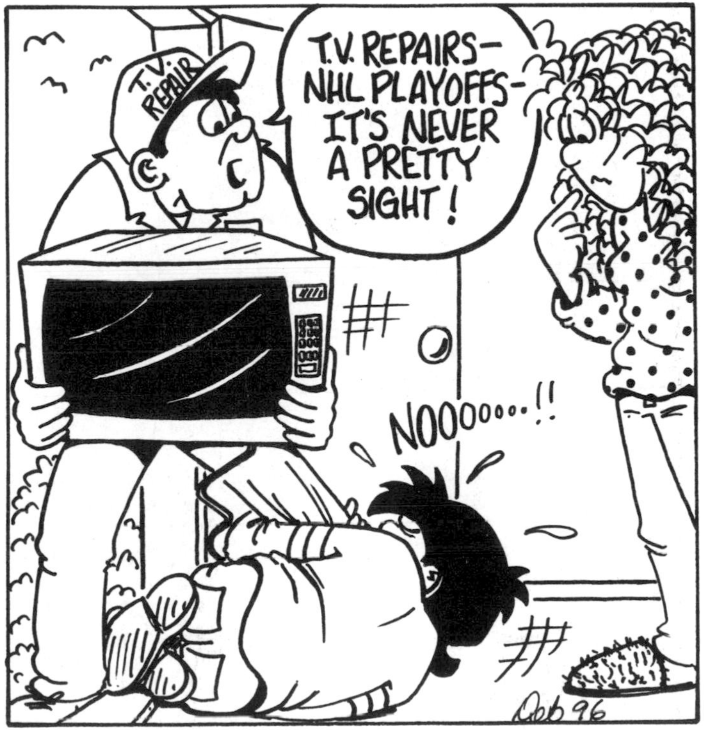
T.V. REPAIR
T.V. REPAIRS- NHL PLAYOFFS- IT'S NEVER A PRETTY SIGHT!
NOOOooo..!!
Deb 96

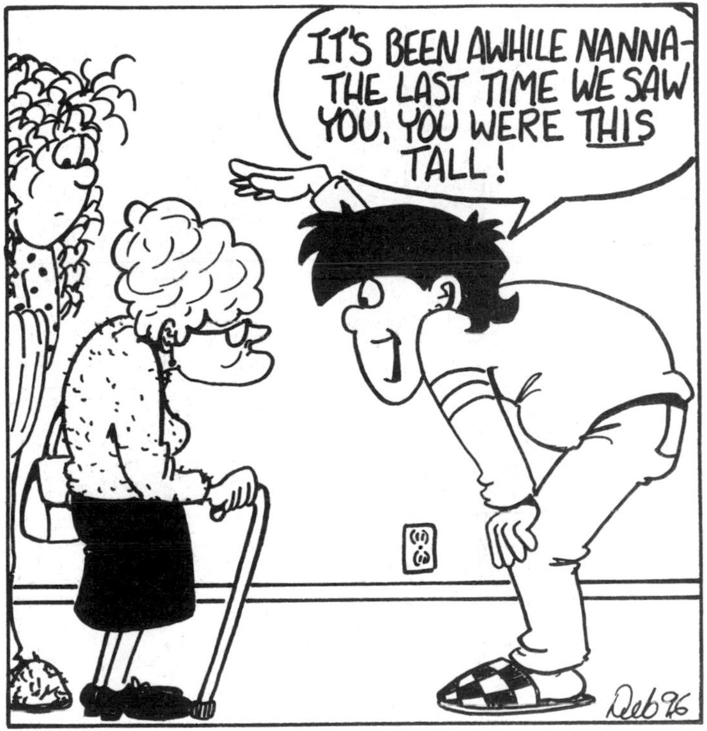
IT'S BEEN AWHILE NANNA- THE LAST TIME WE SAW YOU, YOU WERE THIS TALL!
Deb 96

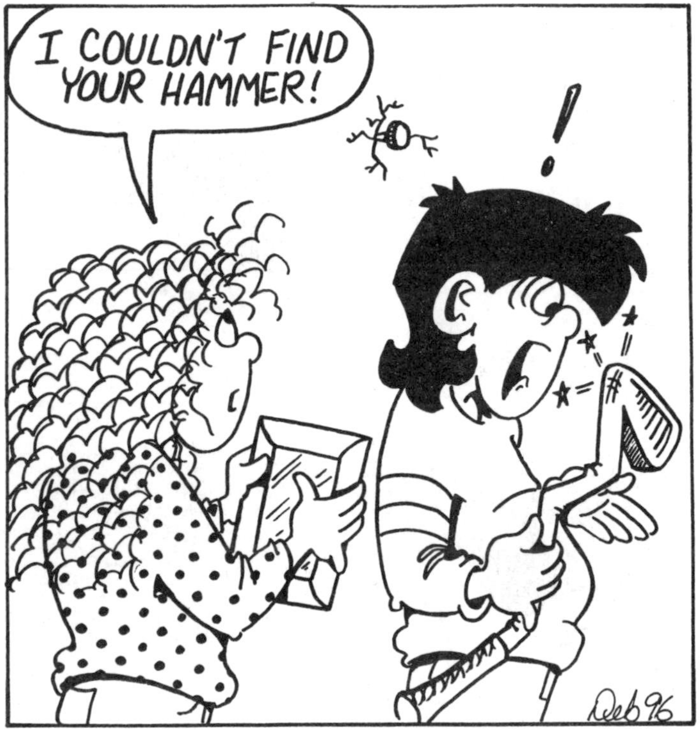
I COULDN'T FIND YOUR HAMMER!
!
Deb 96

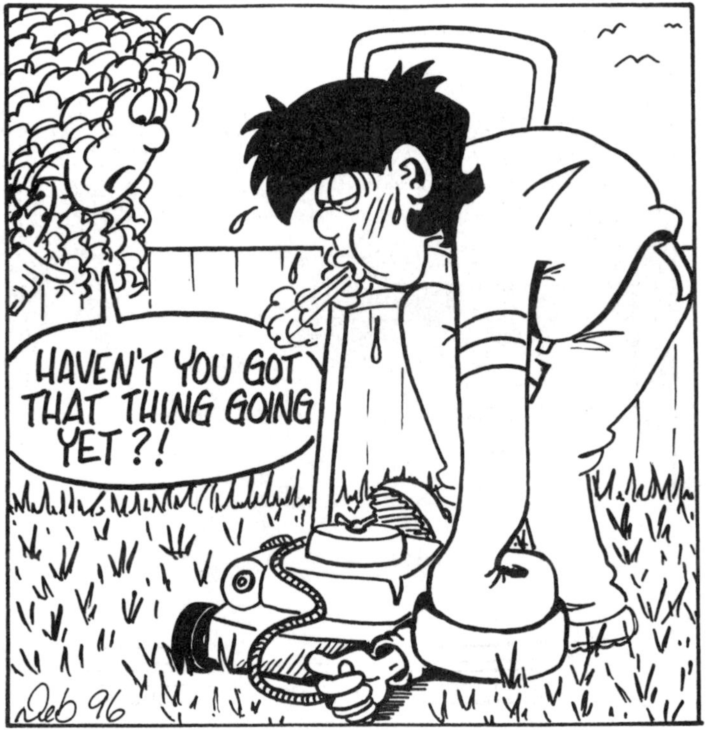
HAVEN'T YOU GOT THAT THING GOING YET?!
Deb 96

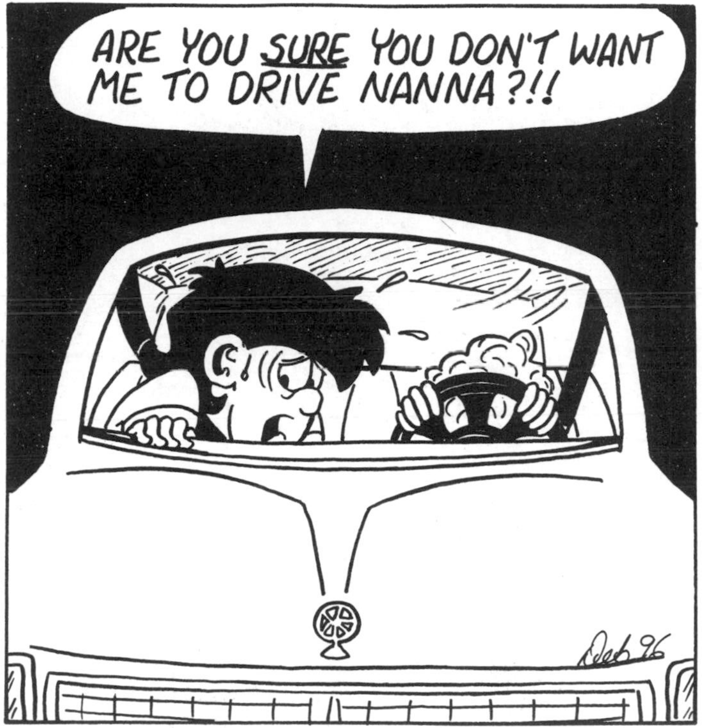
ARE YOU SURE YOU DON'T WANT ME TO DRIVE NANNA?!!
Deb 96

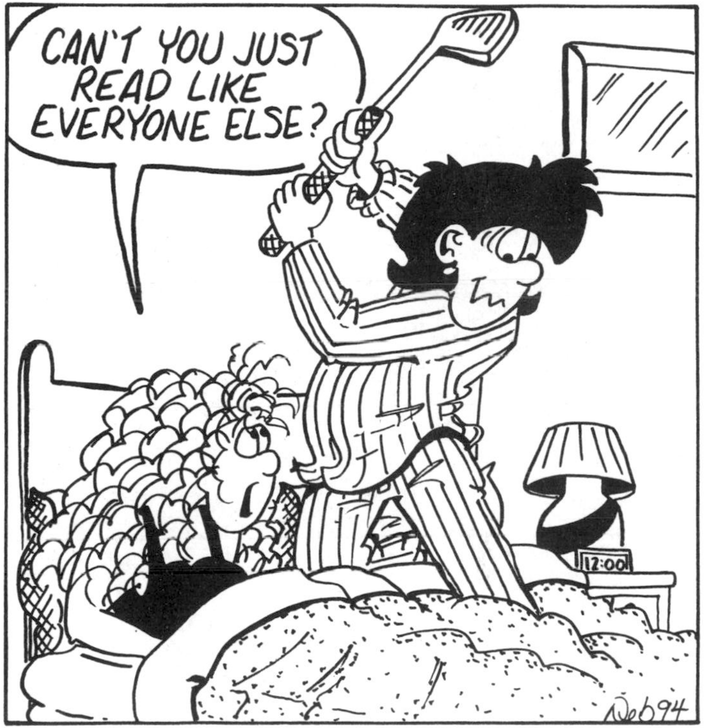
CAN'T YOU JUST READ LIKE EVERYONE ELSE?
12:00
Deb 94

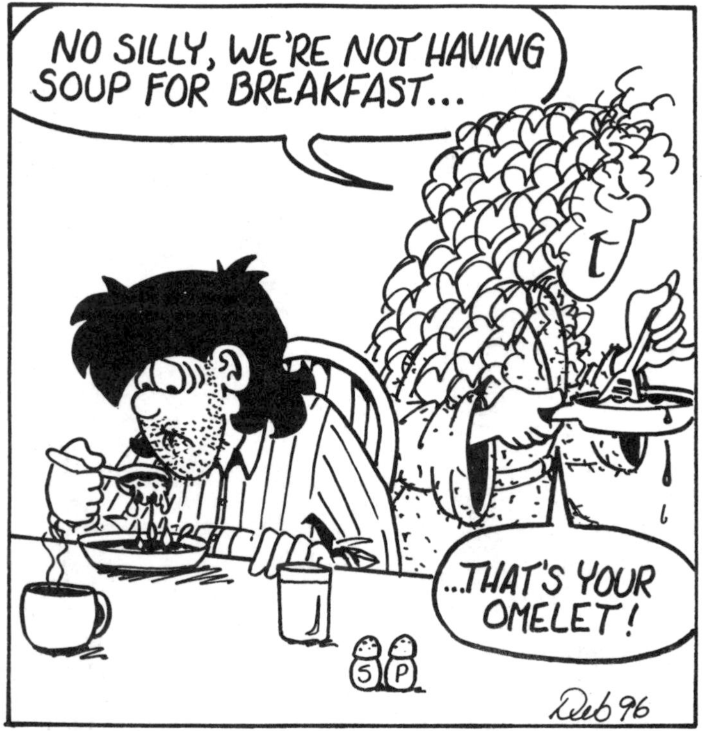
NO SILLY, WE'RE NOT HAVING SOUP FOR BREAKFAST...
...THAT'S YOUR OMELET!
S
P
Deb 96

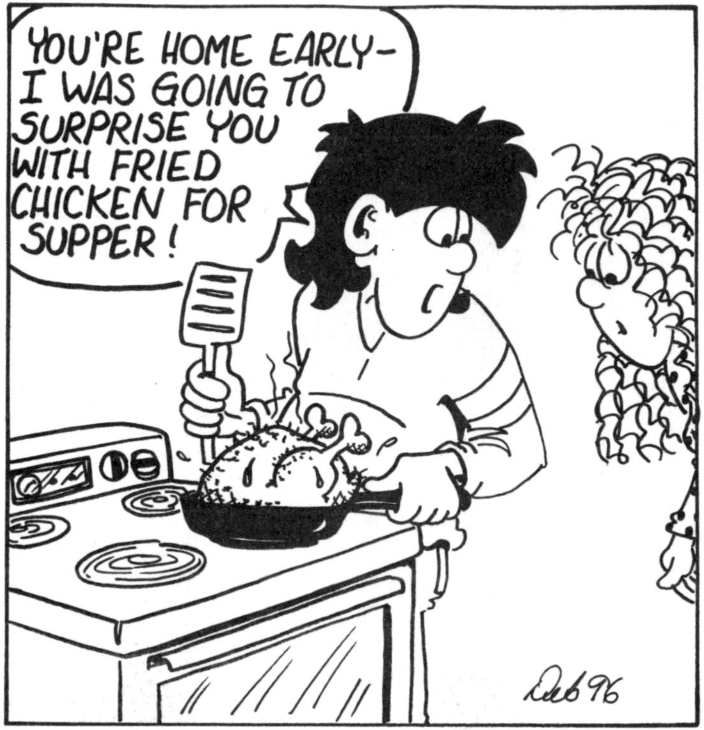
YOU'RE HOME EARLY- I WAS GOING TO SURPRISE YOU WITH FRIED CHICKEN FOR SUPPER!
Deb 96

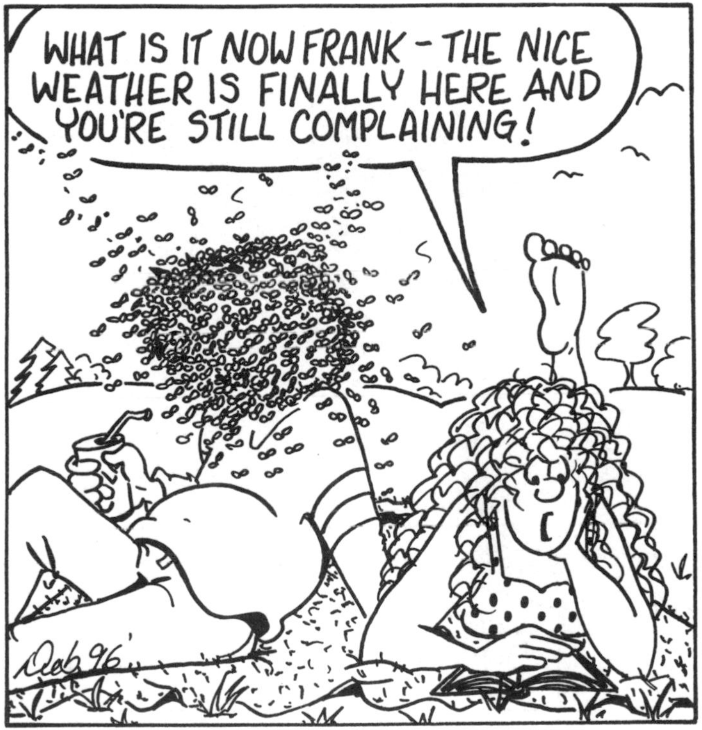
WHAT IS IT NOW FRANK - THE NICE WEATHER IS FINALLY HERE AND YOU'RE STILL COMPLAINING!
Deb 96

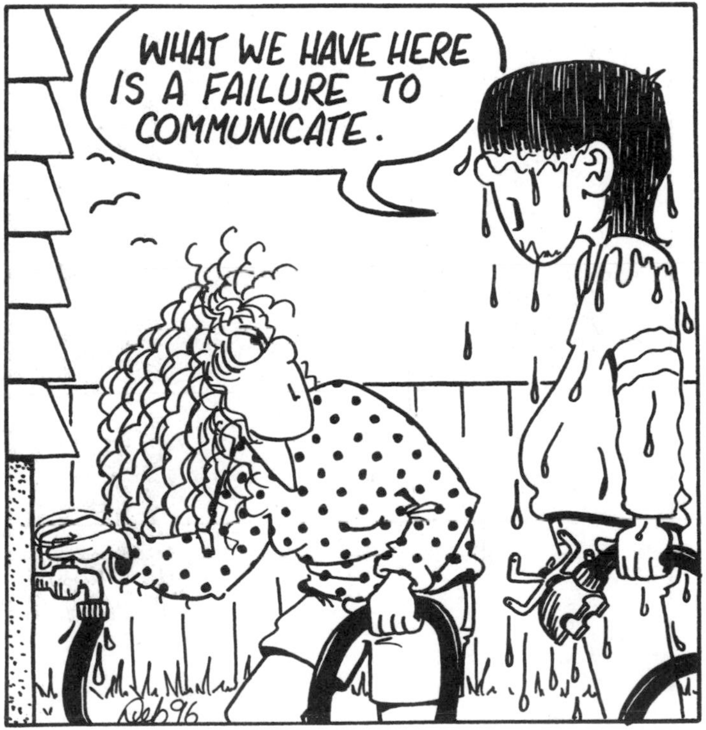
WHAT WE HAVE HERE IS A FAILURE TO COMMUNICATE.
Deb 96

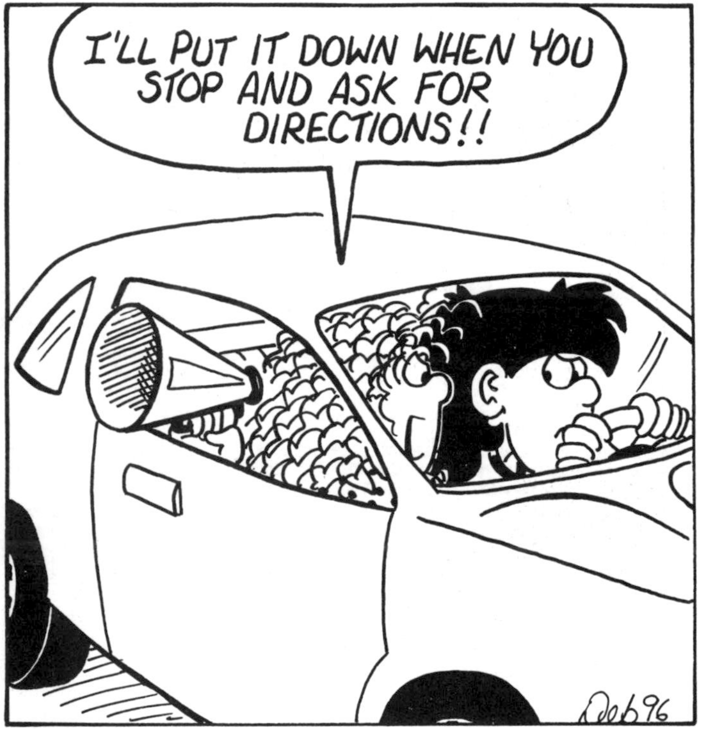
I'LL PUT IT DOWN WHEN YOU STOP AND ASK FOR DIRECTIONS!!
Deb96

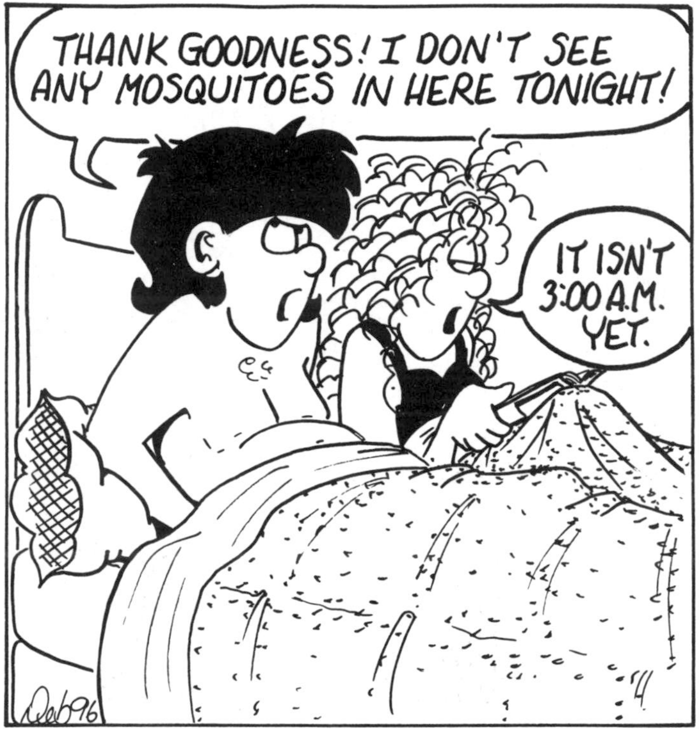
THANK GOODNESS! I DON'T SEE ANY MOSQUITOES IN HERE TONIGHT!
IT ISN'T 3:00 A.M. YET.
Deb96

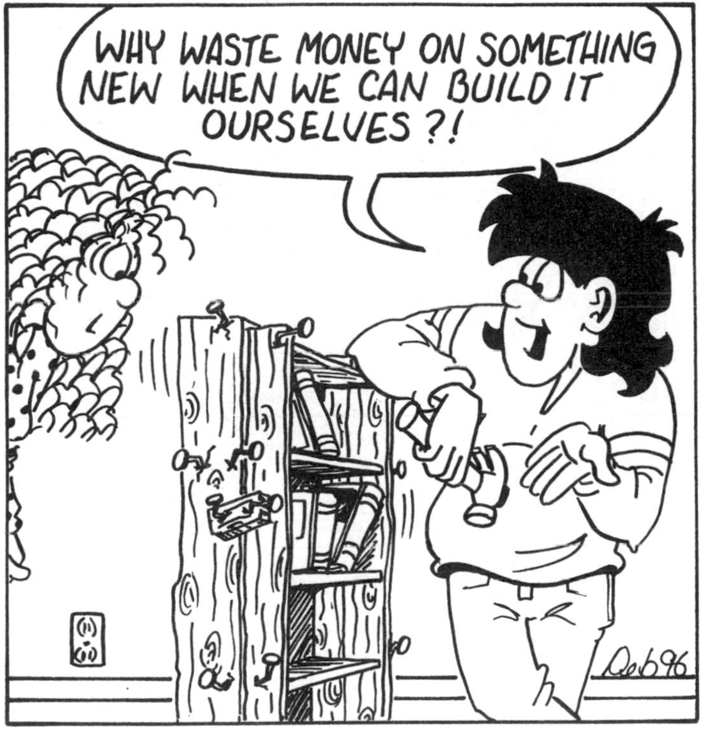
WHY WASTE MONEY ON SOMETHING NEW WHEN WE CAN BUILD IT OURSELVES ?!
Deb96

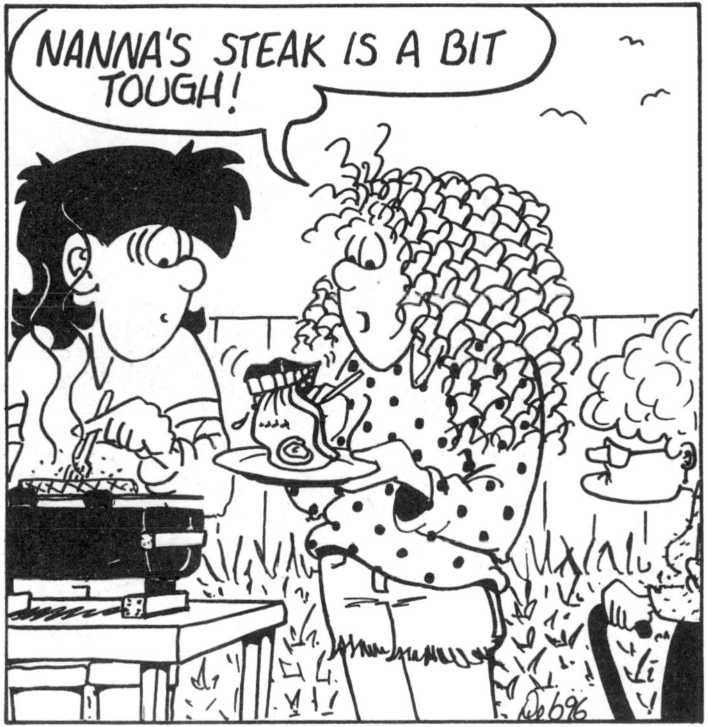
NANNA'S STEAK IS A BIT TOUGH!
Deb96

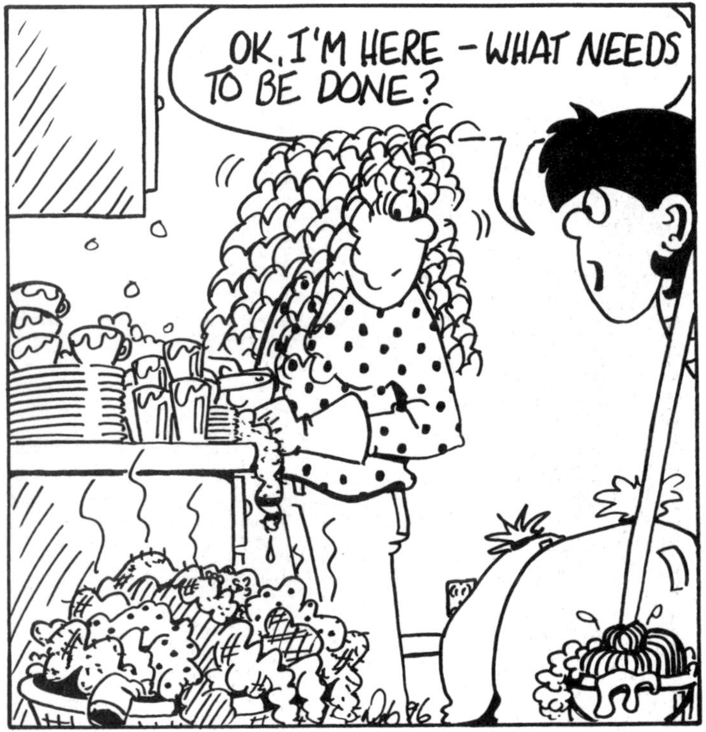
OK, I'M HERE - WHAT NEEDS TO BE DONE?
Dab96

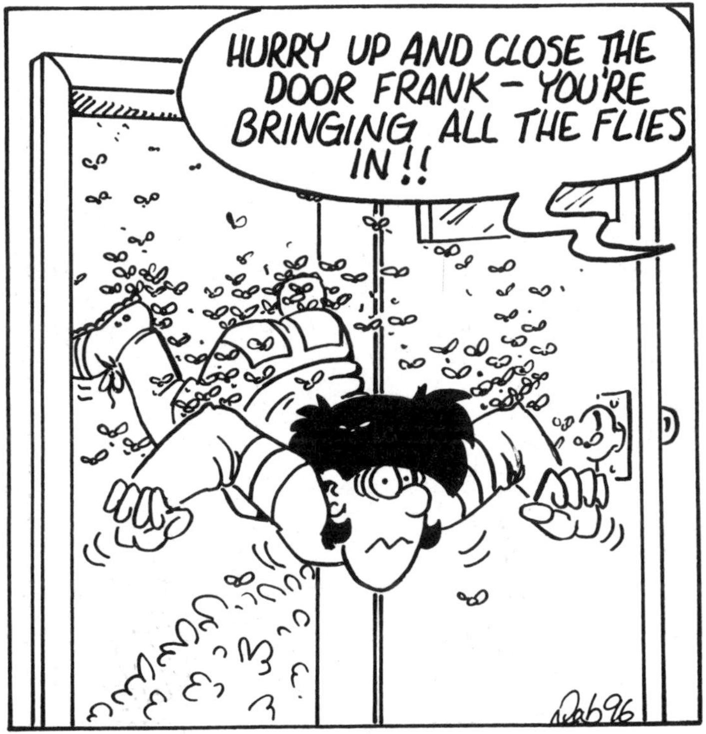
HURRY UP AND CLOSE THE DOOR FRANK - YOU'RE BRINGING ALL THE FLIES IN!!
Dab96

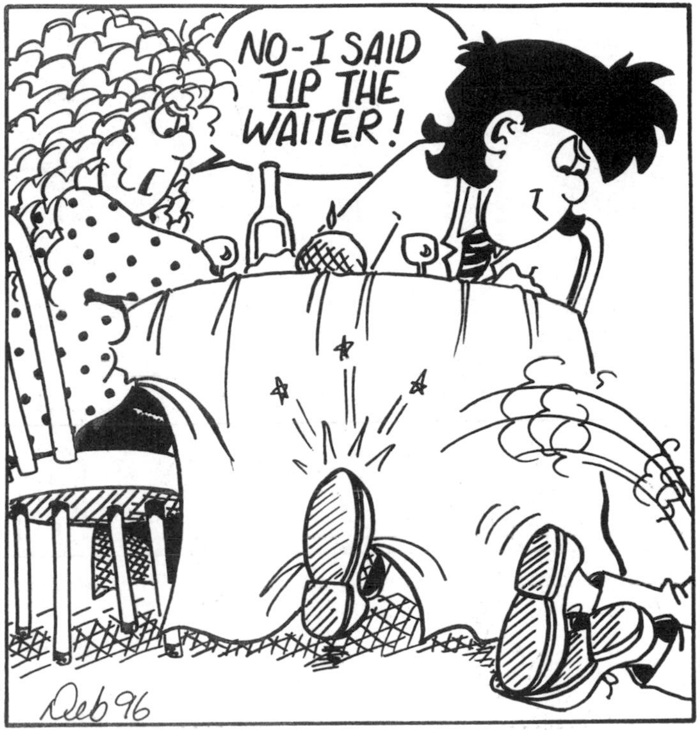
NO-I SAID TIP THE WAITER!
Deb 96

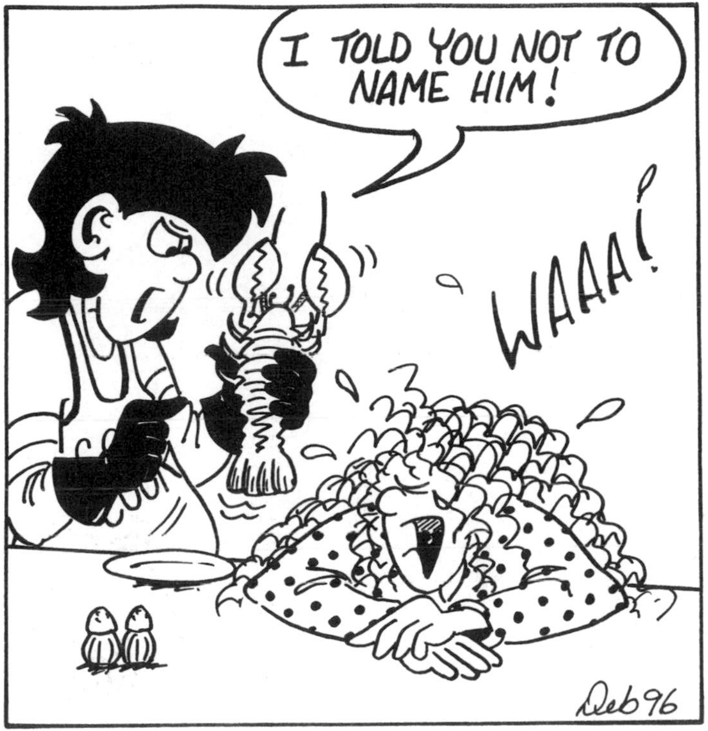
I TOLD YOU NOT TO NAME HIM!
WAAA!
Deb 96

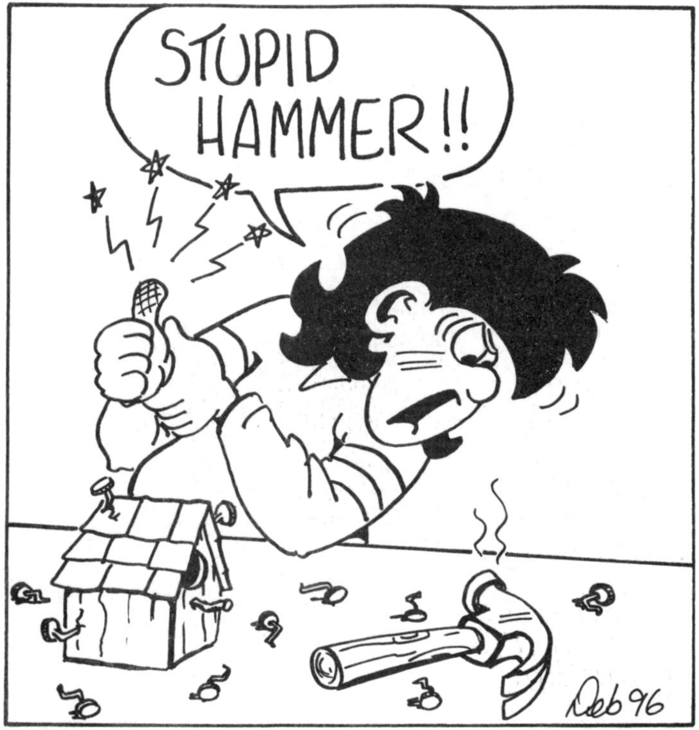
STUPID HAMMER!!
Deb 96

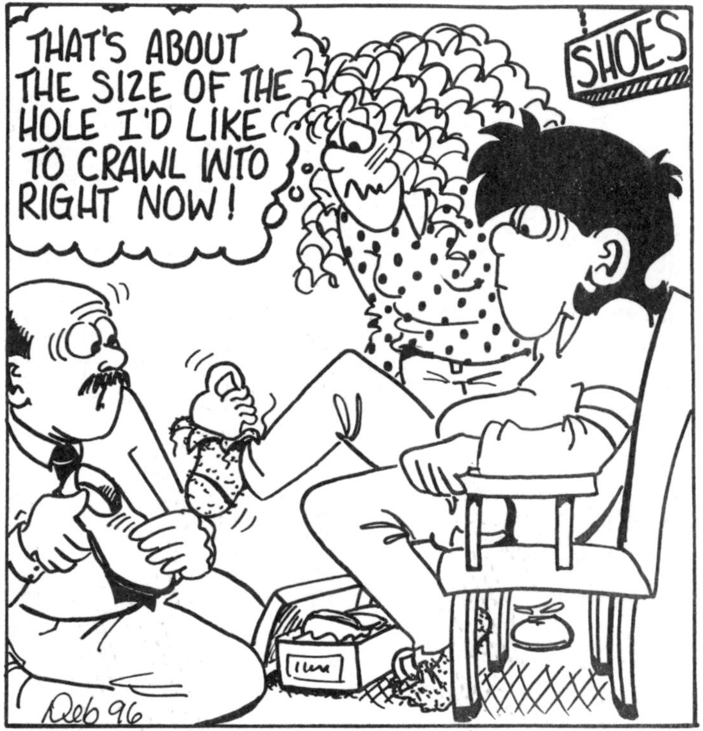
THAT'S ABOUT THE SIZE OF THE HOLE I'D LIKE TO CRAWL INTO RIGHT NOW!
SHOES
Deb 96

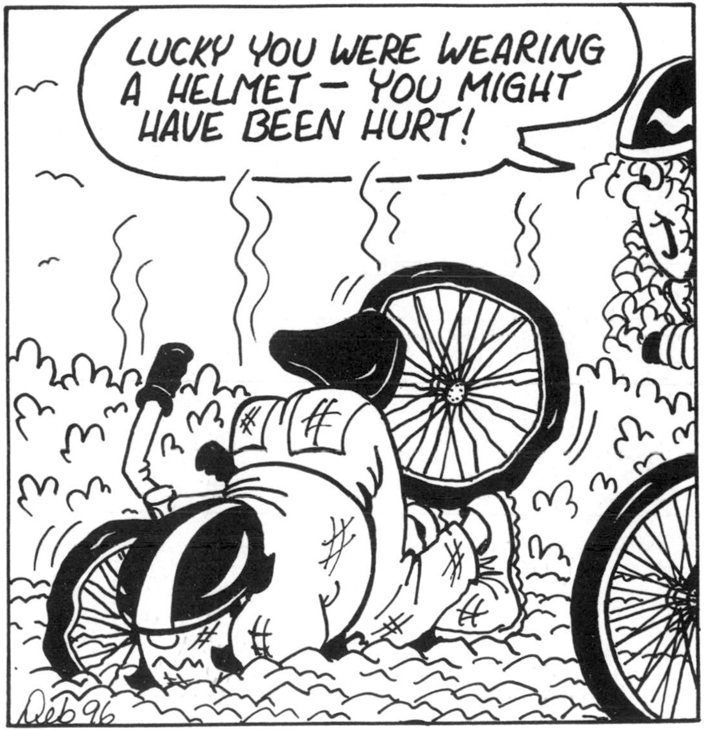
LUCKY YOU WERE WEARING A HELMET — YOU MIGHT HAVE BEEN HURT!
Deb 96

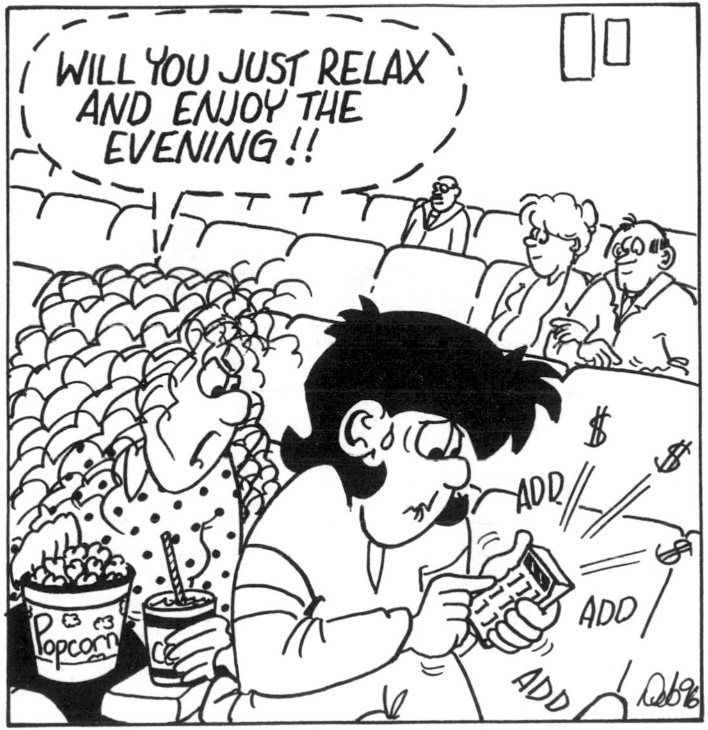
WILL YOU JUST RELAX AND ENJOY THE EVENING!!
Popcorn
ADD
ADD
ADD
$
$
$
Deb 96

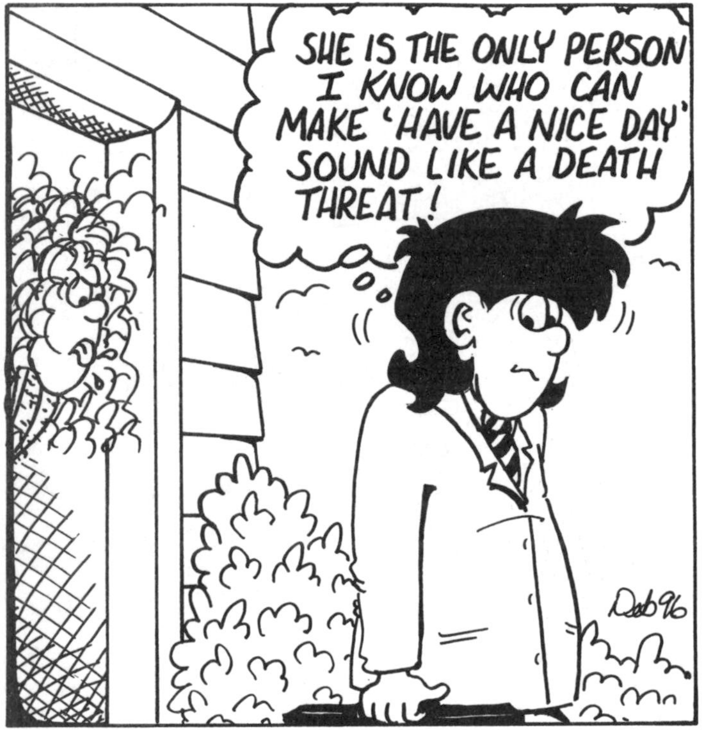
SHE IS THE ONLY PERSON I KNOW WHO CAN MAKE 'HAVE A NICE DAY' SOUND LIKE A DEATH THREAT!
Deb96

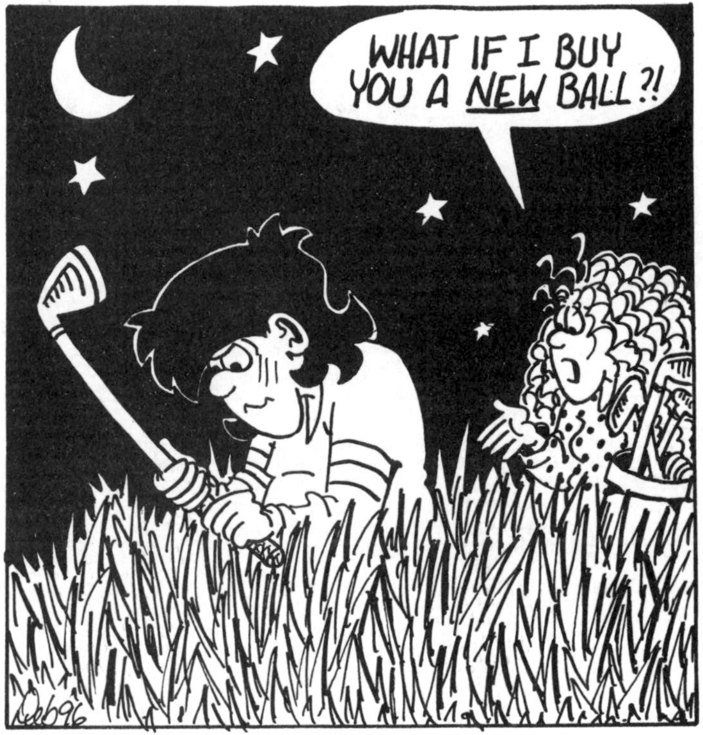
WHAT IF I BUY YOU A NEW BALL?!
Deb96

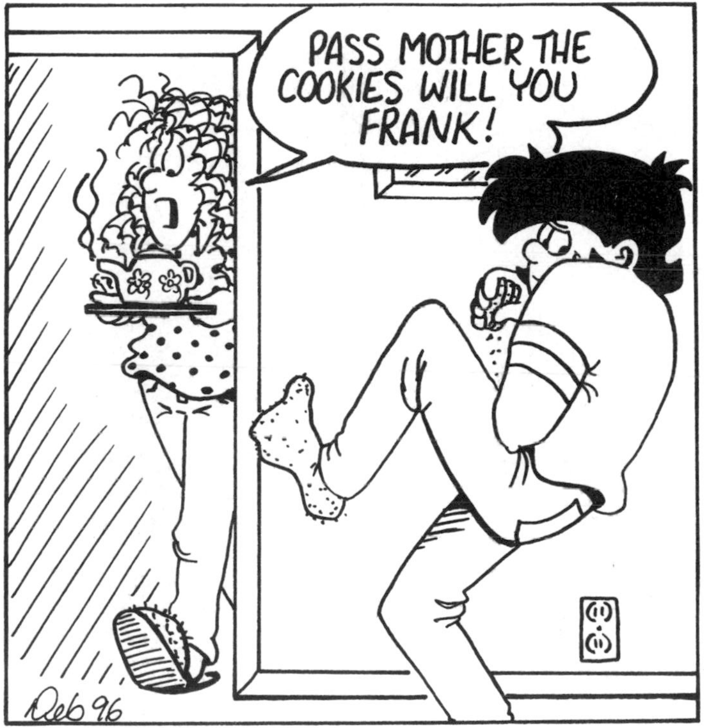
PASS MOTHER THE COOKIES WILL YOU FRANK!
Deb 96

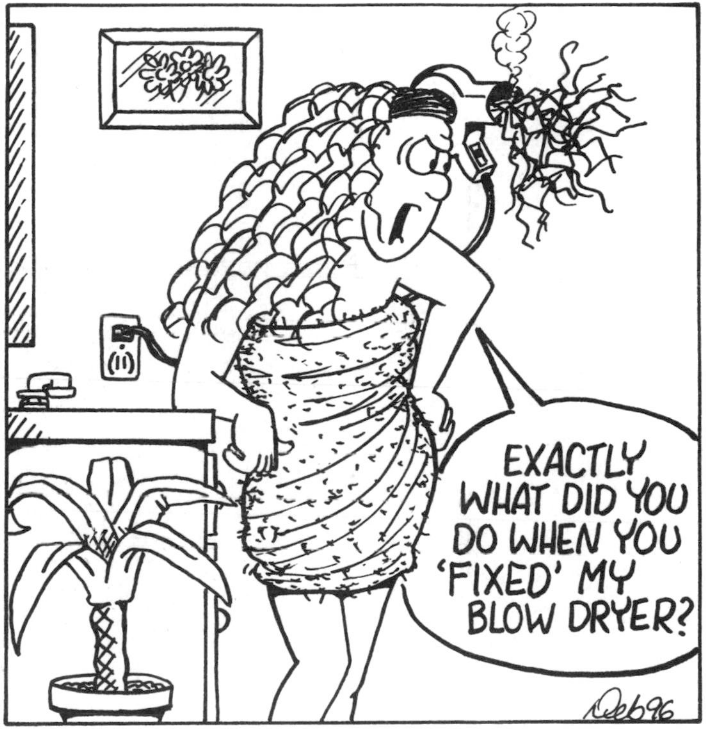
EXACTLY WHAT DID YOU DO WHEN YOU 'FIXED' MY BLOW DRYER?
Deb96

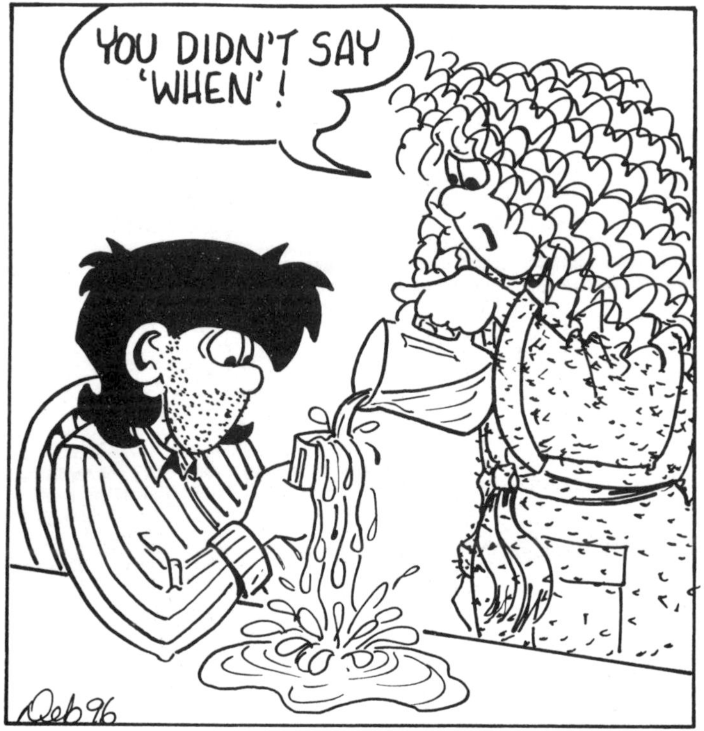
YOU DIDN'T SAY 'WHEN'!
Deb96

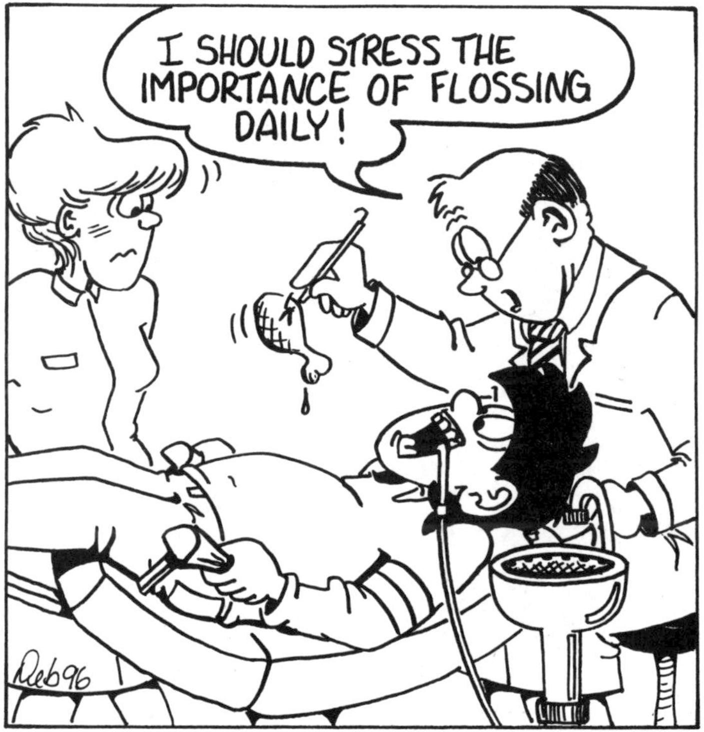
I SHOULD STRESS THE IMPORTANCE OF FLOSSING DAILY!
Deb96

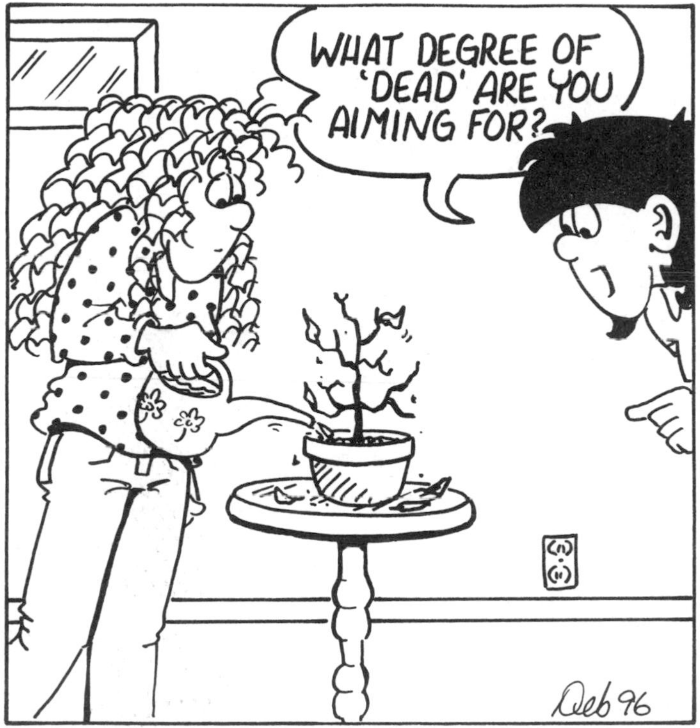
WHAT DEGREE OF 'DEAD' ARE YOU AIMING FOR?
Deb 96

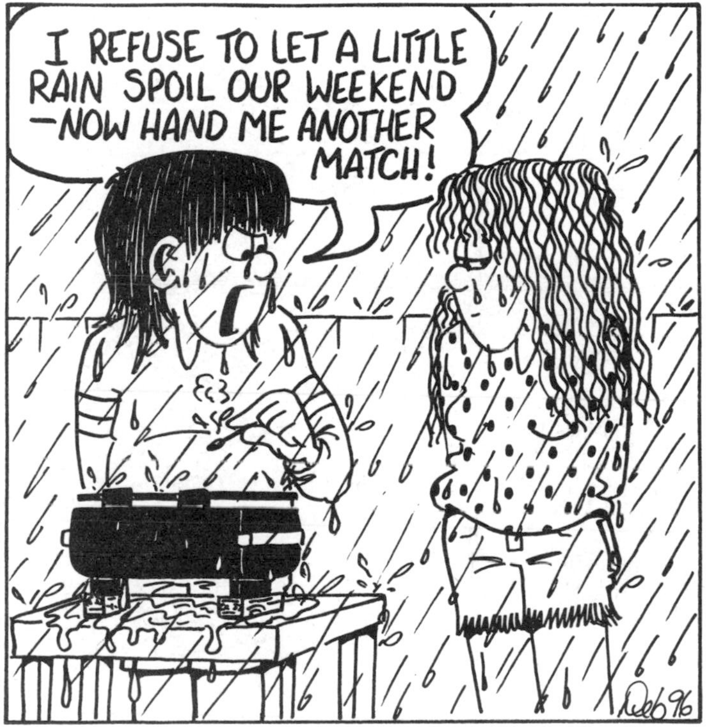
I REFUSE TO LET A LITTLE RAIN SPOIL OUR WEEKEND —NOW HAND ME ANOTHER MATCH!
Deb 96

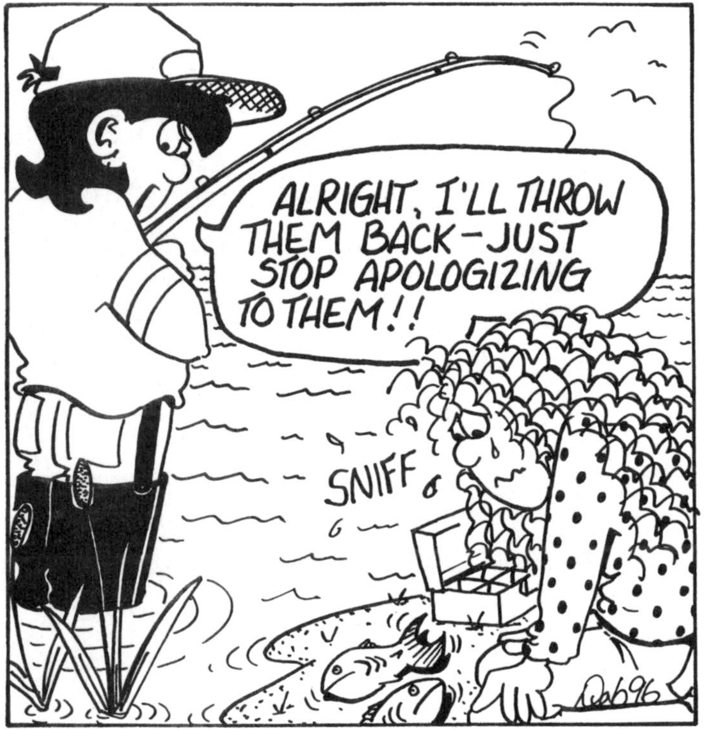
ALRIGHT, I'LL THROW THEM BACK - JUST STOP APOLOGIZING TO THEM!!
SNIFF
Dab96

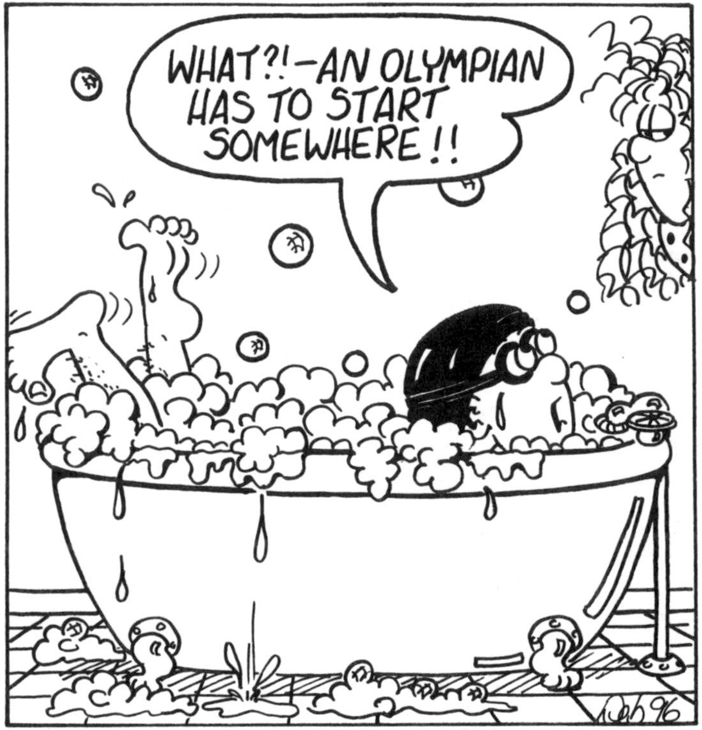
WHAT?! - AN OLYMPIAN HAS TO START SOMEWHERE!!
Dab96

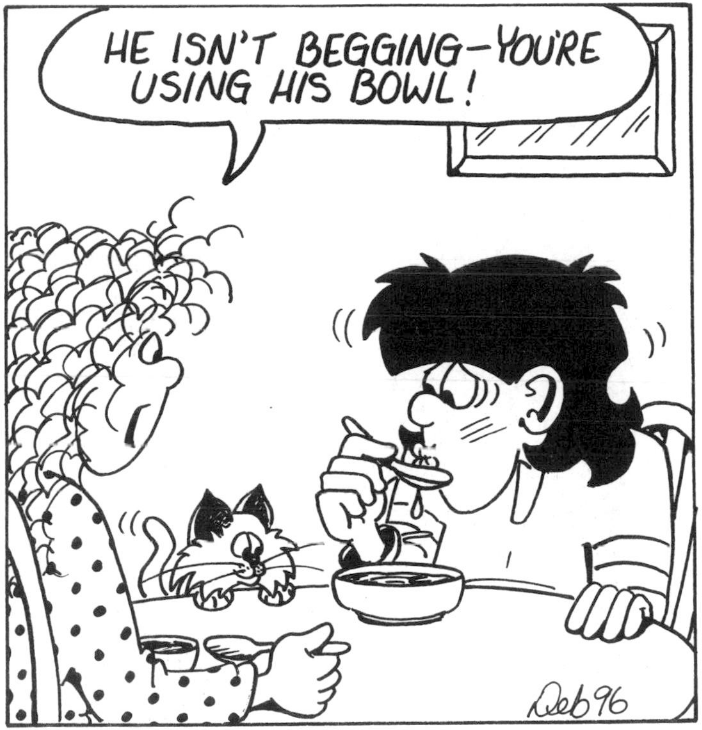
HE ISN'T BEGGING—YOU'RE USING HIS BOWL!
Deb96

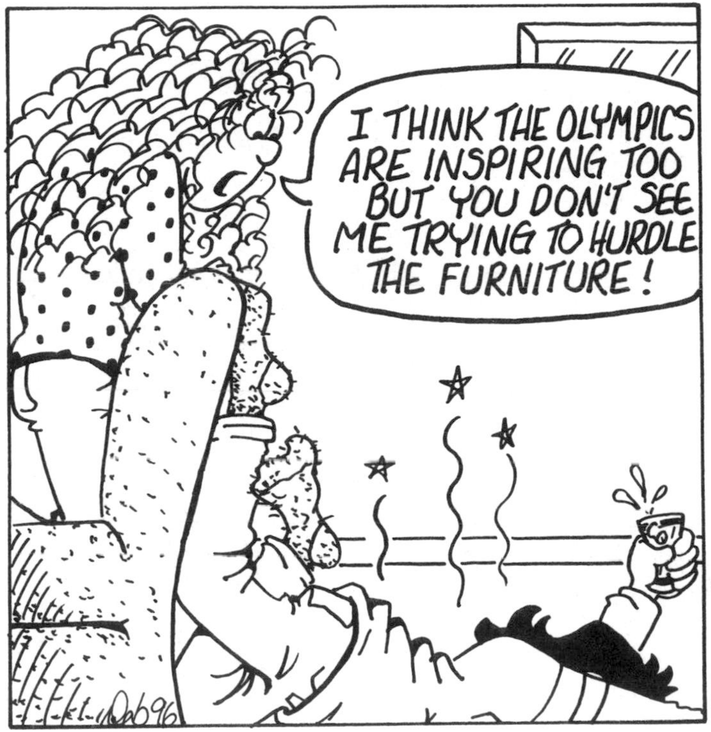
I THINK THE OLYMPICS ARE INSPIRING TOO BUT YOU DON'T SEE ME TRYING TO HURDLE THE FURNITURE!
Deb96

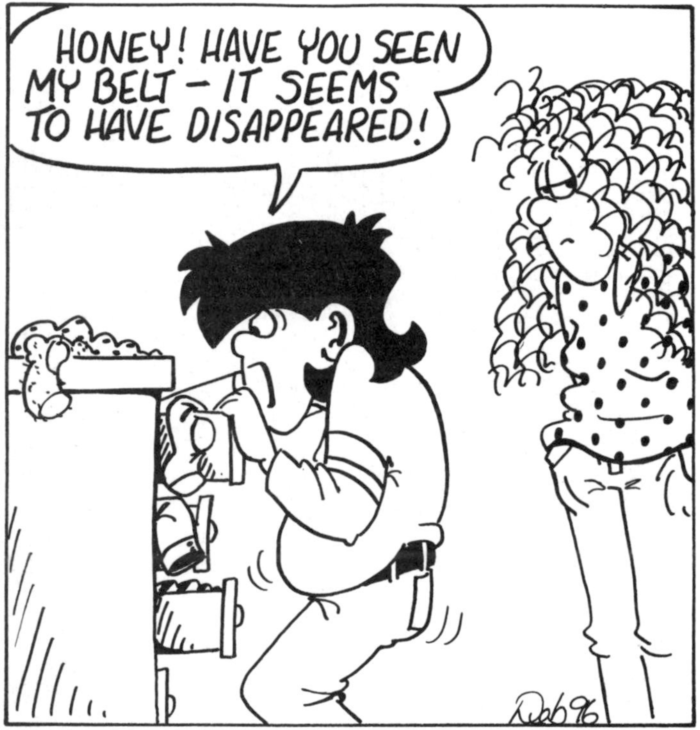
HONEY! HAVE YOU SEEN MY BELT – IT SEEMS TO HAVE DISAPPEARED!
Deb 96

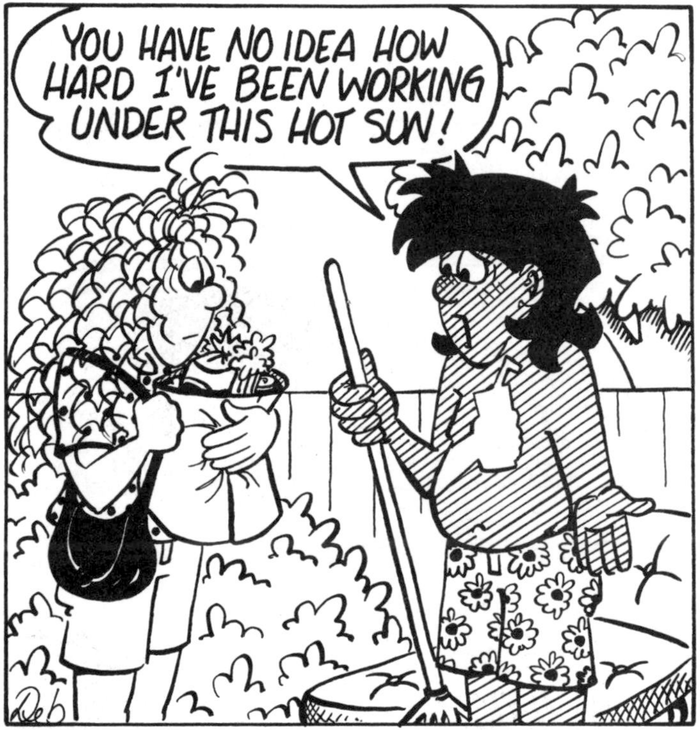
YOU HAVE NO IDEA HOW HARD I'VE BEEN WORKING UNDER THIS HOT SUN!
Deb

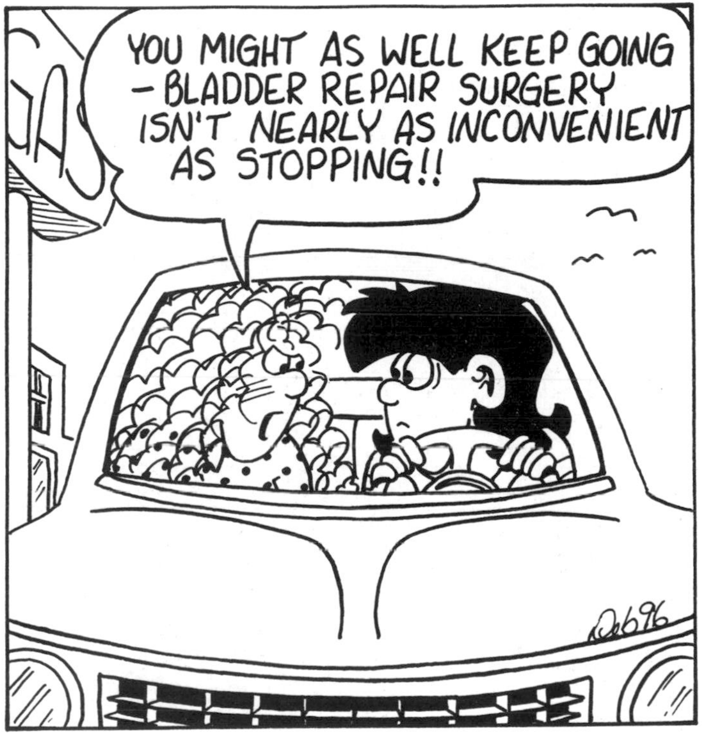
GAS
YOU MIGHT AS WELL KEEP GOING - BLADDER REPAIR SURGERY ISN'T NEARLY AS INCONVENIENT AS STOPPING!!
Deb96

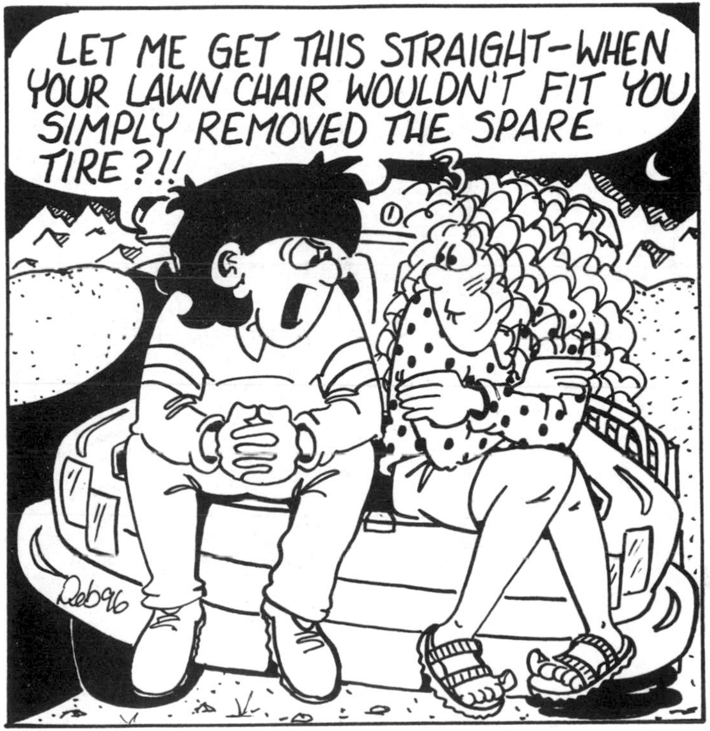
LET ME GET THIS STRAIGHT—WHEN YOUR LAWN CHAIR WOULDN'T FIT YOU SIMPLY REMOVED THE SPARE TIRE?!!
Deb96

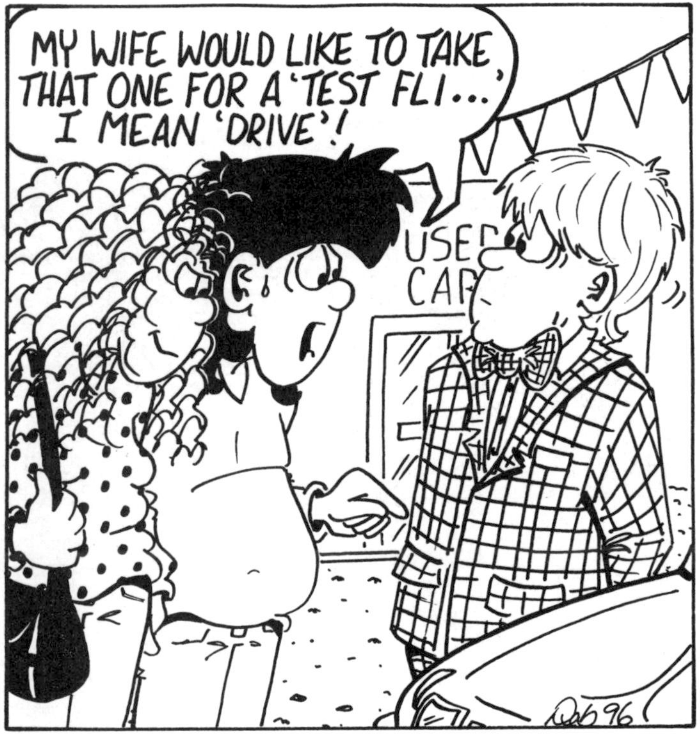
MY WIFE WOULD LIKE TO TAKE THAT ONE FOR A 'TEST FLI...' I MEAN 'DRIVE'!
USED CAR

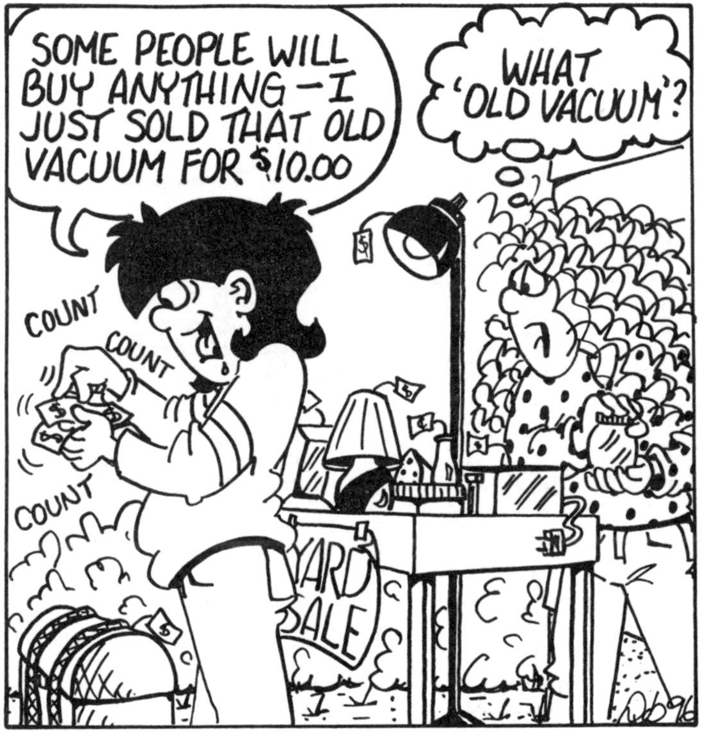
SOME PEOPLE WILL BUY ANYTHING – I JUST SOLD THAT OLD VACUUM FOR $10.00
WHAT 'OLD VACUUM'?
COUNT
COUNT
COUNT
YARD SALE

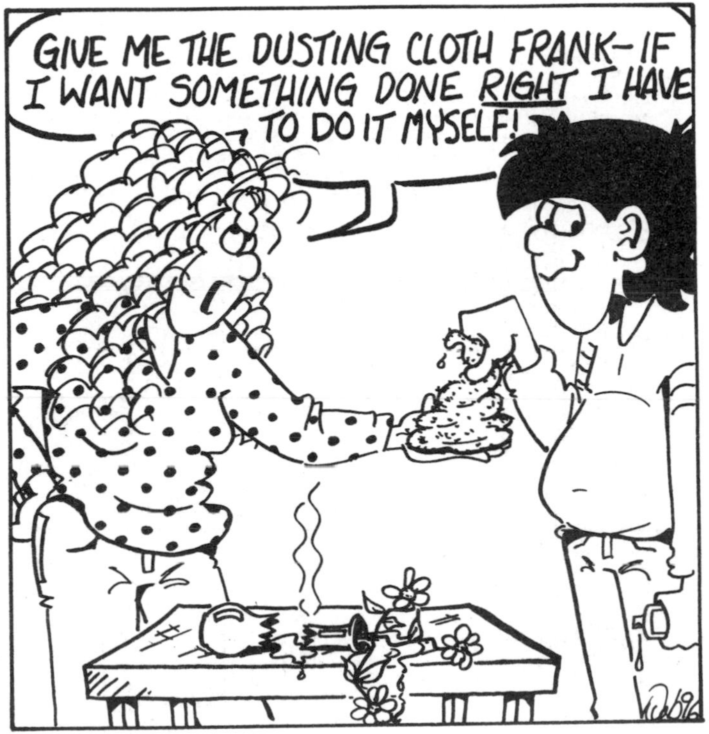
GIVE ME THE DUSTING CLOTH FRANK– IF I WANT SOMETHING DONE RIGHT I HAVE TO DO IT MYSELF!

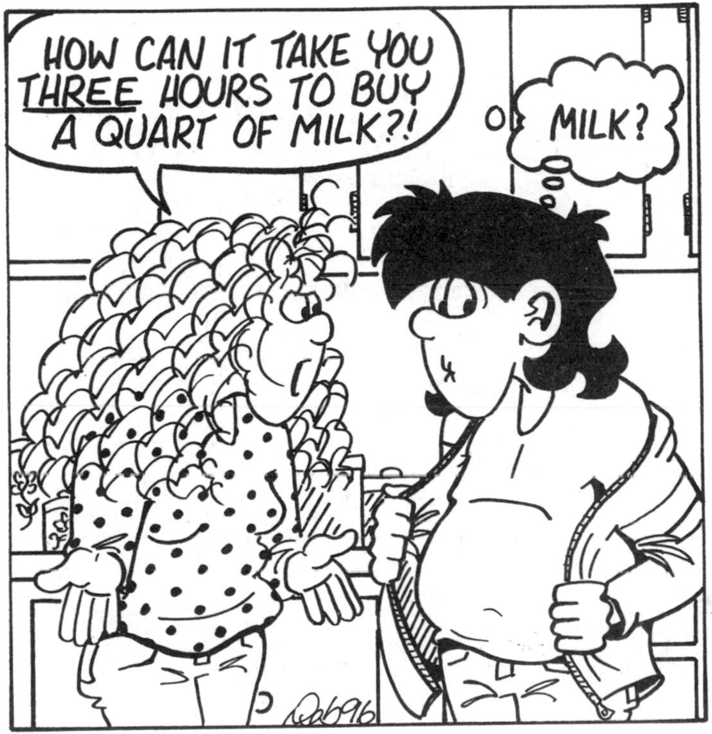
HOW CAN IT TAKE YOU THREE HOURS TO BUY A QUART OF MILK?!
MILK?

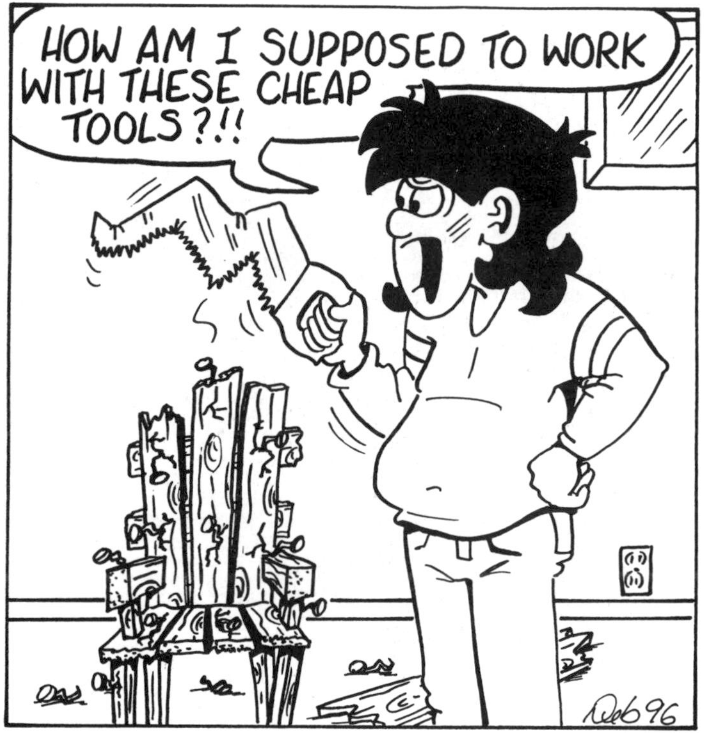
HOW AM I SUPPOSED TO WORK WITH THESE CHEAP TOOLS?!!
Deb 96

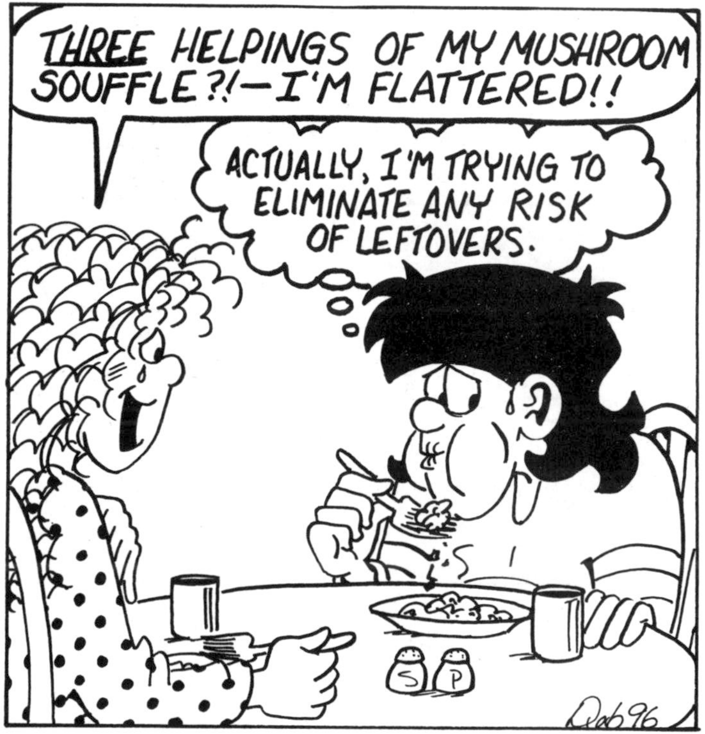
THREE HELPINGS OF MY MUSHROOM SOUFFLE?!—I'M FLATTERED!!
ACTUALLY, I'M TRYING TO ELIMINATE ANY RISK OF LEFTOVERS.
S
P
Deb 96

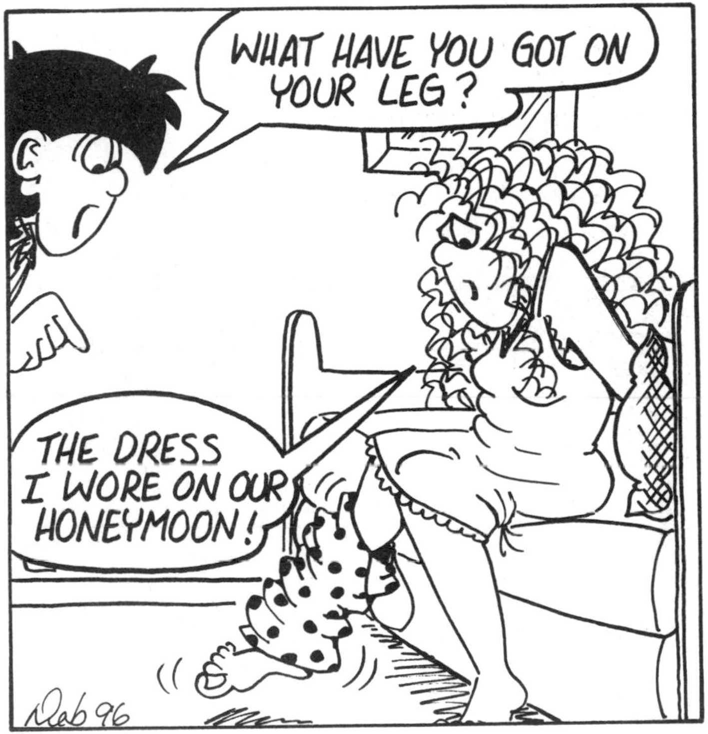
WHAT HAVE YOU GOT ON YOUR LEG?
THE DRESS I WORE ON OUR HONEYMOON!
Deb 96

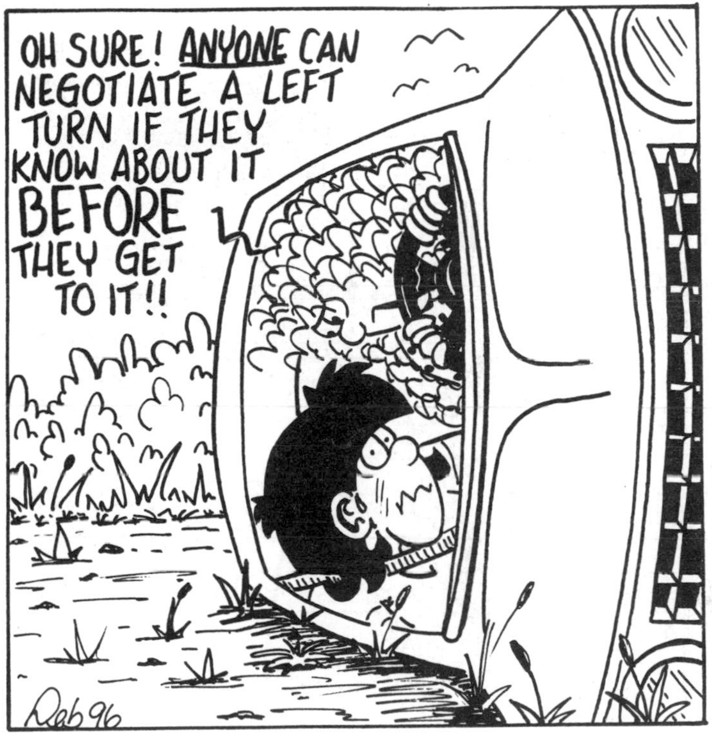
OH SURE! ANYONE CAN NEGOTIATE A LEFT TURN IF THEY KNOW ABOUT IT BEFORE THEY GET TO IT!!
Deb 96

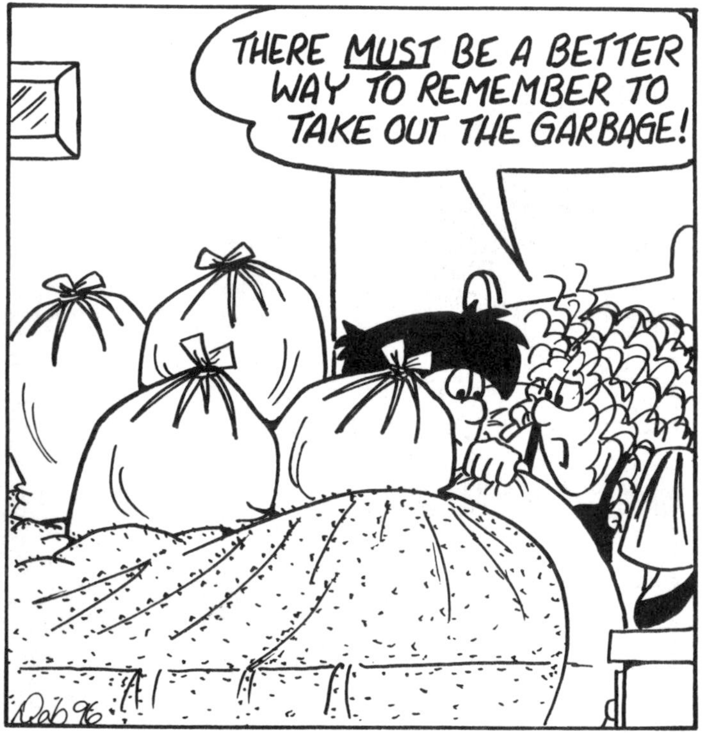
THERE MUST BE A BETTER WAY TO REMEMBER TO TAKE OUT THE GARBAGE!
Deb 96

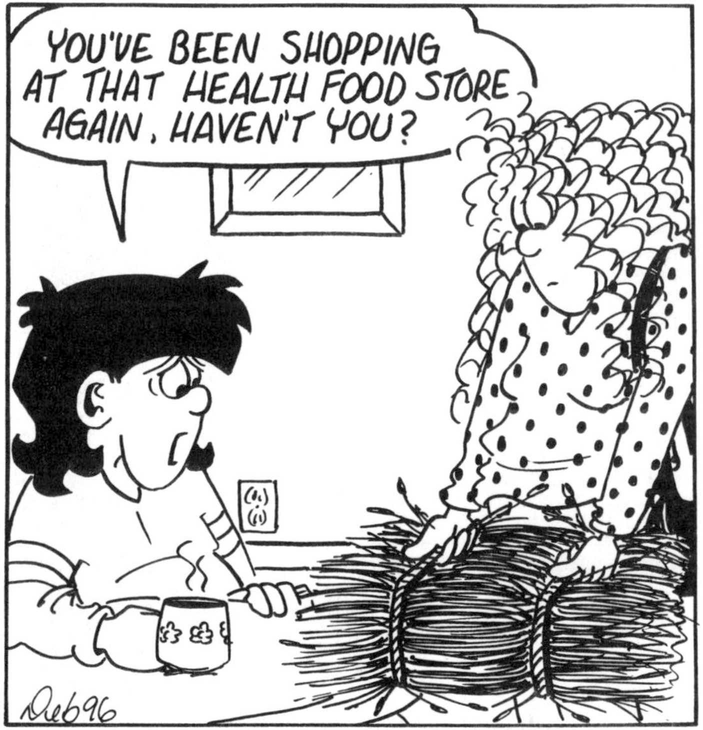
YOU'VE BEEN SHOPPING AT THAT HEALTH FOOD STORE AGAIN, HAVEN'T YOU?
Deb 96

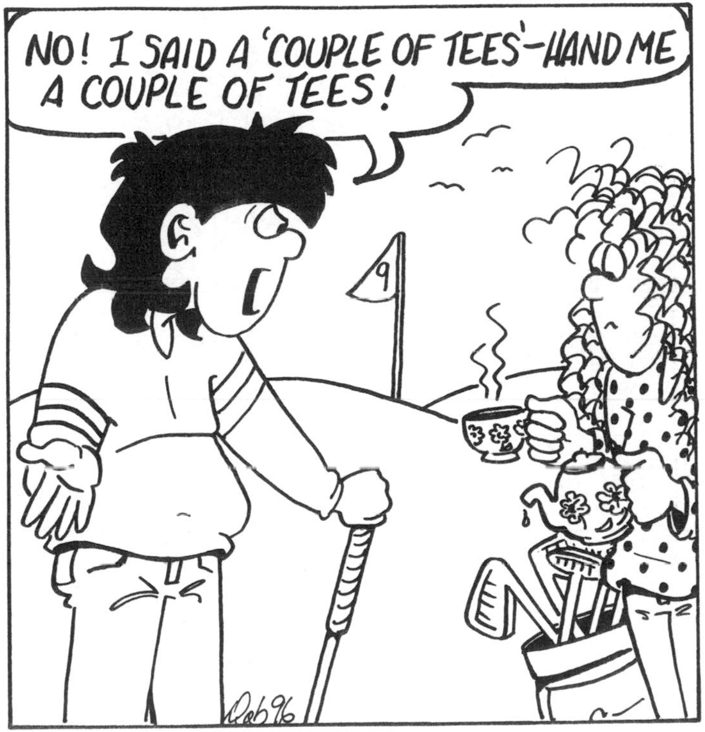
NO! I SAID A 'COUPLE OF TEES'-HAND ME A COUPLE OF TEES!

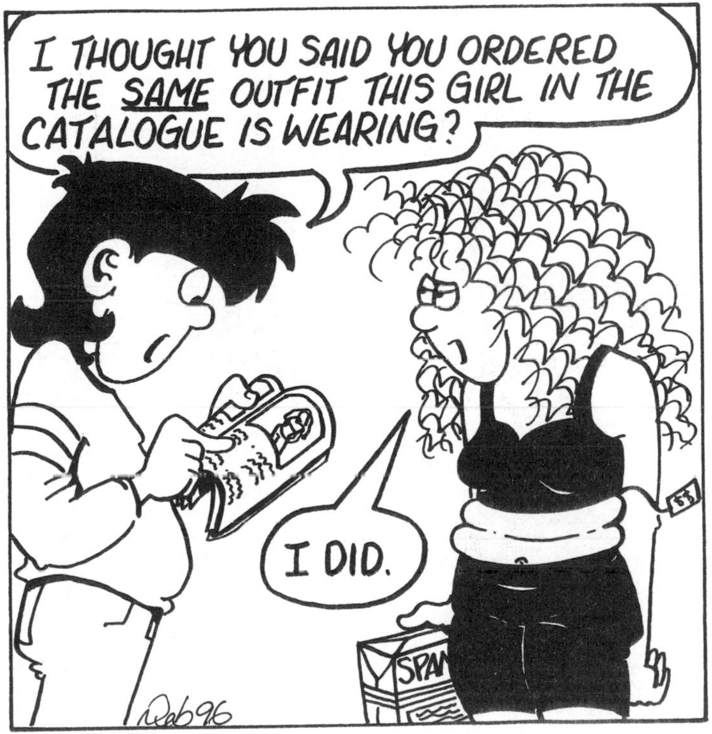
I THOUGHT YOU SAID YOU ORDERED THE SAME OUTFIT THIS GIRL IN THE CATALOGUE IS WEARING?
I DID.

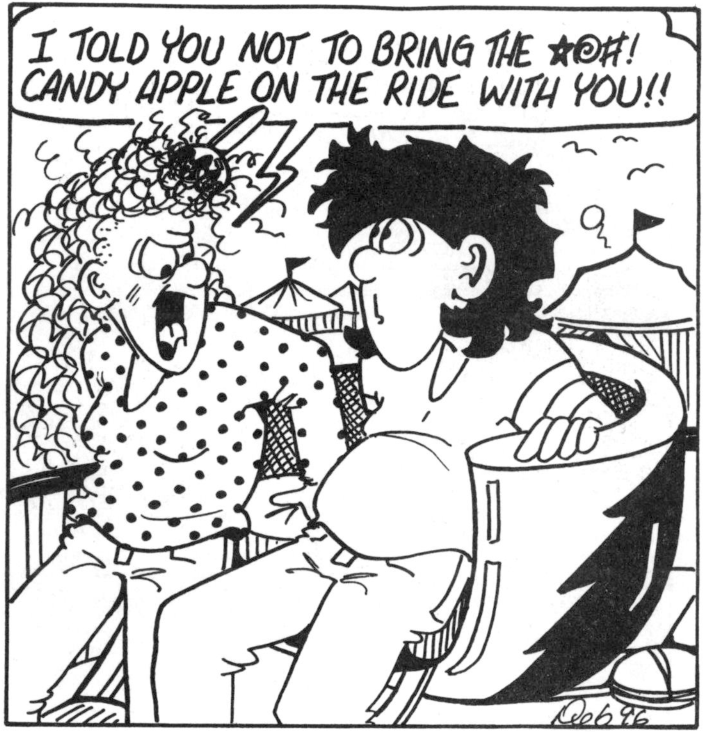
I TOLD YOU NOT TO BRING THE *@#! CANDY APPLE ON THE RIDE WITH YOU!!
Deb 96

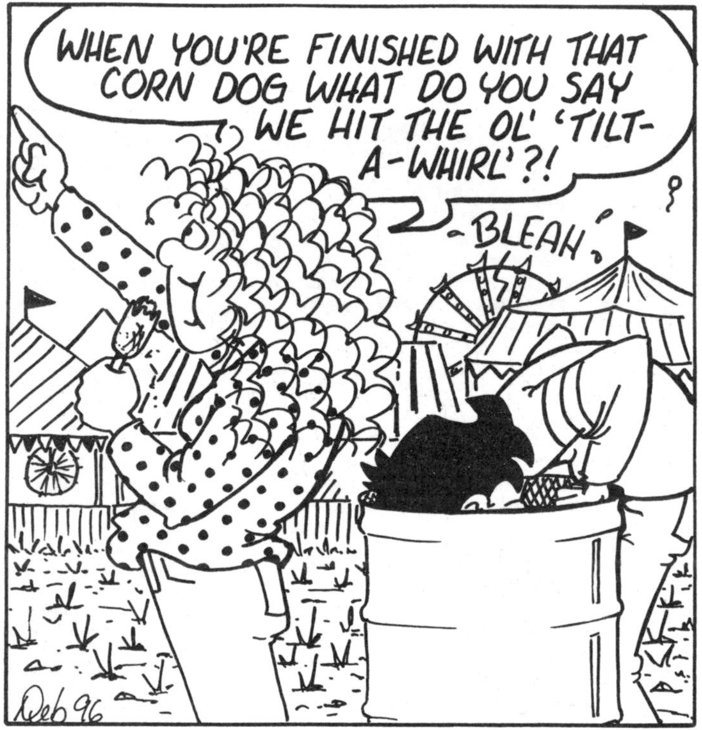
WHEN YOU'RE FINISHED WITH THAT CORN DOG WHAT DO YOU SAY WE HIT THE OL' 'TILT-A-WHIRL'?!
-BLEAH-
Deb 96

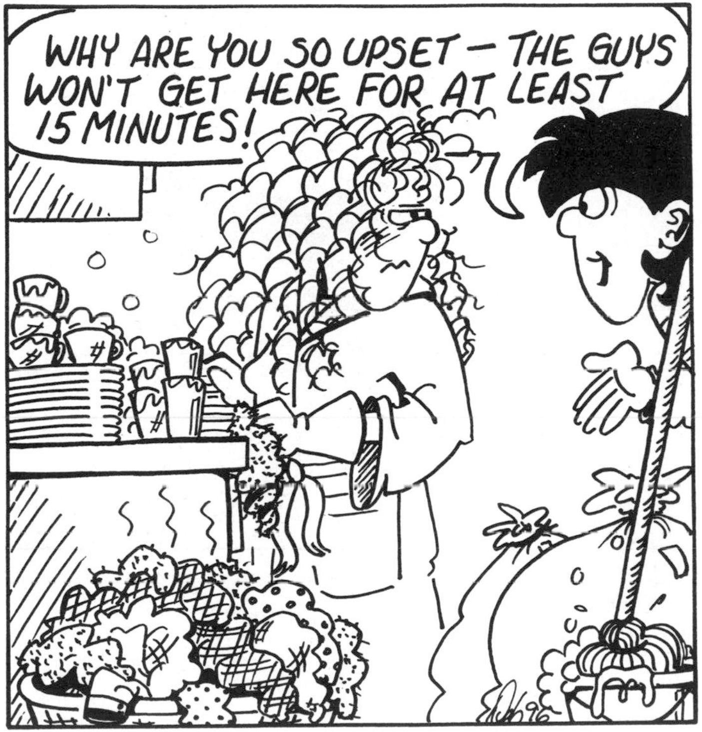
WHY ARE YOU SO UPSET — THE GUYS WON'T GET HERE FOR AT LEAST 15 MINUTES!

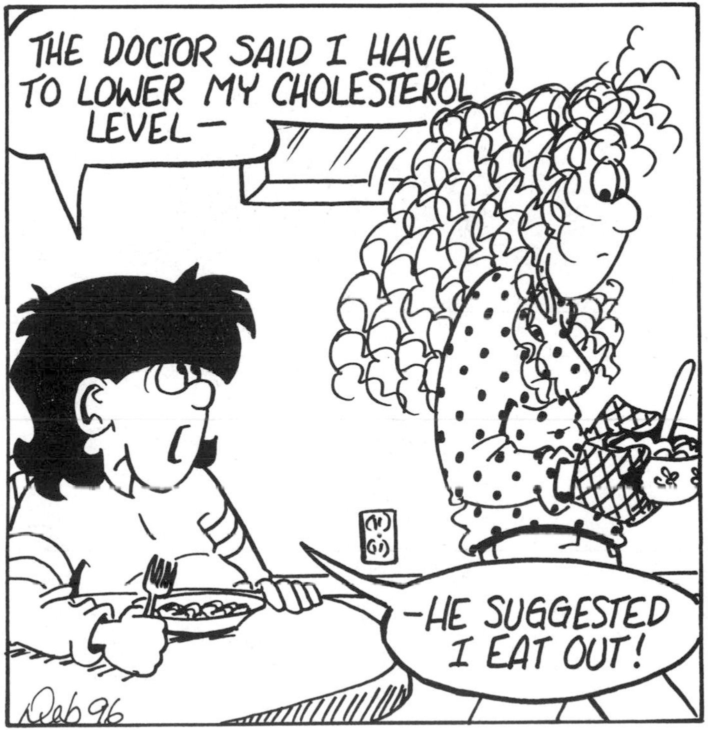
THE DOCTOR SAID I HAVE TO LOWER MY CHOLESTEROL LEVEL —
—HE SUGGESTED I EAT OUT!

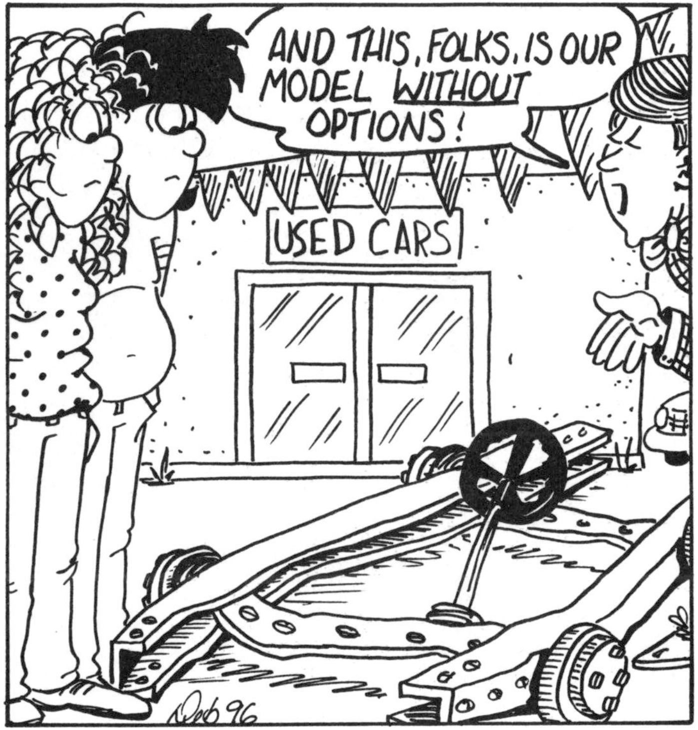
AND THIS, FOLKS, IS OUR MODEL WITHOUT OPTIONS!
USED CARS

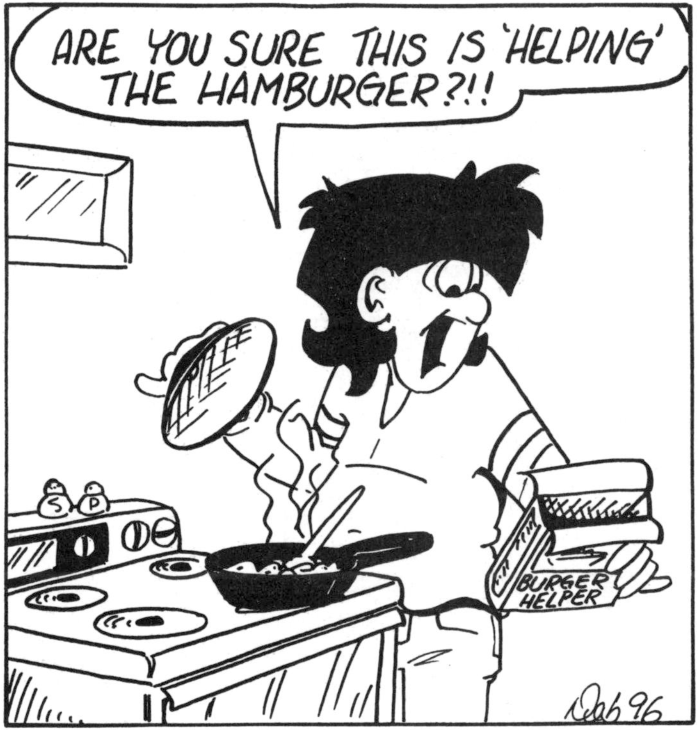
ARE YOU SURE THIS IS 'HELPING' THE HAMBURGER?!!
BURGER HELPER

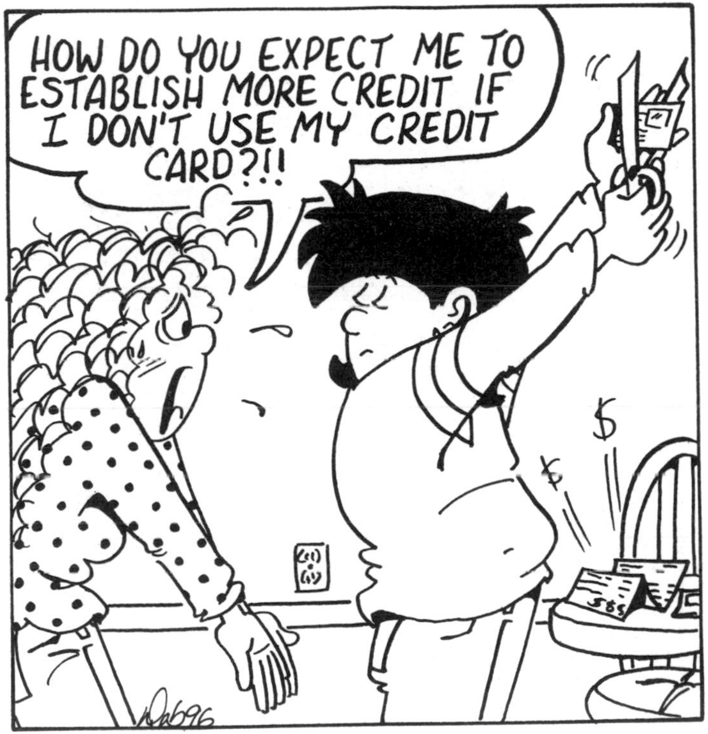
HOW DO YOU EXPECT ME TO ESTABLISH MORE CREDIT IF I DON'T USE MY CREDIT CARD?!!

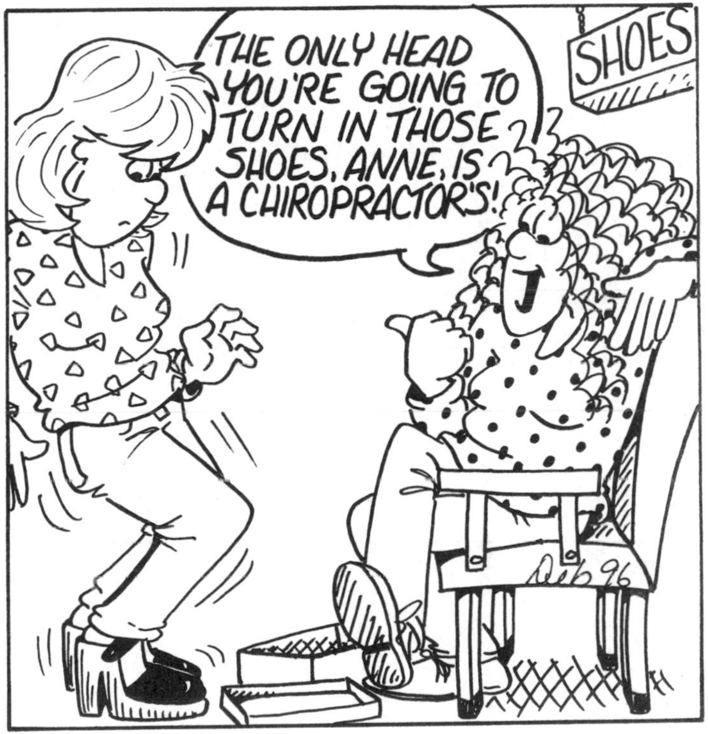
SHOES
THE ONLY HEAD YOU'RE GOING TO TURN IN THOSE SHOES, ANNE, IS A CHIROPRACTOR'S!

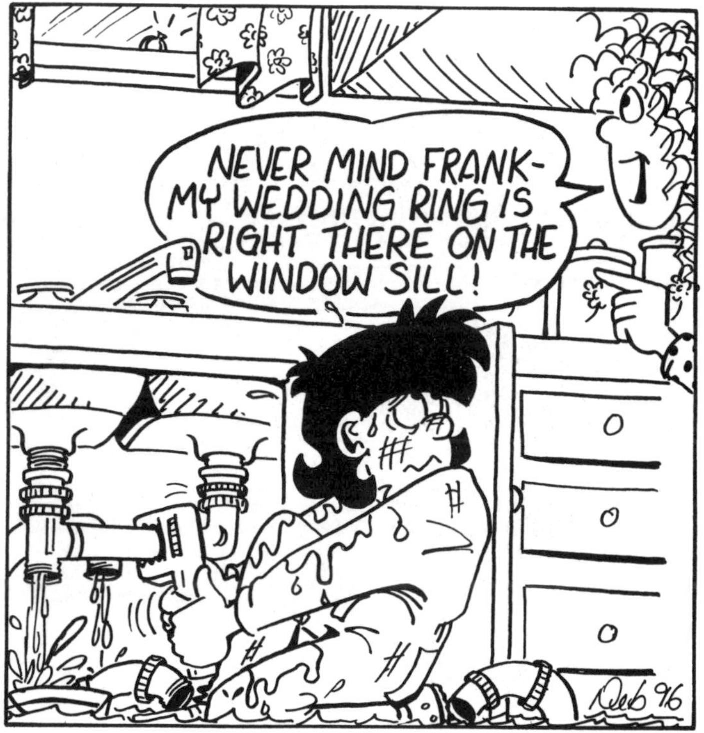
NEVER MIND FRANK- MY WEDDING RING IS RIGHT THERE ON THE WINDOW SILL!
Deb 96

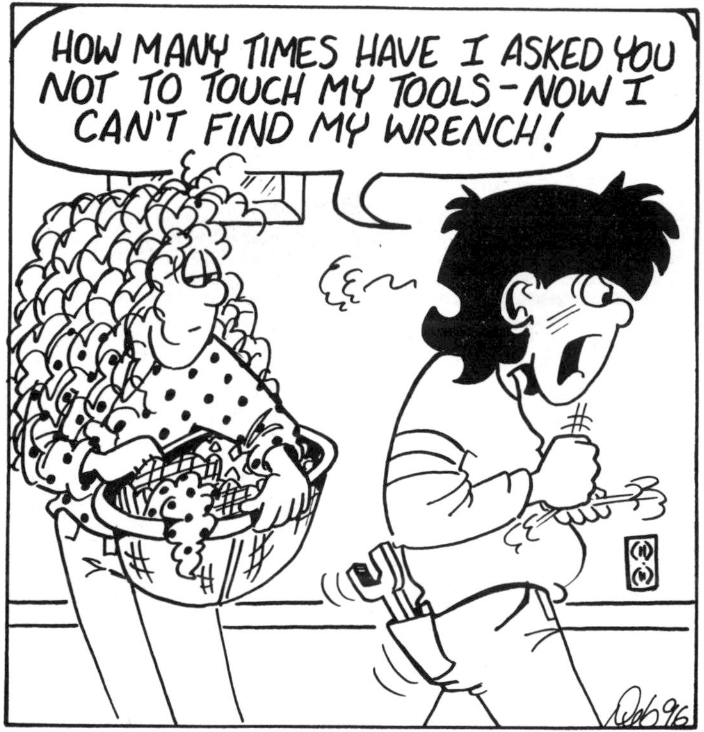
HOW MANY TIMES HAVE I ASKED YOU NOT TO TOUCH MY TOOLS - NOW I CAN'T FIND MY WRENCH!
Deb 96

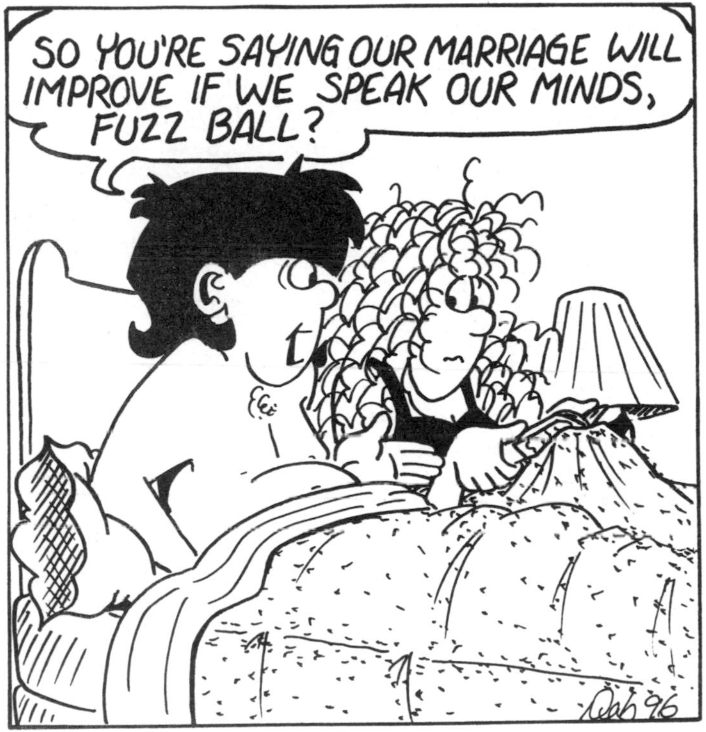
SO YOU'RE SAYING OUR MARRIAGE WILL IMPROVE IF WE SPEAK OUR MINDS, FUZZ BALL?

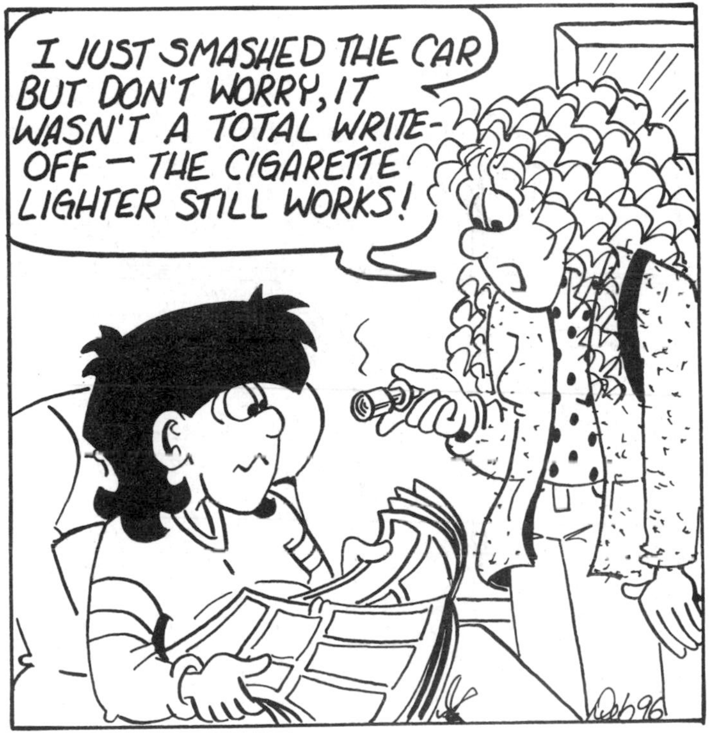
I JUST SMASHED THE CAR BUT DON'T WORRY, IT WASN'T A TOTAL WRITE-OFF — THE CIGARETTE LIGHTER STILL WORKS!

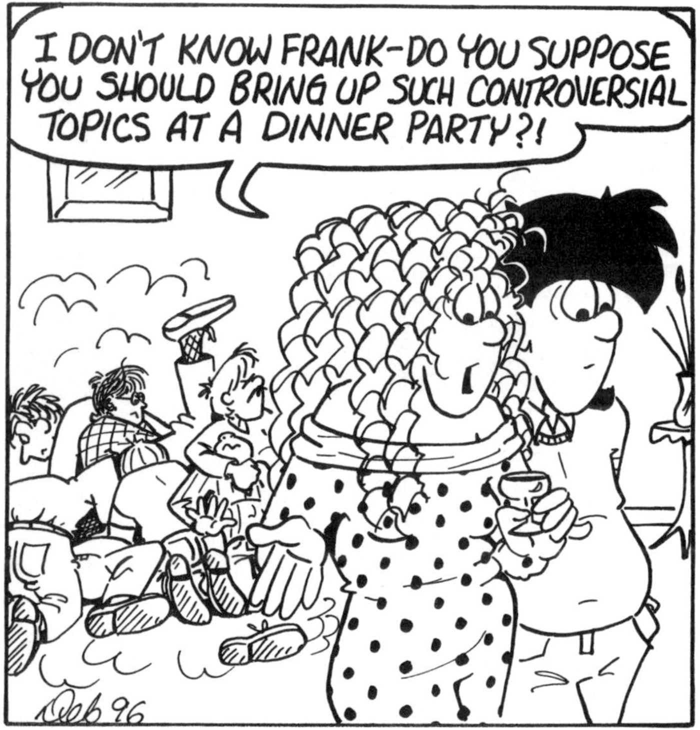
I DON'T KNOW FRANK-DO YOU SUPPOSE YOU SHOULD BRING UP SUCH CONTROVERSIAL TOPICS AT A DINNER PARTY?!
Deb 96

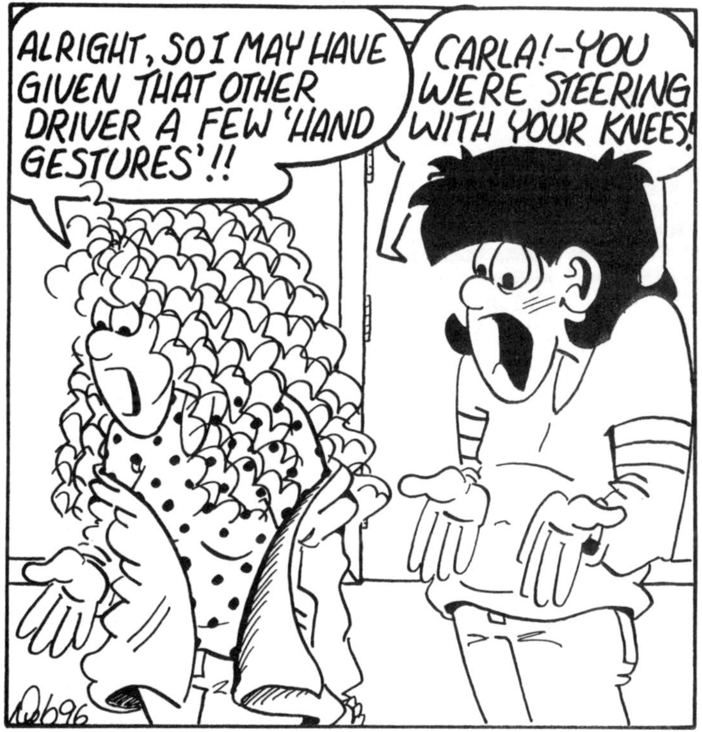
ALRIGHT, SO I MAY HAVE GIVEN THAT OTHER DRIVER A FEW 'HAND GESTURES'!!
CARLA!-YOU WERE STEERING WITH YOUR KNEES!
Deb96

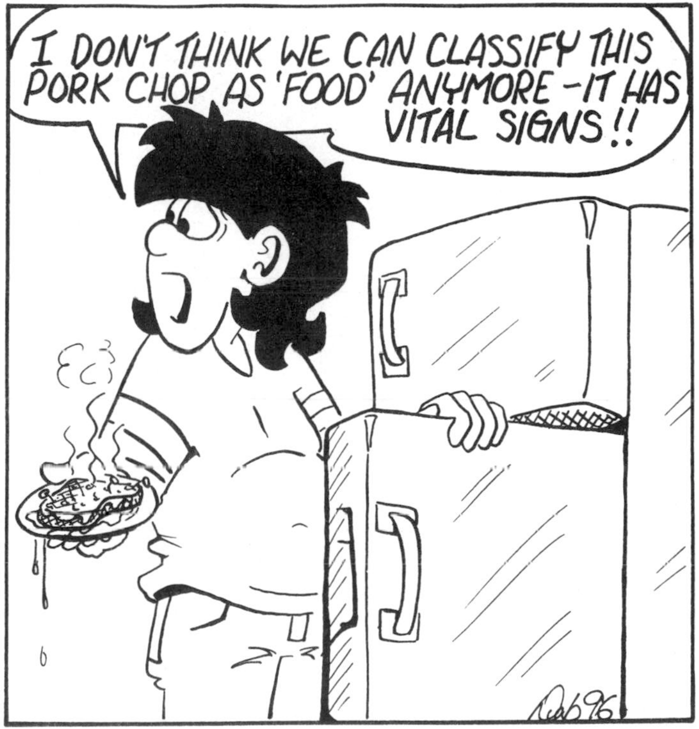
I DON'T THINK WE CAN CLASSIFY THIS PORK CHOP AS 'FOOD' ANYMORE - IT HAS VITAL SIGNS!!
Deb96

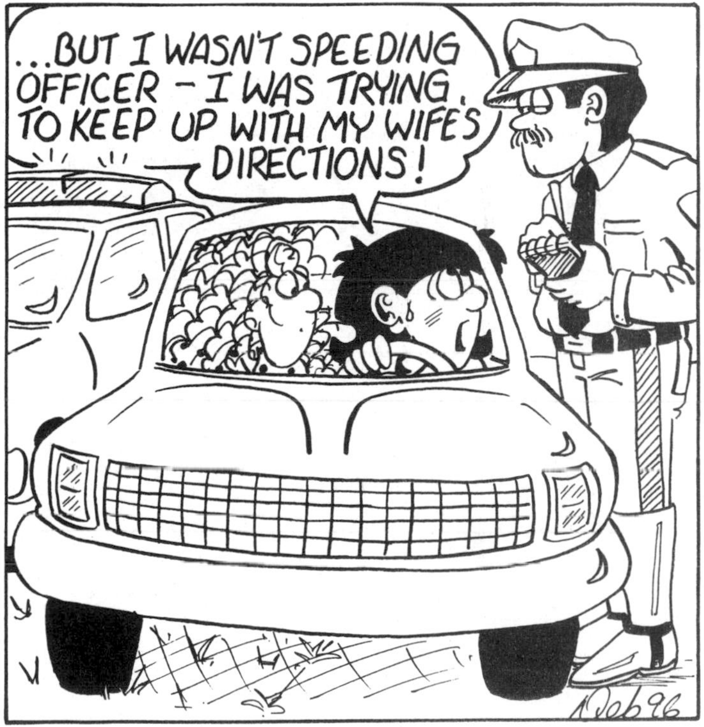
...BUT I WASN'T SPEEDING OFFICER - I WAS TRYING TO KEEP UP WITH MY WIFE'S DIRECTIONS!
Deb96

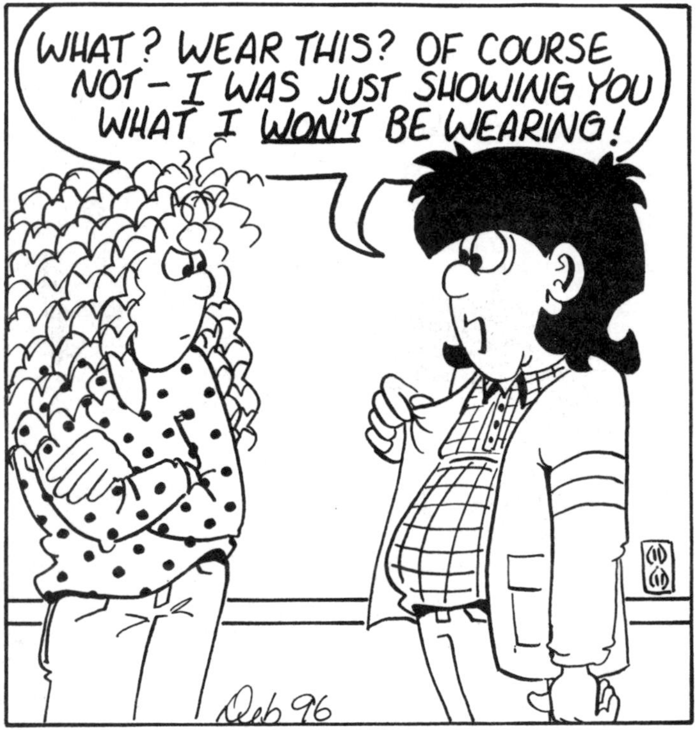
WHAT? WEAR THIS? OF COURSE NOT– I WAS JUST SHOWING YOU WHAT I WON'T BE WEARING!
Deb 96

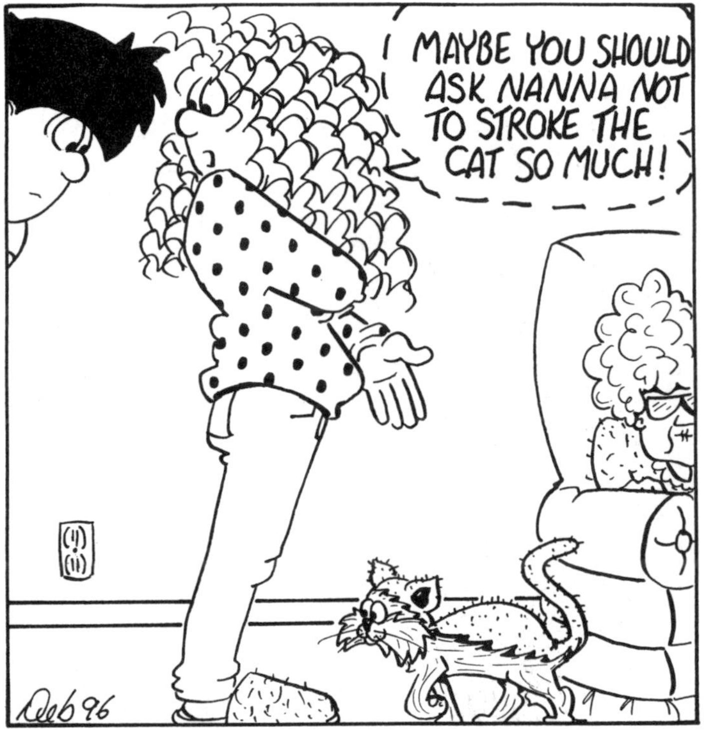
MAYBE YOU SHOULD ASK NANNA NOT TO STROKE THE CAT SO MUCH!
Deb 96

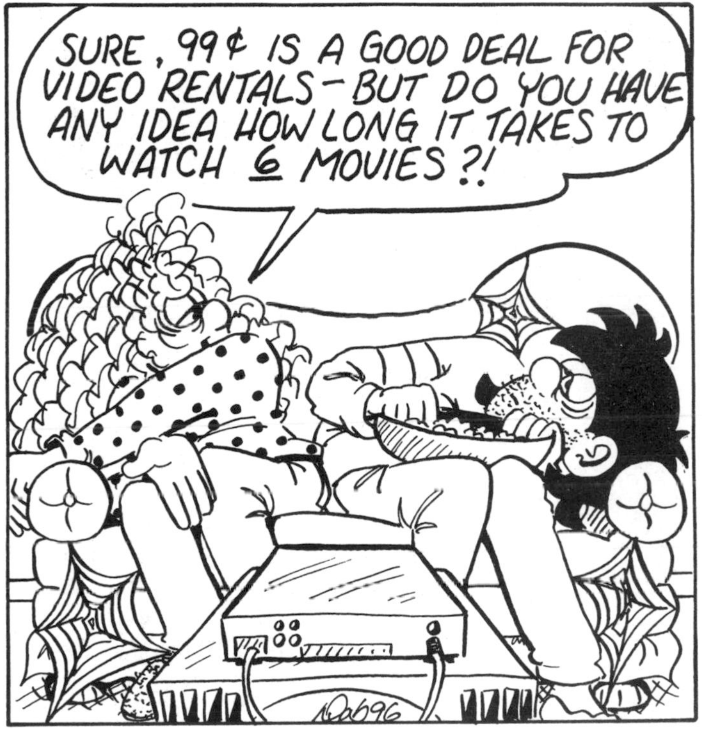
SURE, 99¢ IS A GOOD DEAL FOR VIDEO RENTALS – BUT DO YOU HAVE ANY IDEA HOW LONG IT TAKES TO WATCH 6 MOVIES ?!

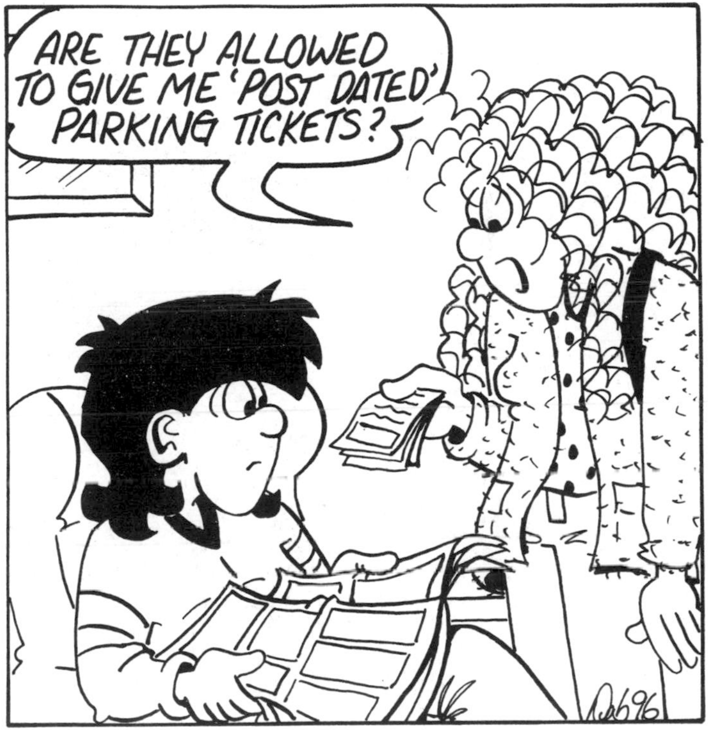
ARE THEY ALLOWED TO GIVE ME 'POST DATED' PARKING TICKETS?

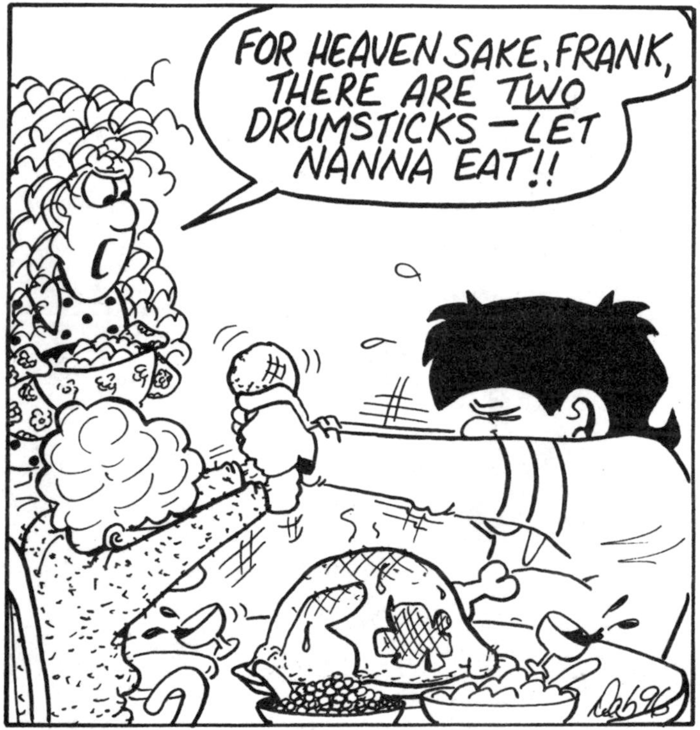
FOR HEAVEN SAKE, FRANK, THERE ARE TWO DRUMSTICKS—LET NANNA EAT!!

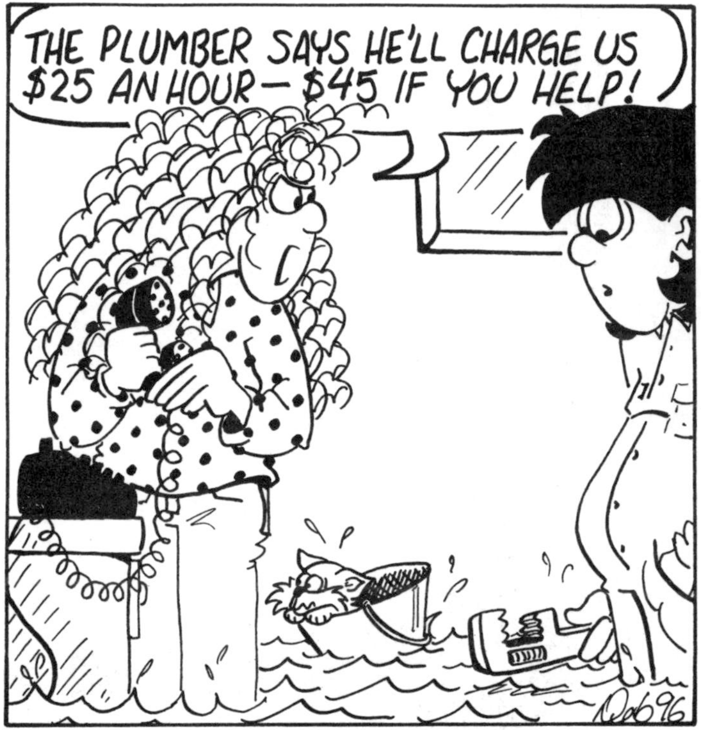
THE PLUMBER SAYS HE'LL CHARGE US $25 AN HOUR—$45 IF YOU HELP!

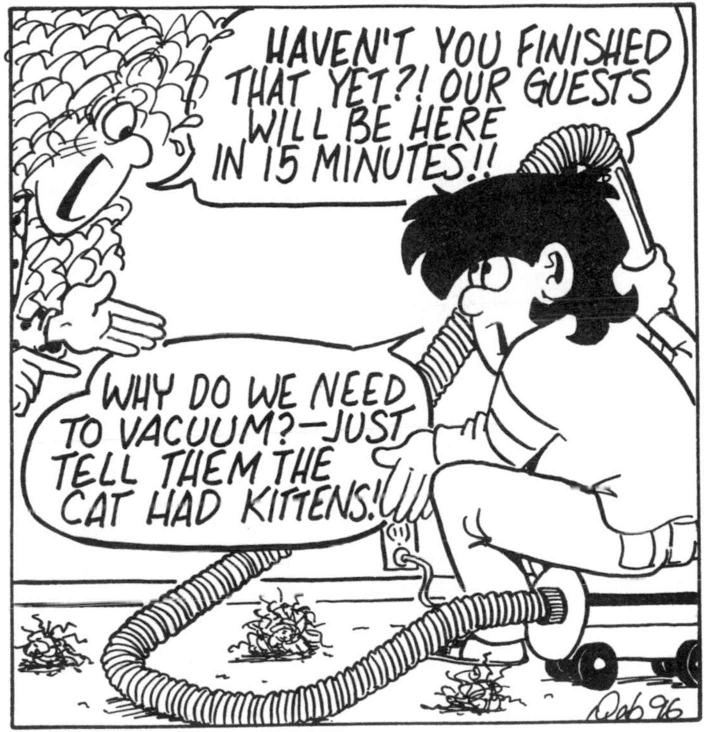
HAVEN'T YOU FINISHED THAT YET?! OUR GUESTS WILL BE HERE IN 15 MINUTES!!
WHY DO WE NEED TO VACUUM?—JUST TELL THEM THE CAT HAD KITTENS!
Deb 96

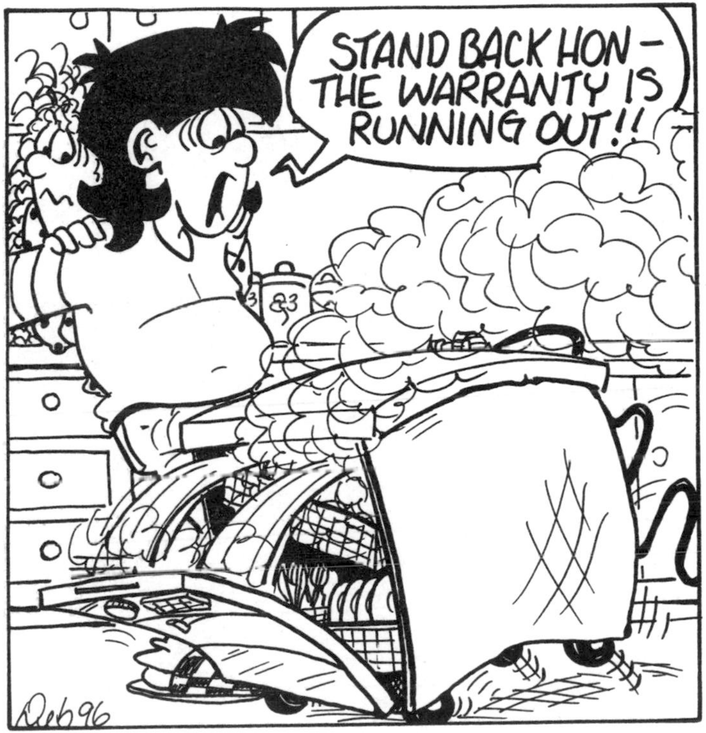
STAND BACK HON—THE WARRANTY IS RUNNING OUT!!
Deb 96

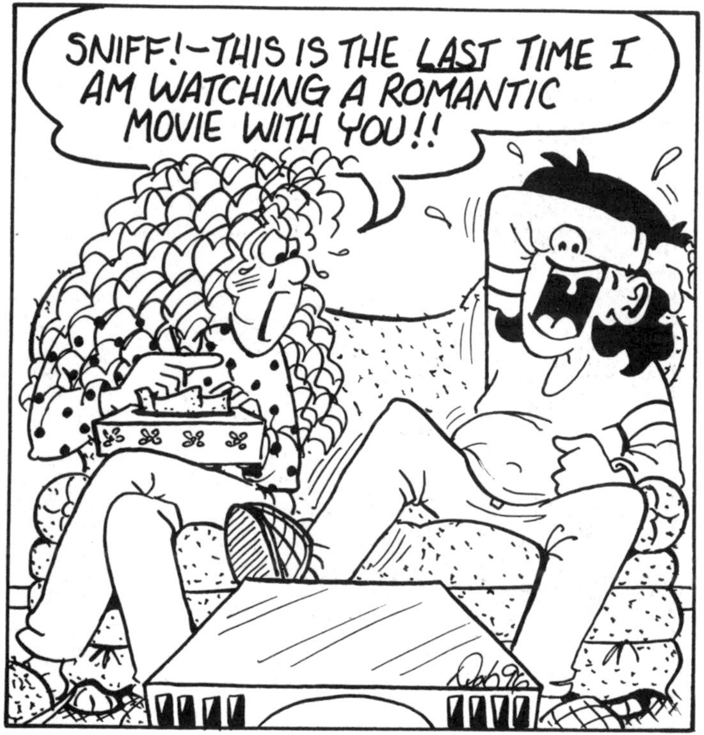
SNIFF!-THIS IS THE LAST TIME I AM WATCHING A ROMANTIC MOVIE WITH YOU!!
Deb96

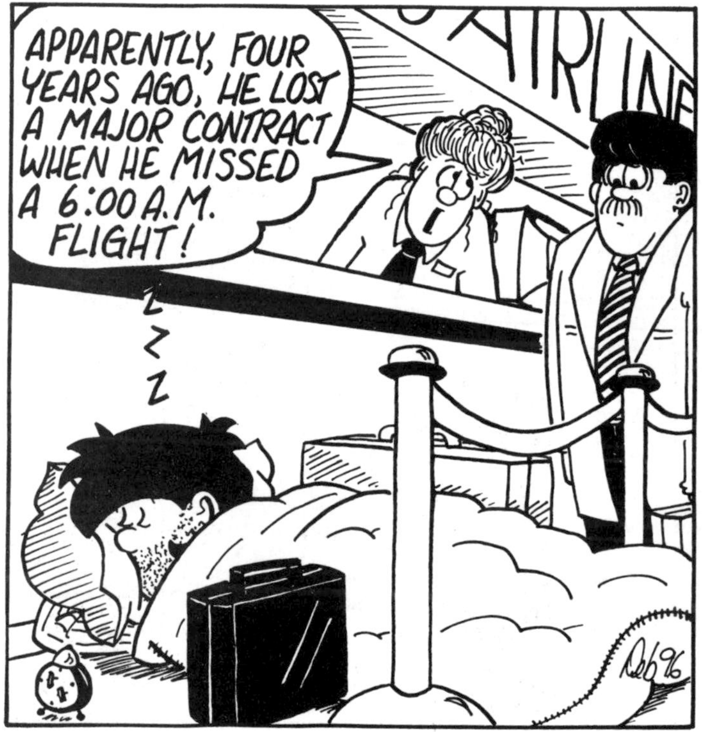
AIRLINE
APPARENTLY, FOUR YEARS AGO, HE LOST A MAJOR CONTRACT WHEN HE MISSED A 6:00 A.M. FLIGHT!
Z Z Z
Deb96

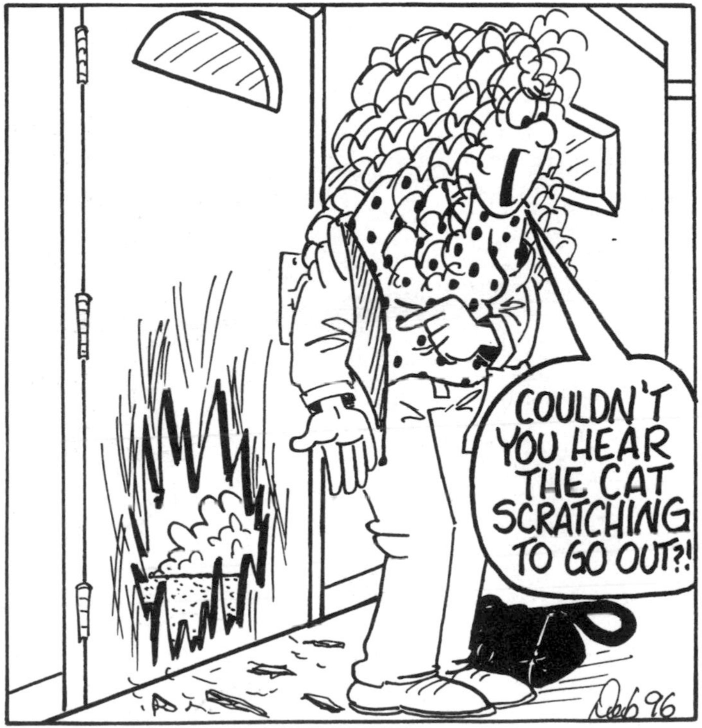
COULDN'T YOU HEAR THE CAT SCRATCHING TO GO OUT?!

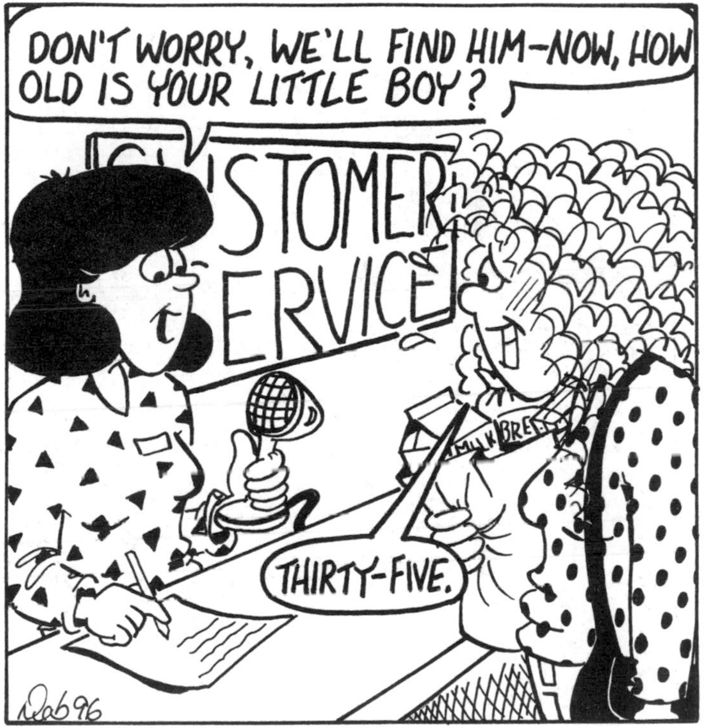
DON'T WORRY, WE'LL FIND HIM—NOW, HOW OLD IS YOUR LITTLE BOY?
THIRTY-FIVE.

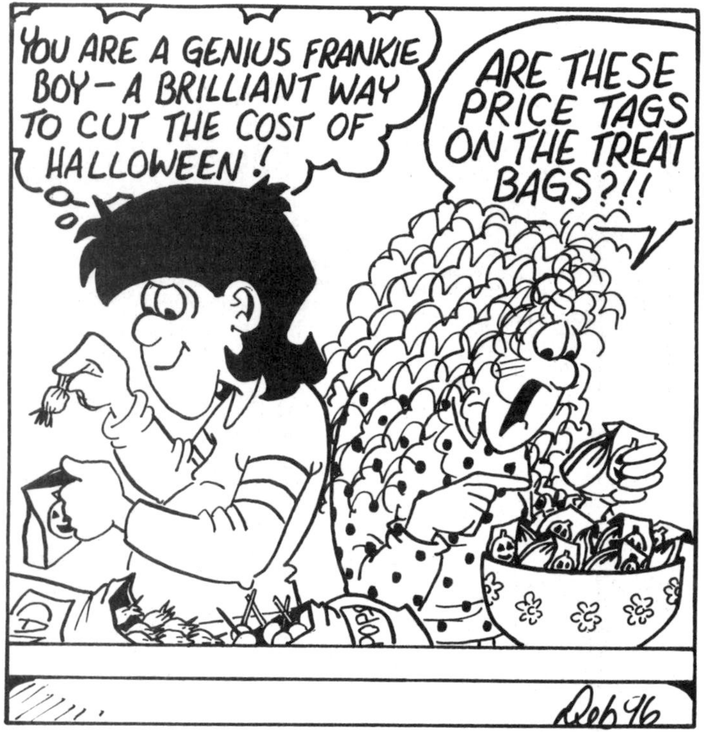
YOU ARE A GENIUS FRANKIE BOY – A BRILLIANT WAY TO CUT THE COST OF HALLOWEEN!
ARE THESE PRICE TAGS ON THE TREAT BAGS?!!

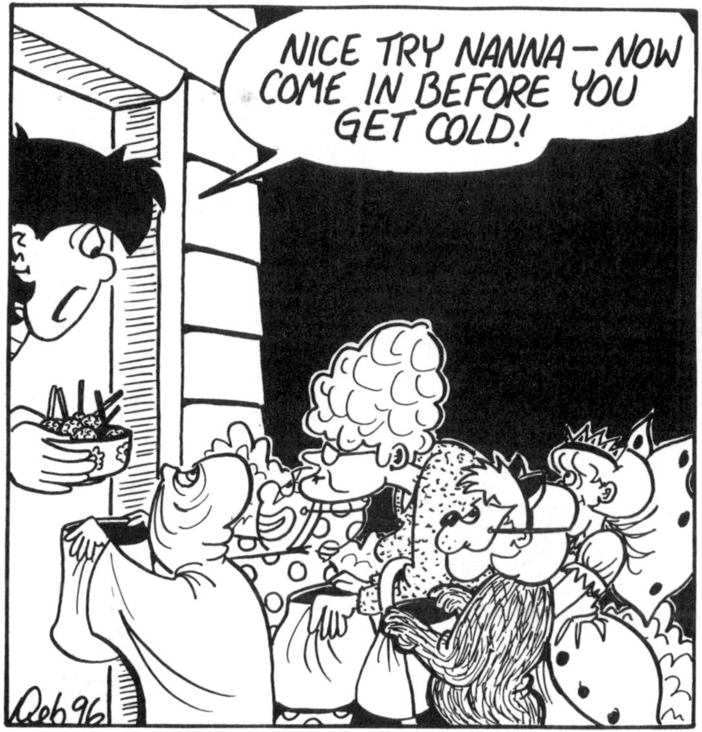
NICE TRY NANNA – NOW COME IN BEFORE YOU GET COLD!

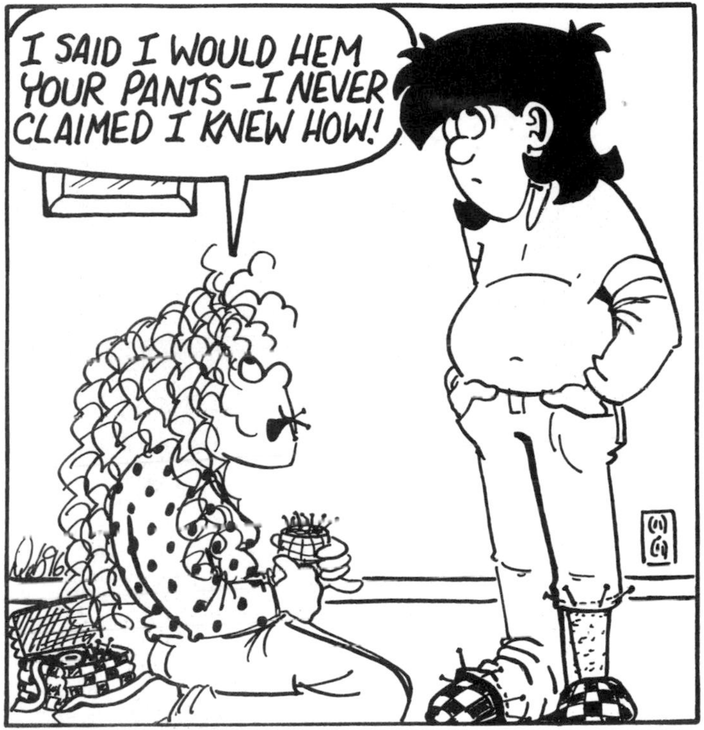
I SAID I WOULD HEM YOUR PANTS - I NEVER CLAIMED I KNEW HOW!
Deb 96

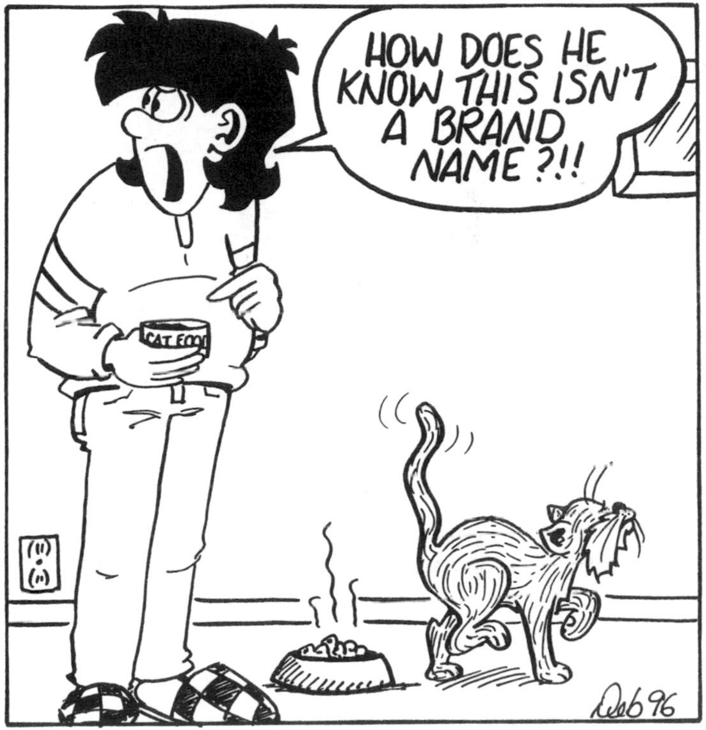
HOW DOES HE KNOW THIS ISN'T A BRAND NAME ?!!
CAT FOOD
Deb 96

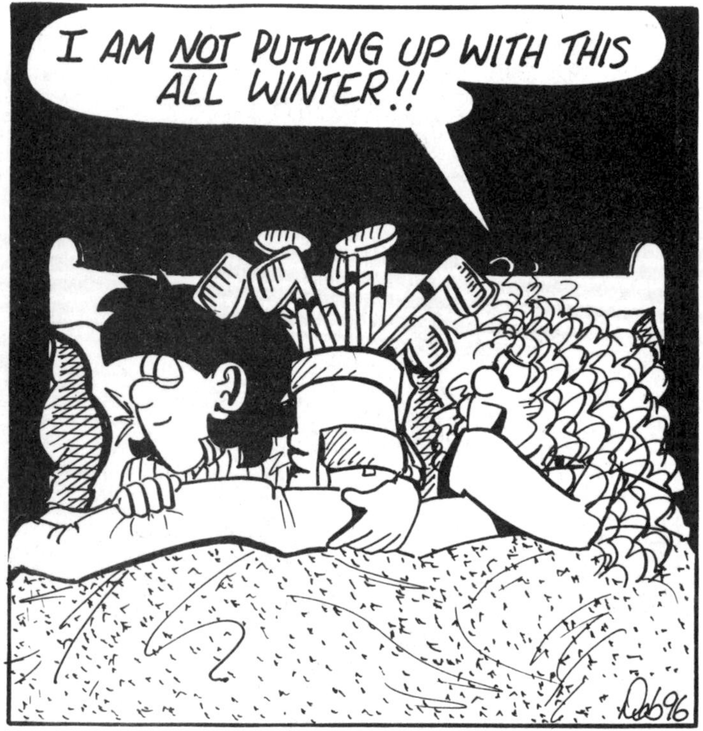
I AM NOT PUTTING UP WITH THIS ALL WINTER!!
Deb96

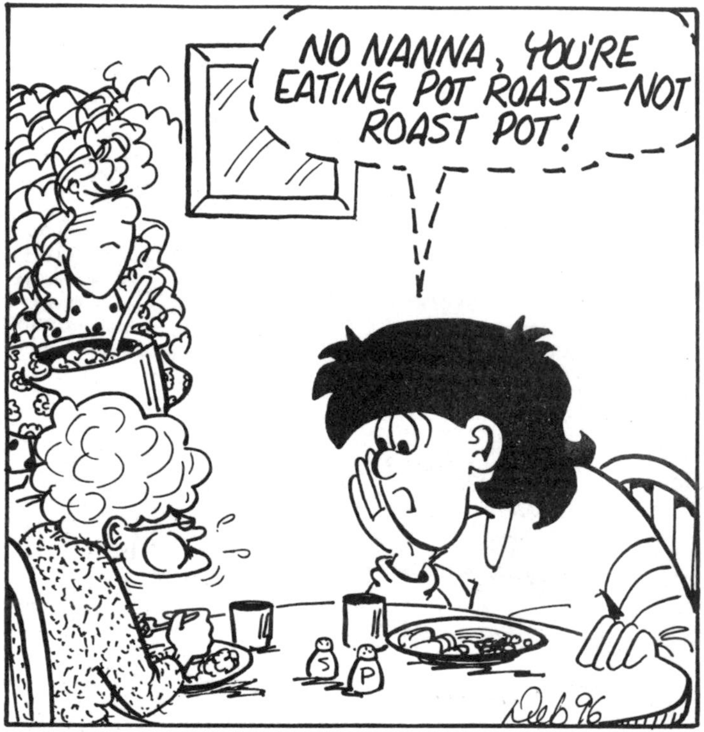
NO NANNA, YOU'RE EATING POT ROAST—NOT ROAST POT!
S
P
Deb96

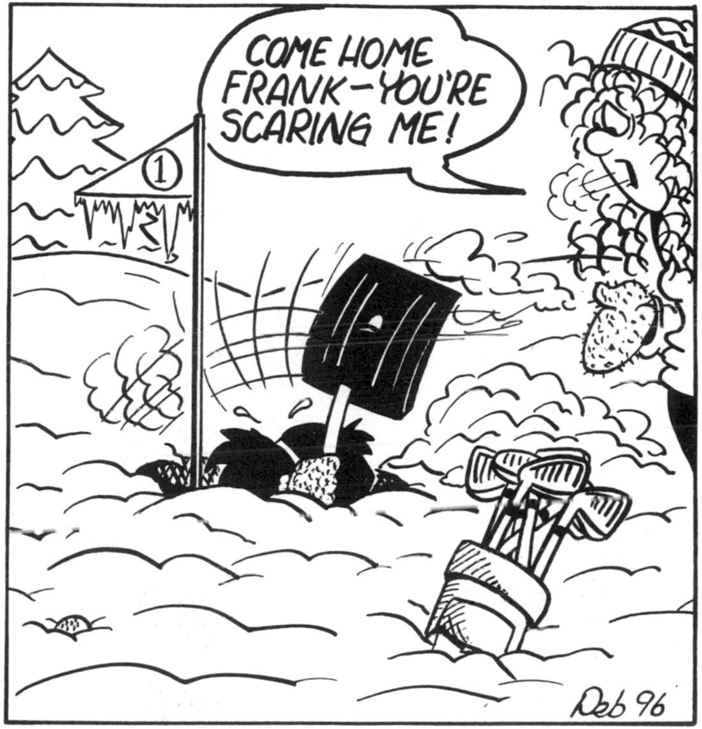
COME HOME FRANK—YOU'RE SCARING ME!
Deb 96

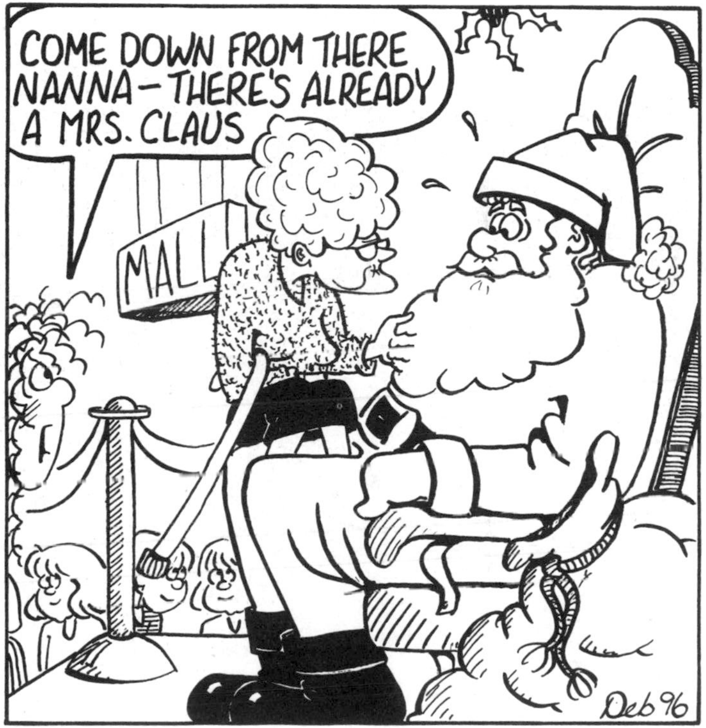
COME DOWN FROM THERE NANNA—THERE'S ALREADY A MRS. CLAUS
MALL
Deb 96

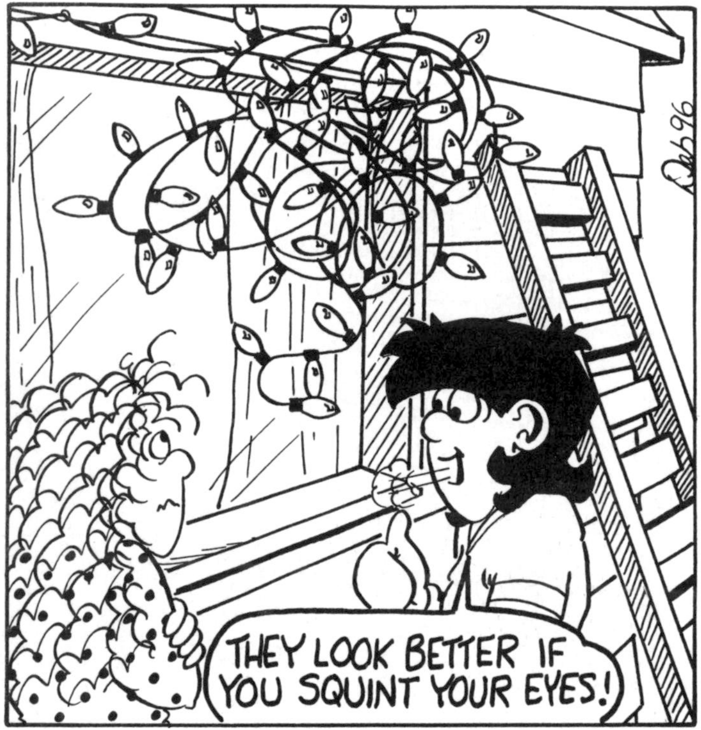
THEY LOOK BETTER IF YOU SQUINT YOUR EYES!
Deb96

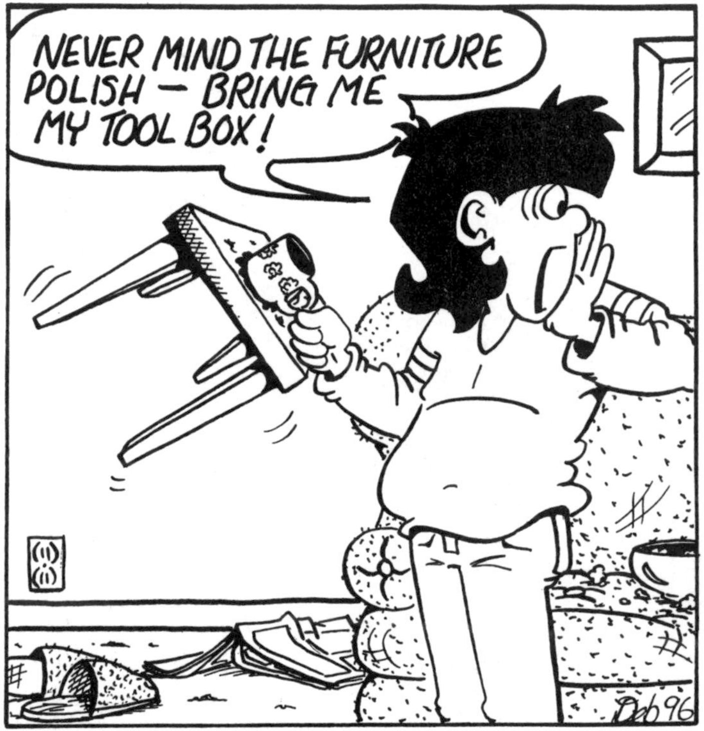
NEVER MIND THE FURNITURE POLISH — BRING ME MY TOOL BOX!
Deb96

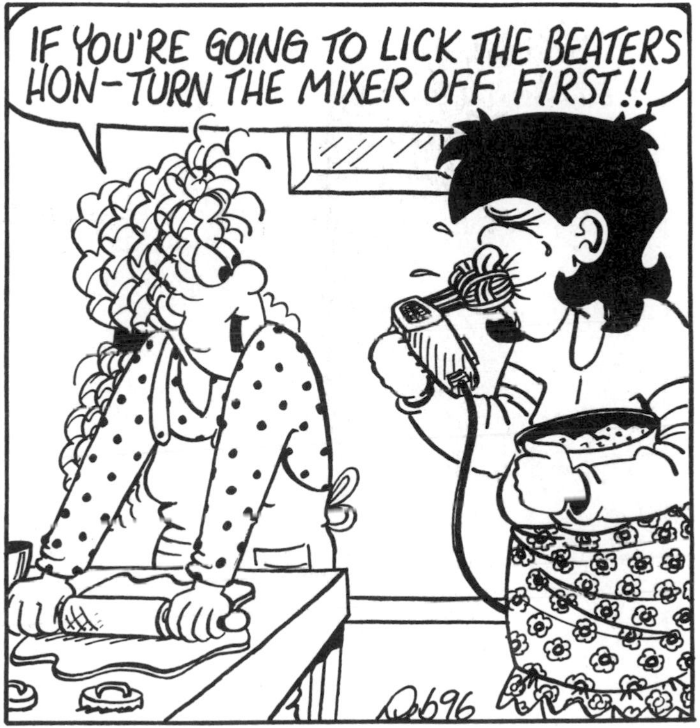
IF YOU'RE GOING TO LICK THE BEATERS HON-TURN THE MIXER OFF FIRST!!
Deb96

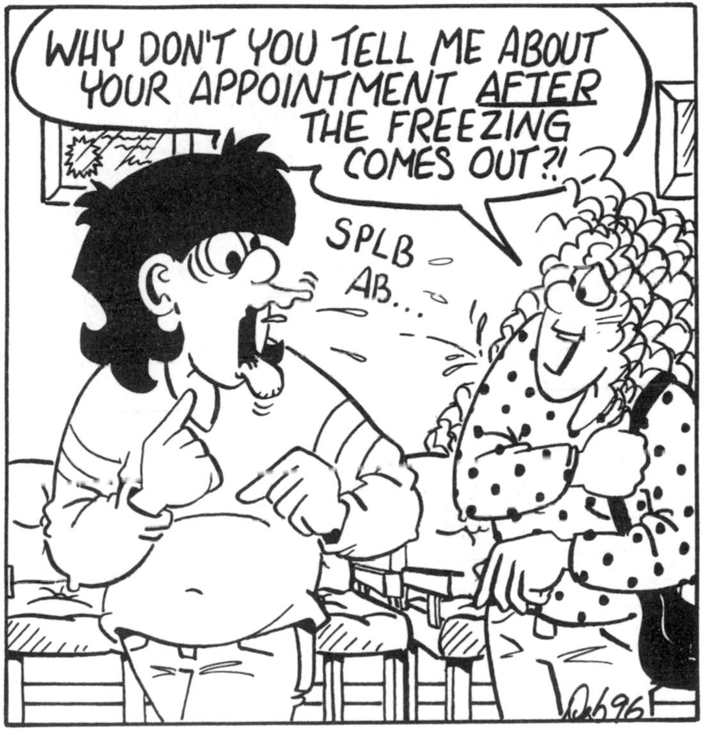
WHY DON'T YOU TELL ME ABOUT YOUR APPOINTMENT AFTER THE FREEZING COMES OUT?!
SPLB AB...
Deb96

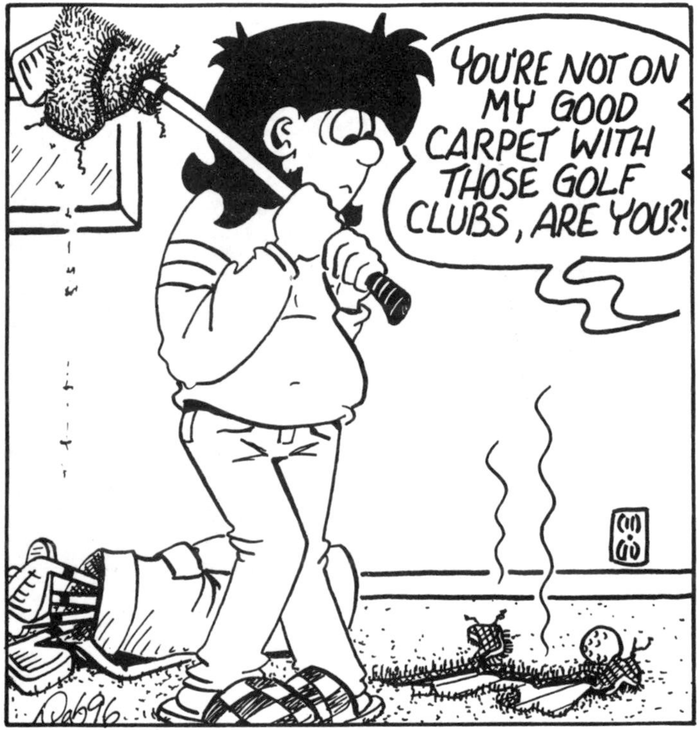
YOU'RE NOT ON MY GOOD CARPET WITH THOSE GOLF CLUBS, ARE YOU?!

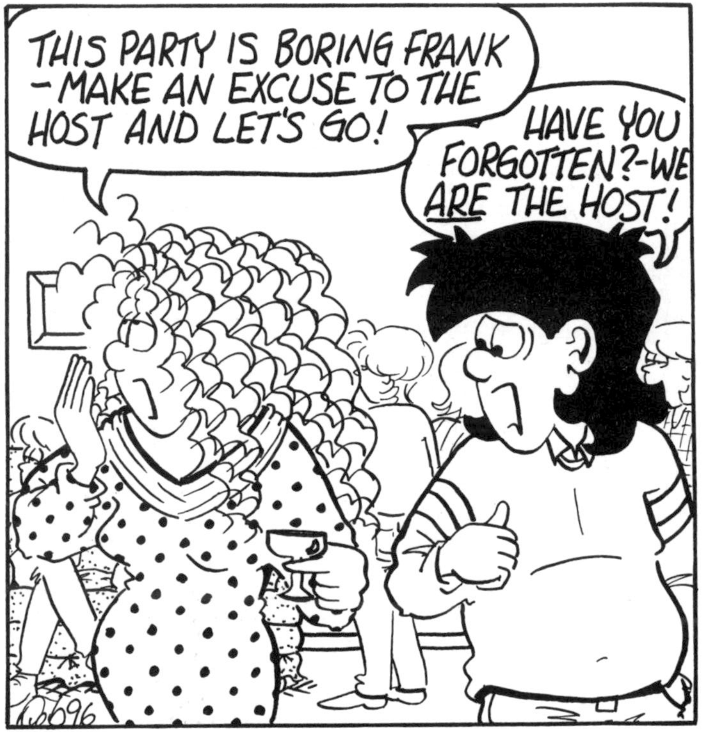
THIS PARTY IS BORING FRANK - MAKE AN EXCUSE TO THE HOST AND LET'S GO!
HAVE YOU FORGOTTEN?-WE ARE THE HOST!

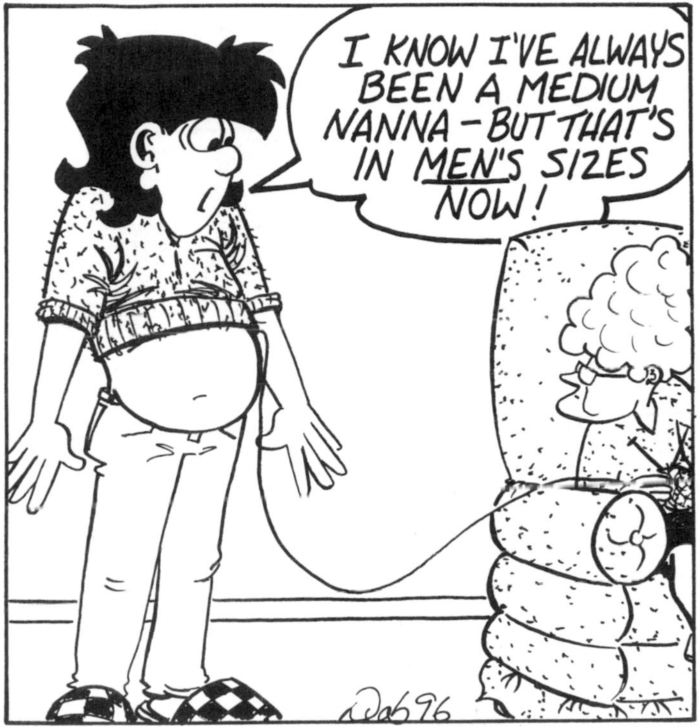
I KNOW I'VE ALWAYS BEEN A MEDIUM NANNA - BUT THAT'S IN MEN'S SIZES NOW!

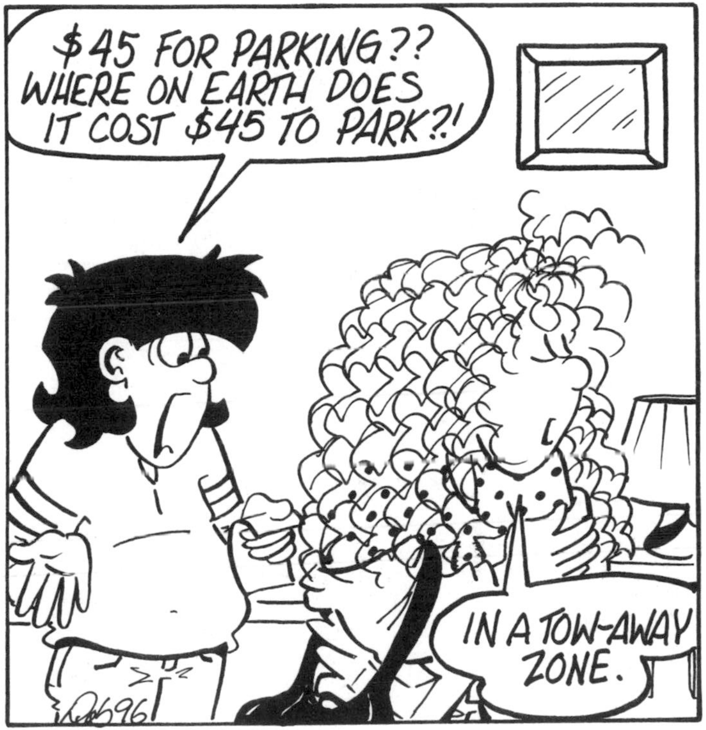
$45 FOR PARKING?? WHERE ON EARTH DOES IT COST $45 TO PARK?!
IN A TOW-AWAY ZONE.

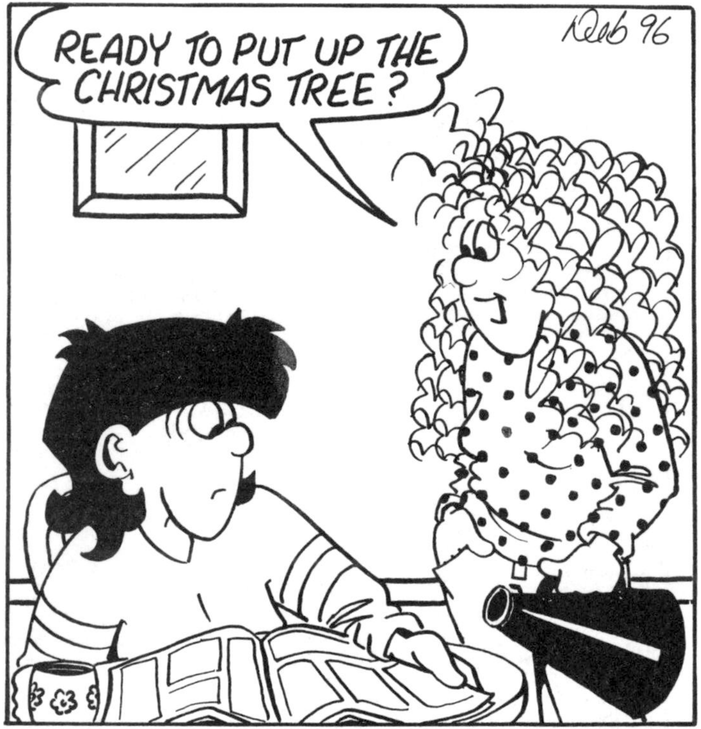
Deb 96
READY TO PUT UP THE CHRISTMAS TREE?

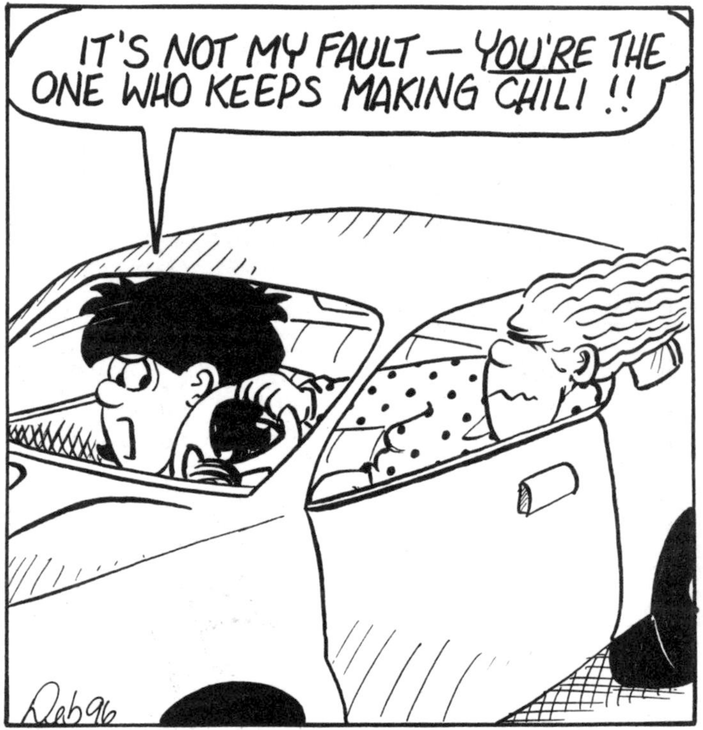
IT'S NOT MY FAULT — YOU'RE THE ONE WHO KEEPS MAKING CHILI !!
Deb 96

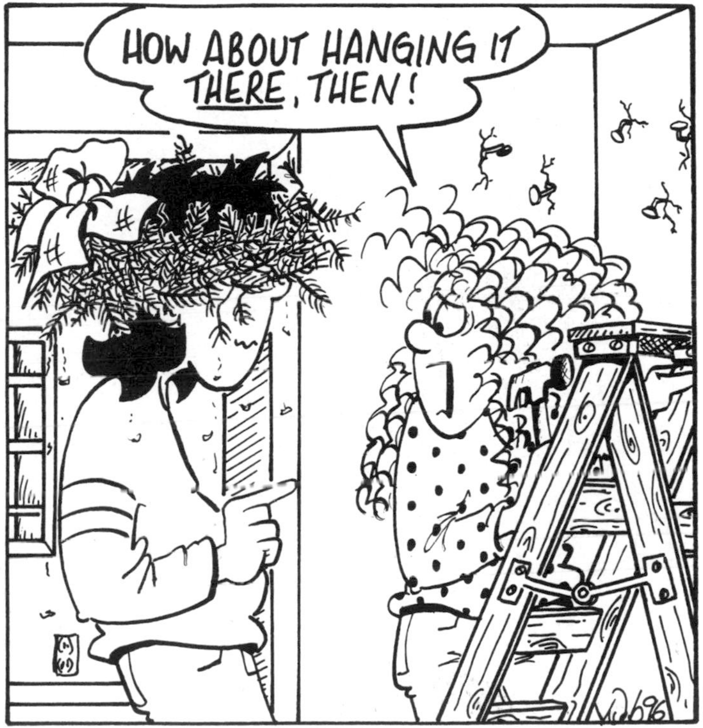
HOW ABOUT HANGING IT THERE, THEN!
Deb96

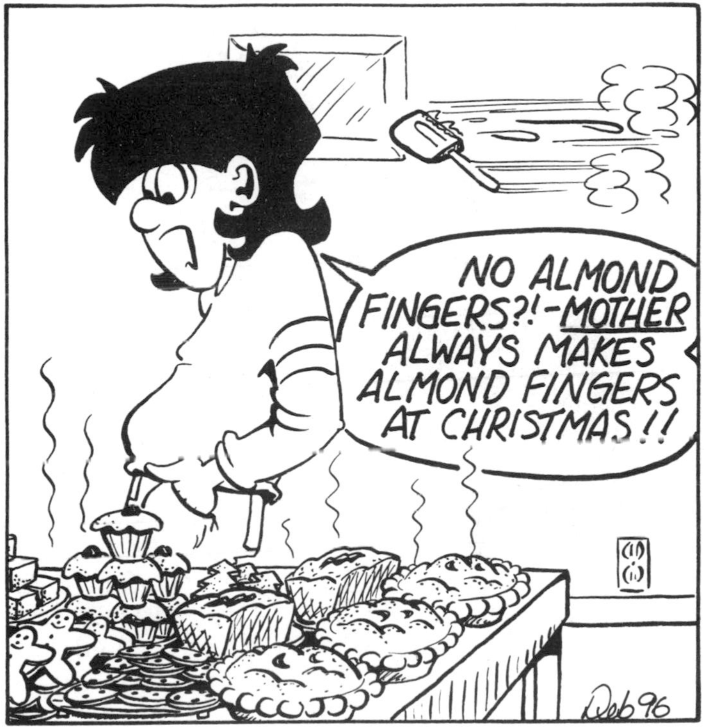
NO ALMOND FINGERS?!-MOTHER ALWAYS MAKES ALMOND FINGERS AT CHRISTMAS!!
Deb96

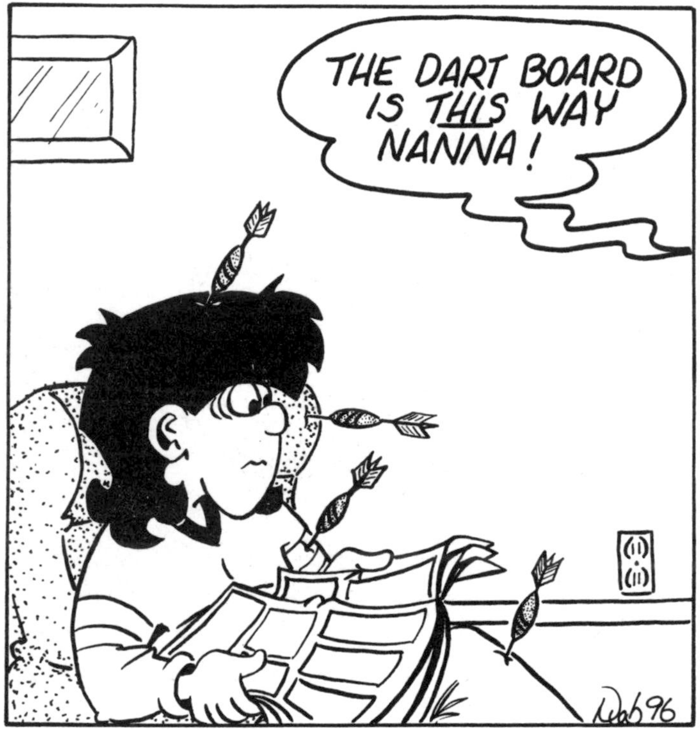
THE DART BOARD IS THIS WAY NANNA!
Wab96

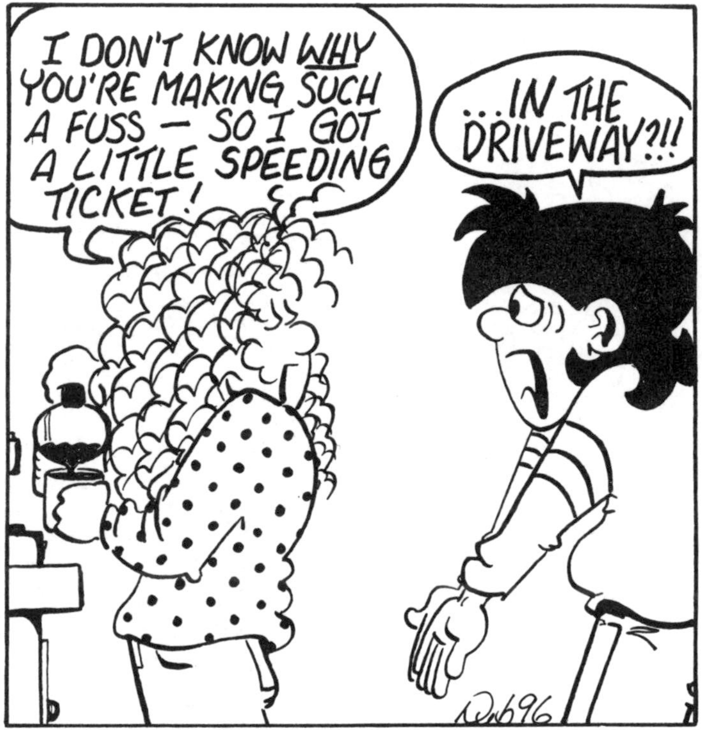
I DON'T KNOW WHY YOU'RE MAKING SUCH A FUSS — SO I GOT A LITTLE SPEEDING TICKET!
...IN THE DRIVEWAY?!!
Wab96

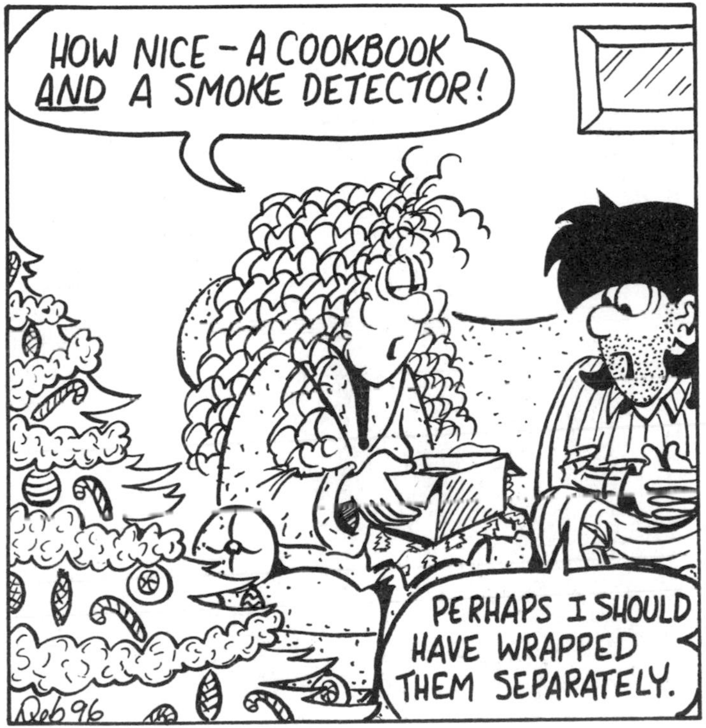
HOW NICE – A COOKBOOK AND A SMOKE DETECTOR!
PERHAPS I SHOULD HAVE WRAPPED THEM SEPARATELY.
Deb 96

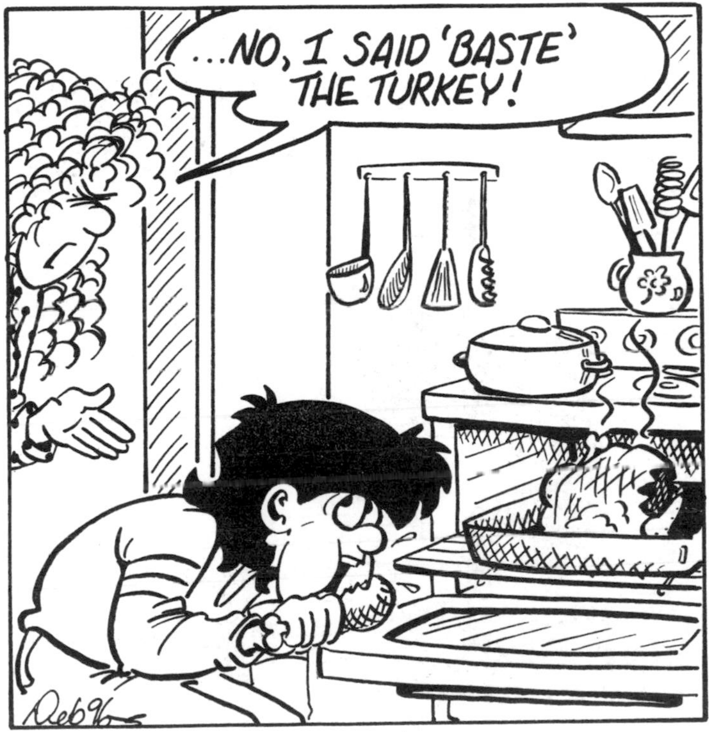
...NO, I SAID 'BASTE' THE TURKEY!
Deb 96

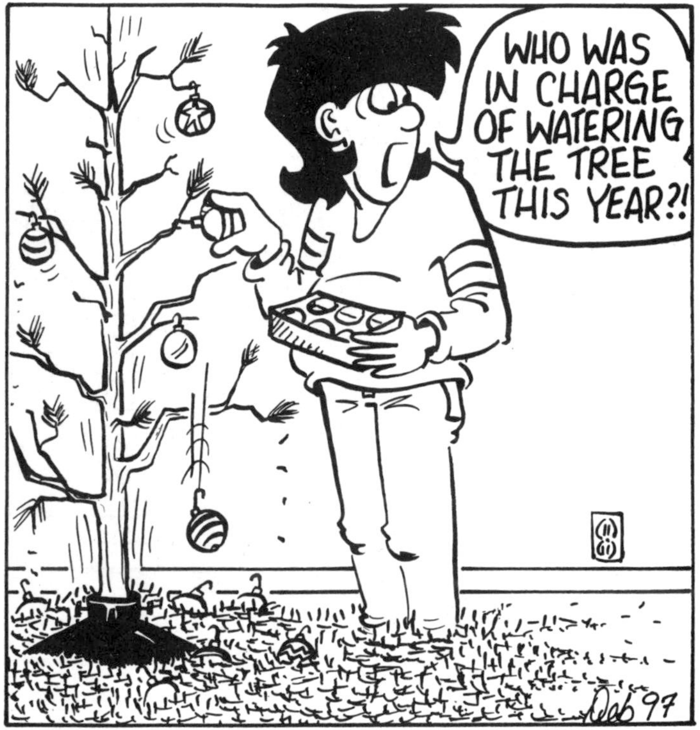
WHO WAS IN CHARGE OF WATERING THE TREE THIS YEAR?!
Deb 97

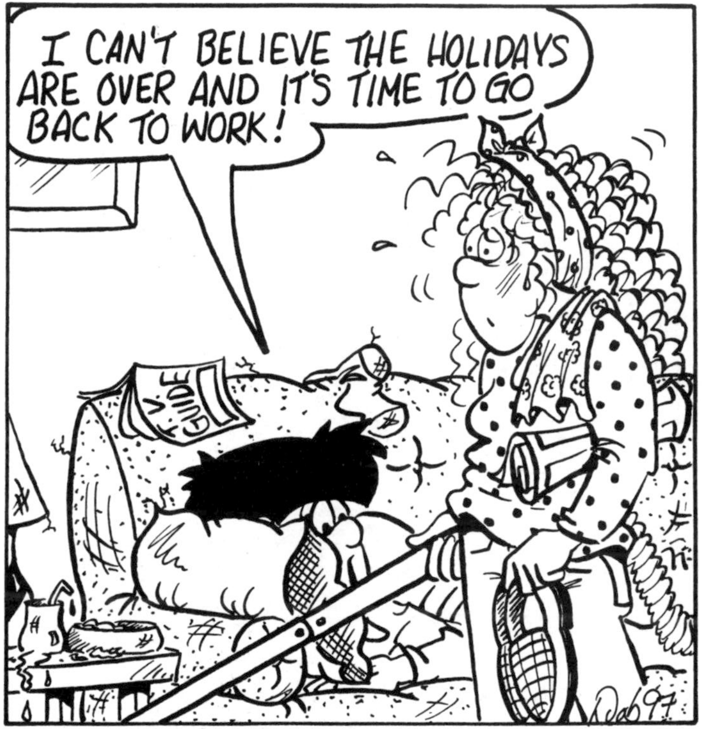
I CAN'T BELIEVE THE HOLIDAYS ARE OVER AND IT'S TIME TO GO BACK TO WORK!
TV GUIDE
Deb 97

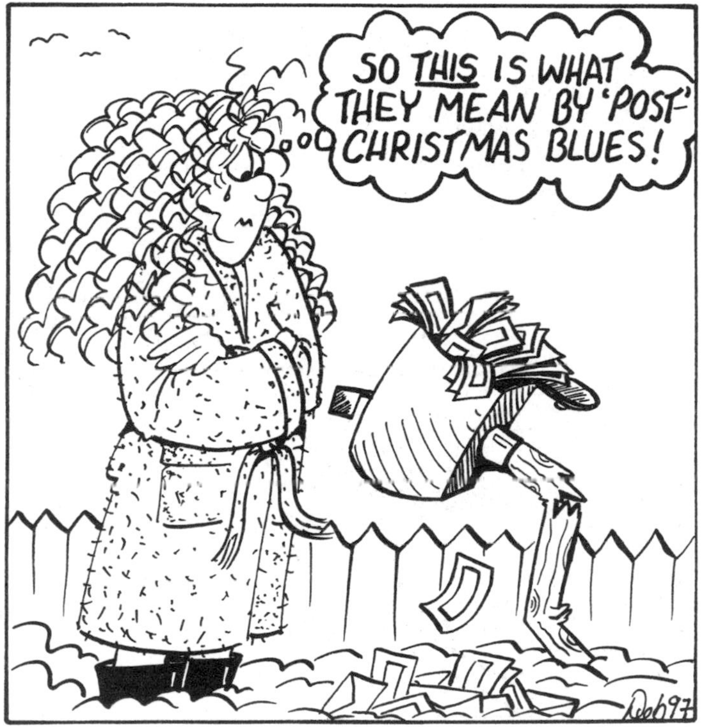
SO THIS IS WHAT THEY MEAN BY 'POST' CHRISTMAS BLUES!
Deb97

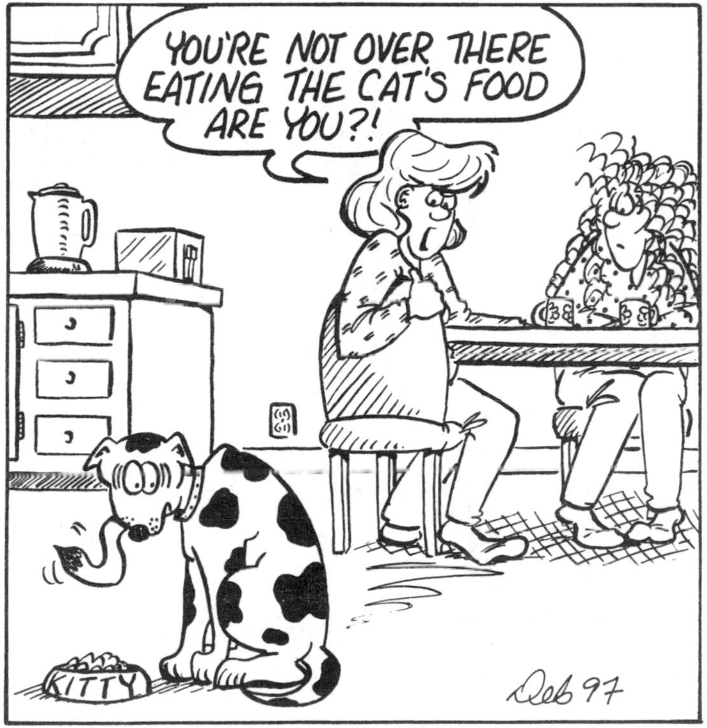
YOU'RE NOT OVER THERE EATING THE CAT'S FOOD ARE YOU?!
KITTY
Deb 97

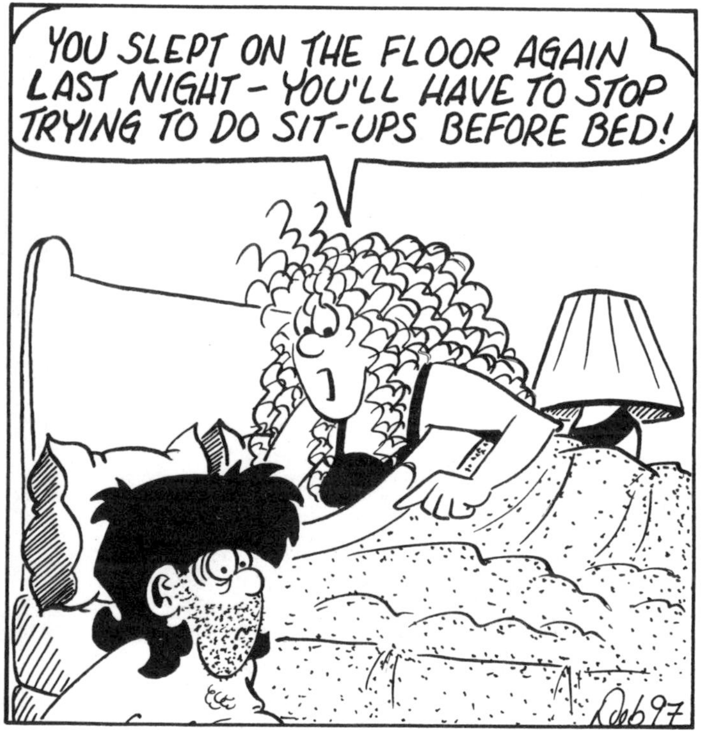
YOU SLEPT ON THE FLOOR AGAIN LAST NIGHT - YOU'LL HAVE TO STOP TRYING TO DO SIT-UPS BEFORE BED!

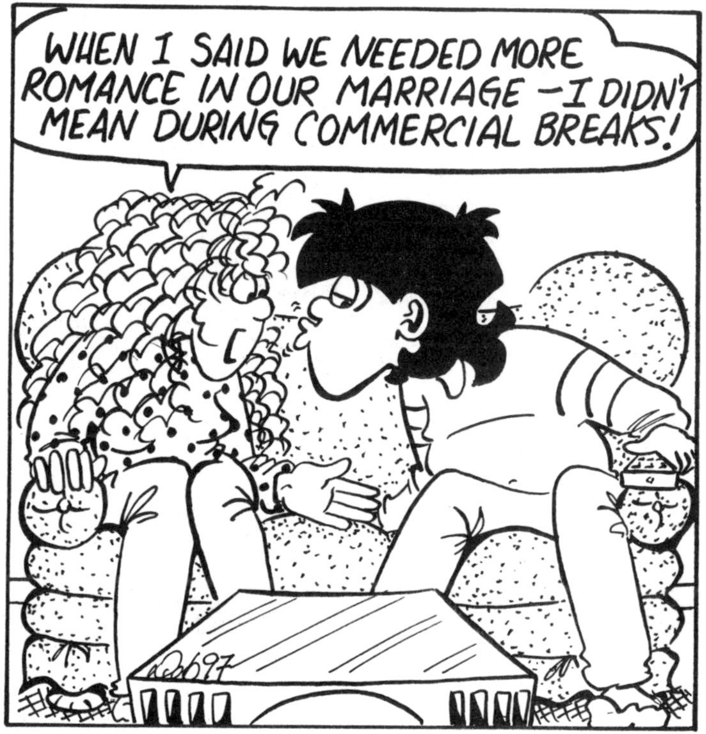
WHEN I SAID WE NEEDED MORE ROMANCE IN OUR MARRIAGE -I DIDN'T MEAN DURING COMMERCIAL BREAKS!

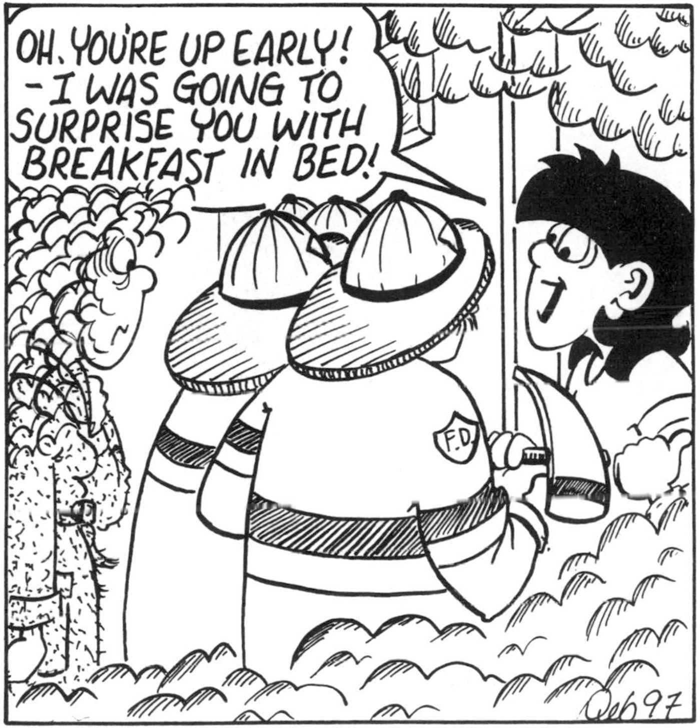
OH, YOU'RE UP EARLY! - I WAS GOING TO SURPRISE YOU WITH BREAKFAST IN BED!
F.D.
Deb 97

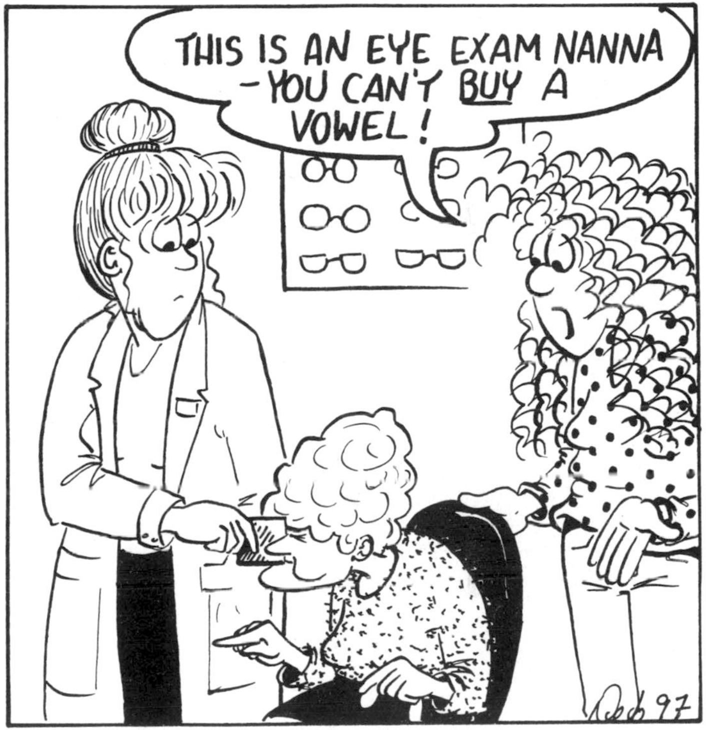
THIS IS AN EYE EXAM NANNA - YOU CAN'T BUY A VOWEL!
Deb 97

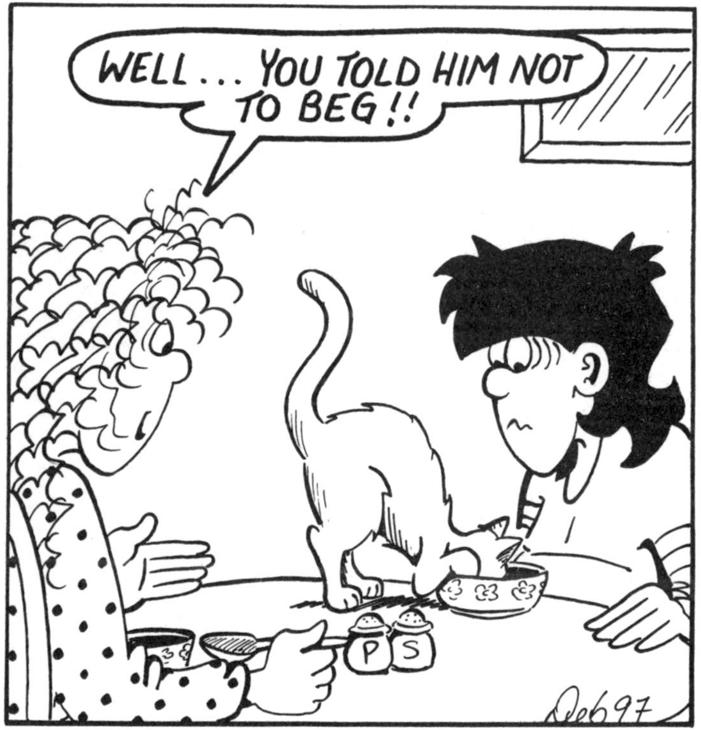
WELL... YOU TOLD HIM NOT TO BEG!!
P
S
Deb97

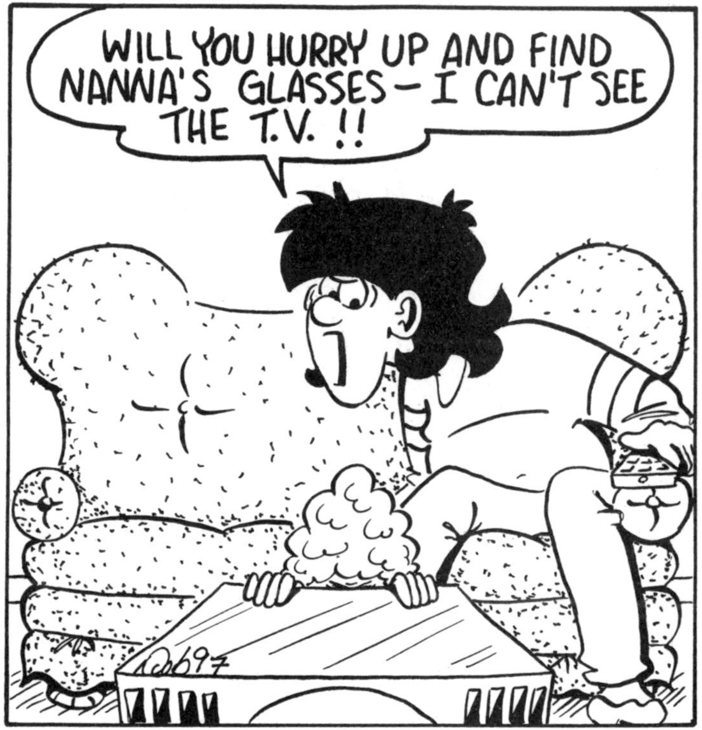
WILL YOU HURRY UP AND FIND NANNA'S GLASSES – I CAN'T SEE THE T.V. !!
Deb97

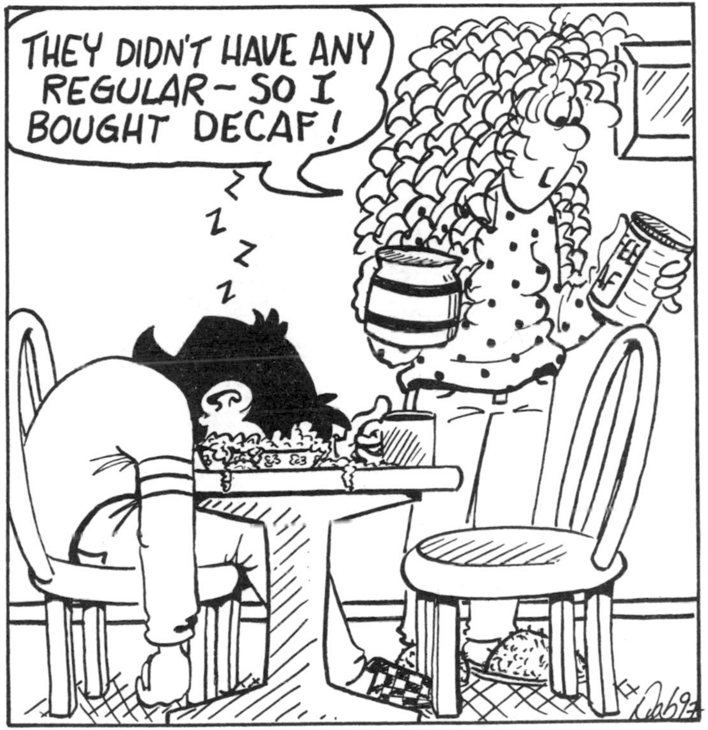
THEY DIDN'T HAVE ANY REGULAR – SO I BOUGHT DECAF!
Z Z Z Z

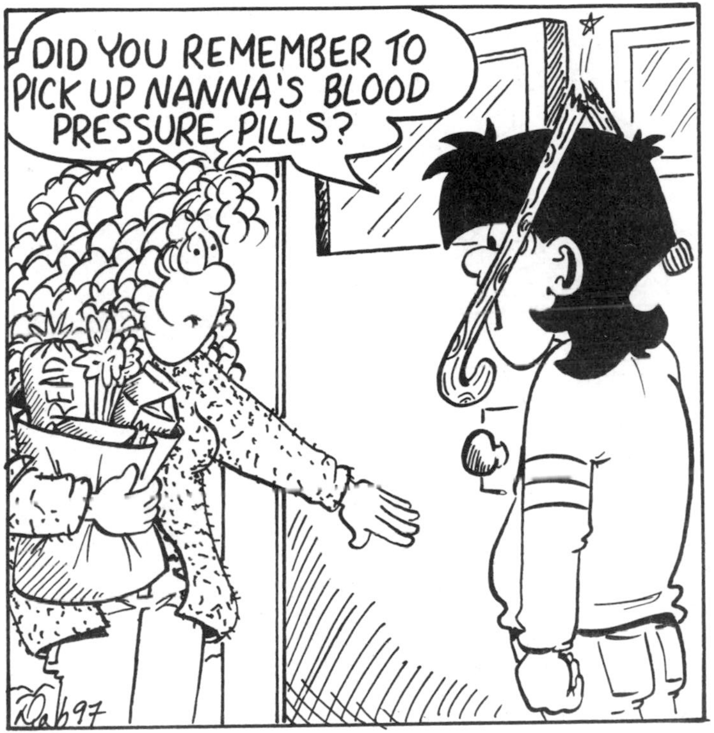
DID YOU REMEMBER TO PICK UP NANNA'S BLOOD PRESSURE PILLS?

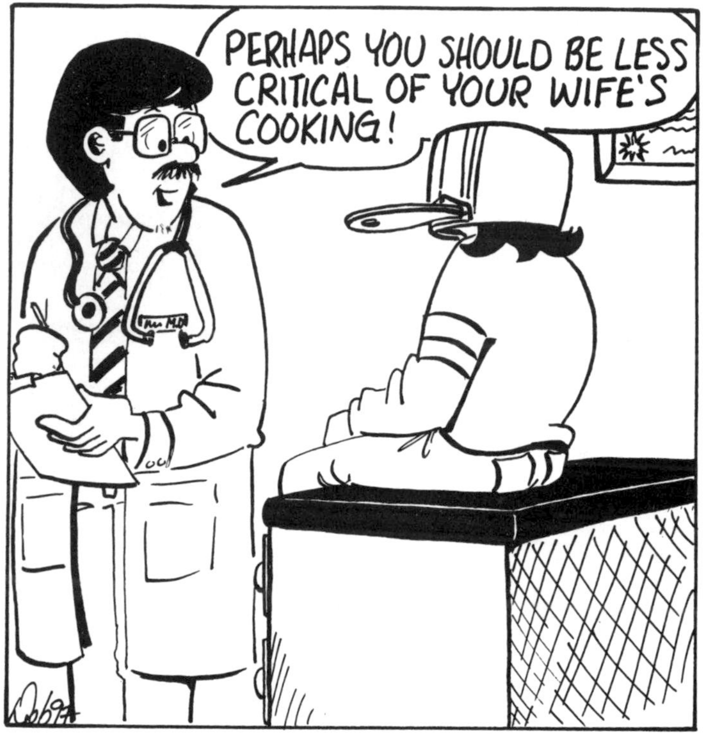
PERHAPS YOU SHOULD BE LESS CRITICAL OF YOUR WIFE'S COOKING!

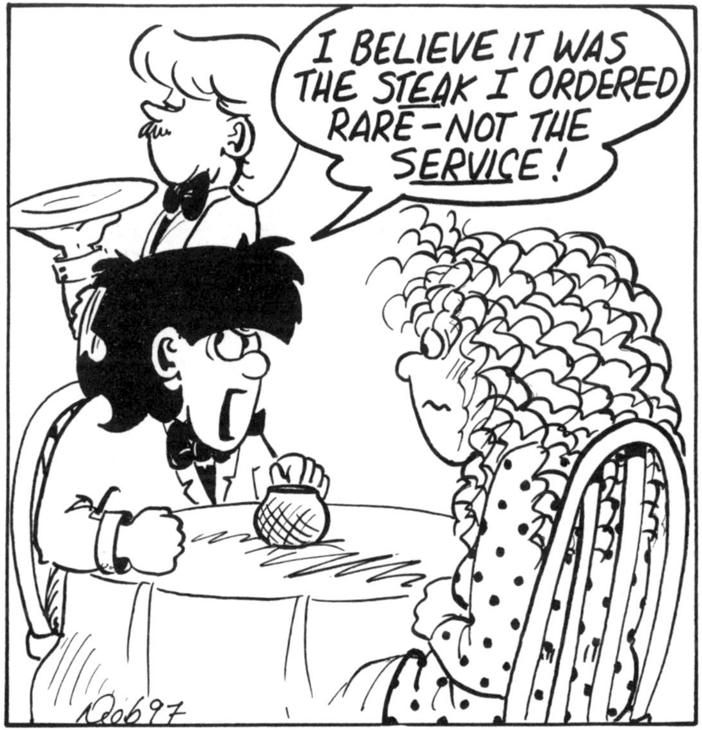
I BELIEVE IT WAS THE STEAK I ORDERED RARE—NOT THE SERVICE!

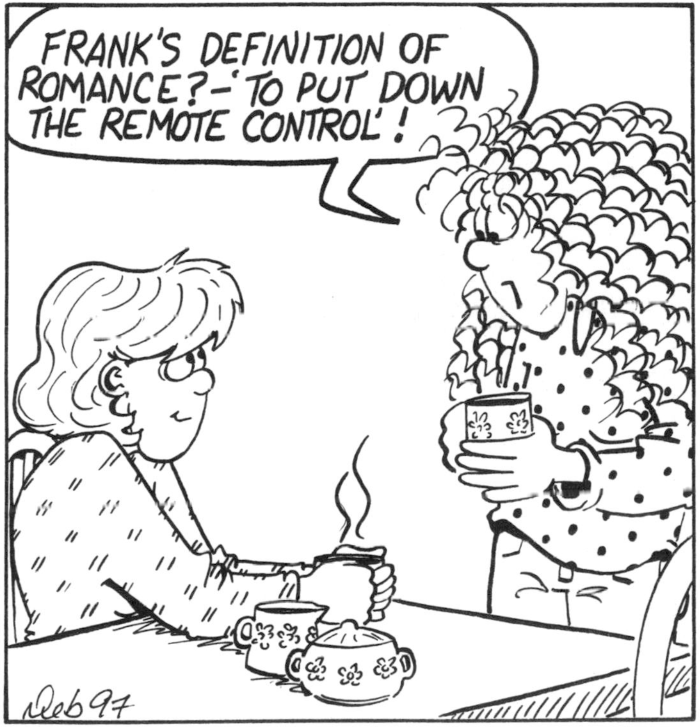
FRANK'S DEFINITION OF ROMANCE?–'TO PUT DOWN THE REMOTE CONTROL'!
Deb97

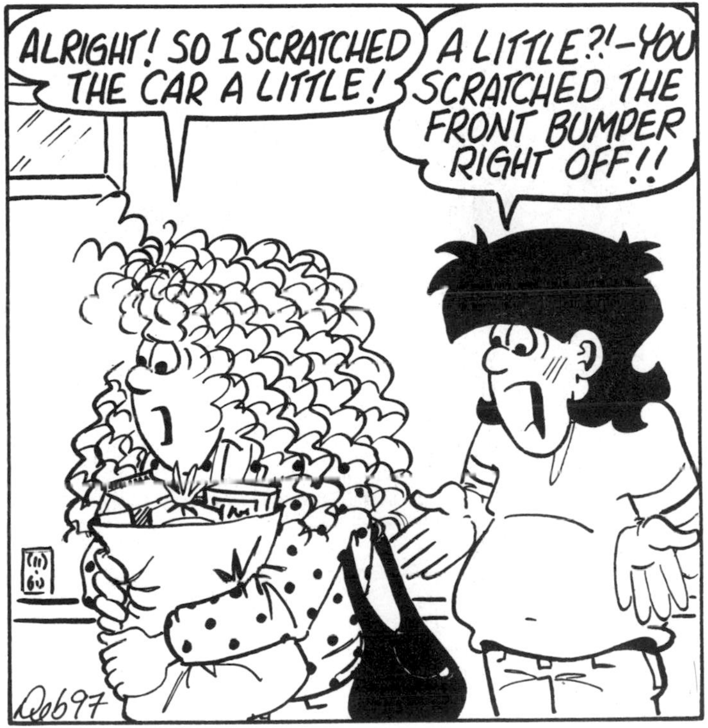
ALRIGHT! SO I SCRATCHED THE CAR A LITTLE!
A LITTLE?!–YOU SCRATCHED THE FRONT BUMPER RIGHT OFF!!
Deb97

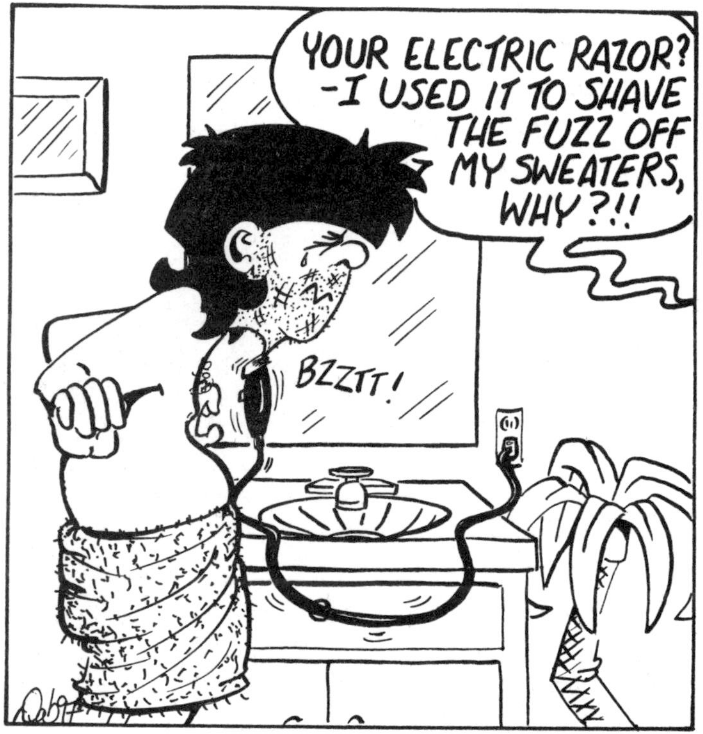
YOUR ELECTRIC RAZOR? -I USED IT TO SHAVE THE FUZZ OFF MY SWEATERS, WHY?!!
BZZTT!

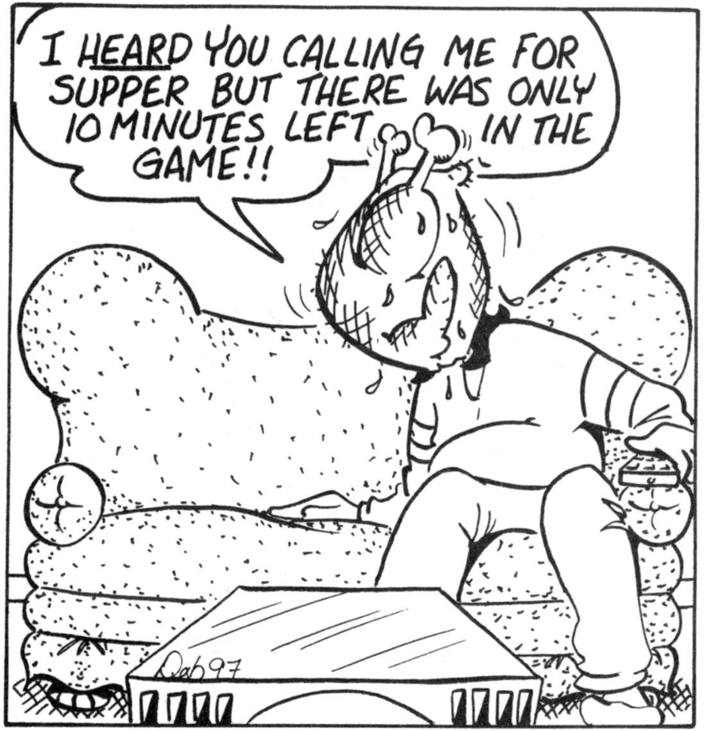
I HEARD YOU CALLING ME FOR SUPPER BUT THERE WAS ONLY 10 MINUTES LEFT IN THE GAME!!

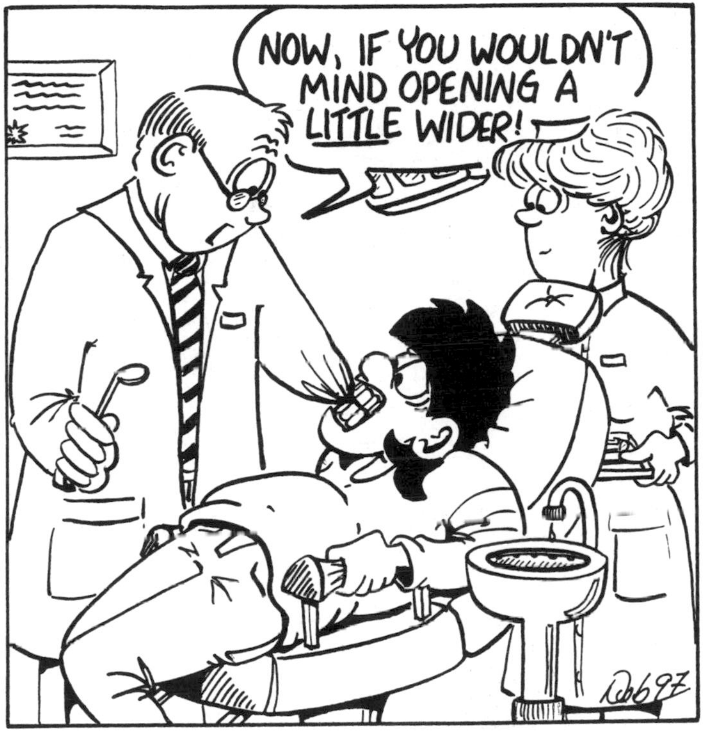
NOW, IF YOU WOULDN'T MIND OPENING A LITTLE WIDER!
Dab 97

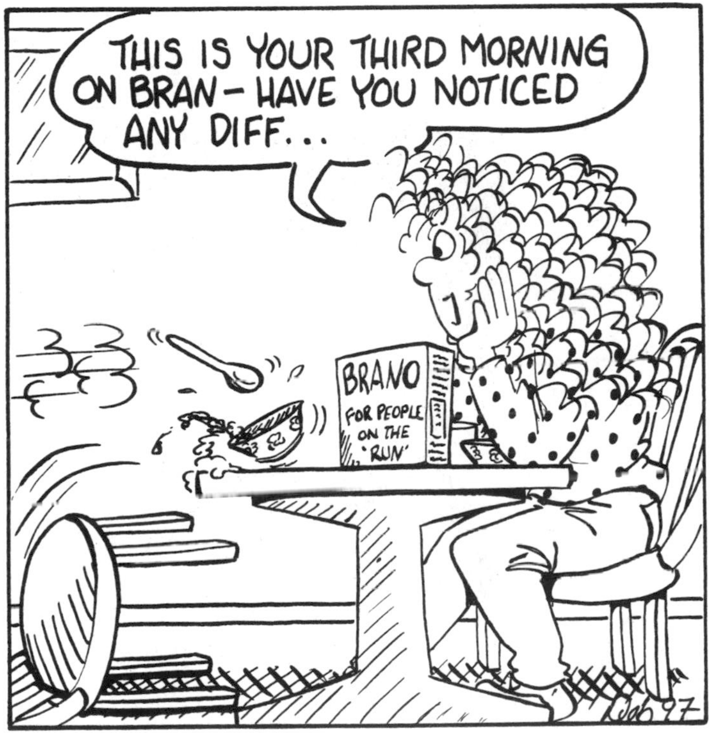
THIS IS YOUR THIRD MORNING ON BRAN – HAVE YOU NOTICED ANY DIFF...
BRANO
FOR PEOPLE ON THE 'RUN'
Dab 97

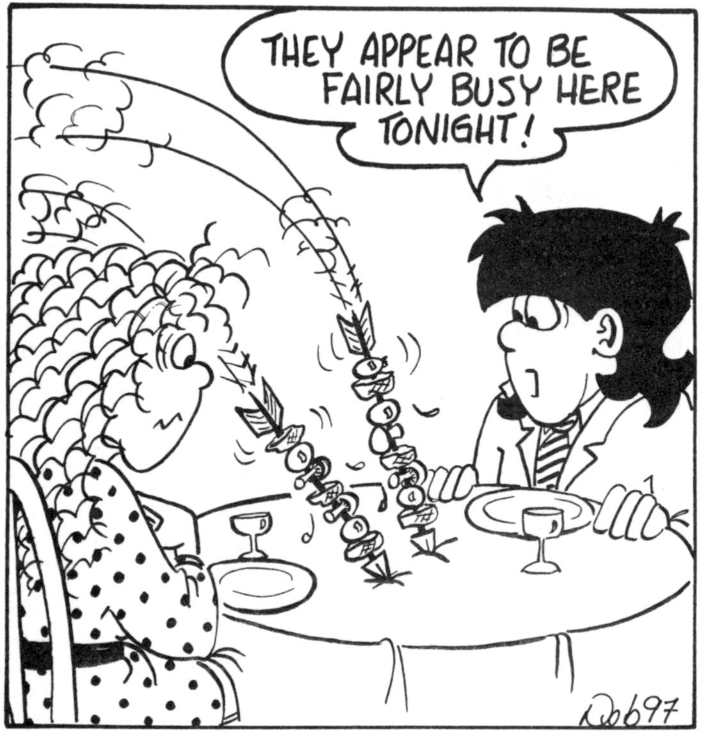
THEY APPEAR TO BE FAIRLY BUSY HERE TONIGHT!
Deb97

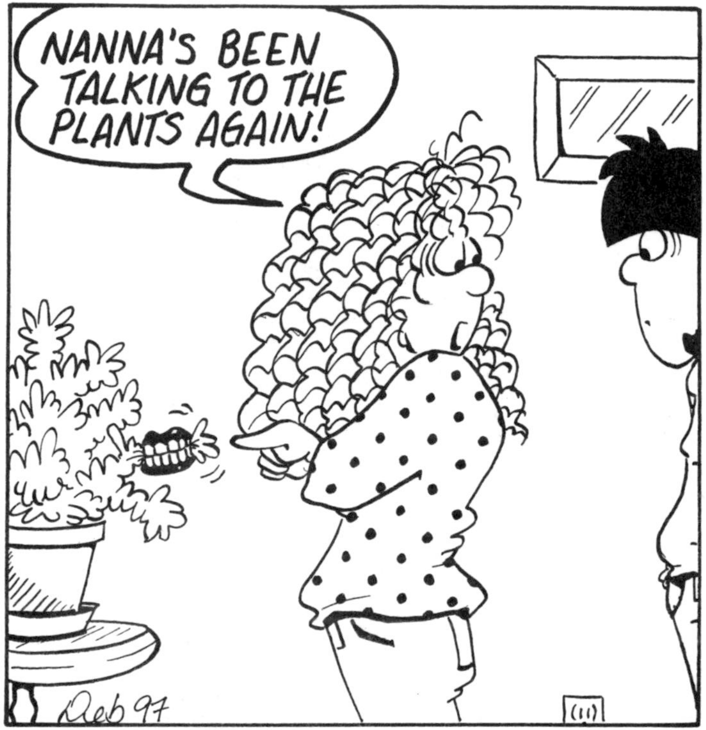
NANNA'S BEEN TALKING TO THE PLANTS AGAIN!
Deb 97
(11)

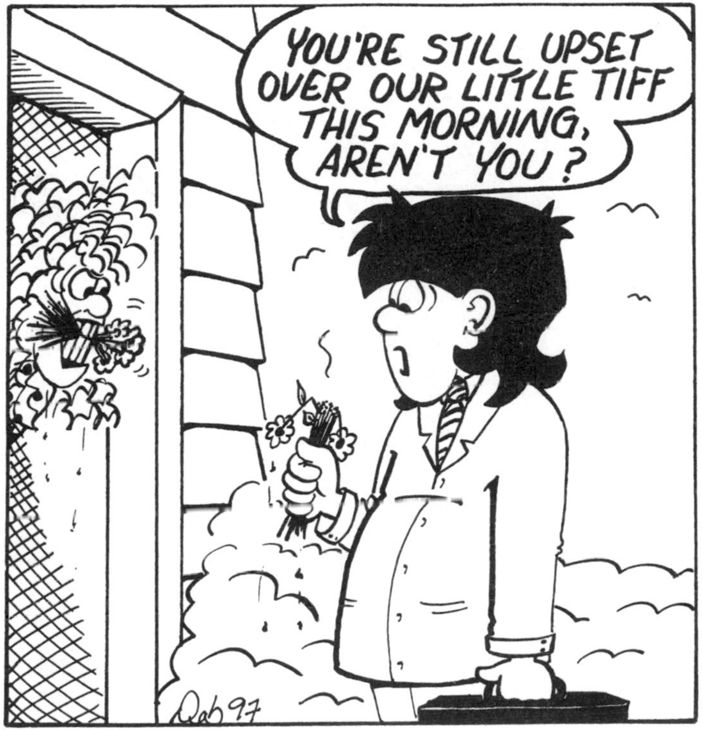
YOU'RE STILL UPSET OVER OUR LITTLE TIFF THIS MORNING, AREN'T YOU?
Deb97

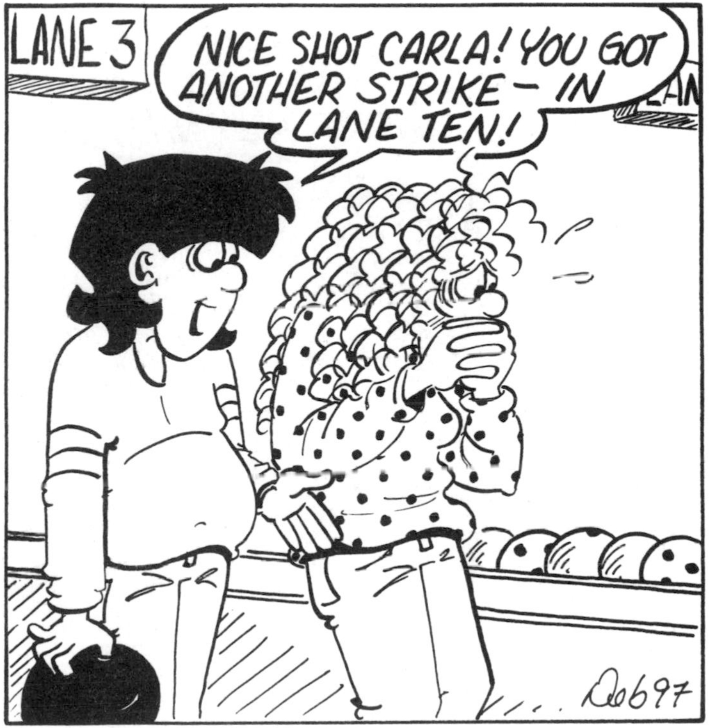
LANE 3
NICE SHOT CARLA! YOU GOT ANOTHER STRIKE— IN LANE TEN!
Deb97

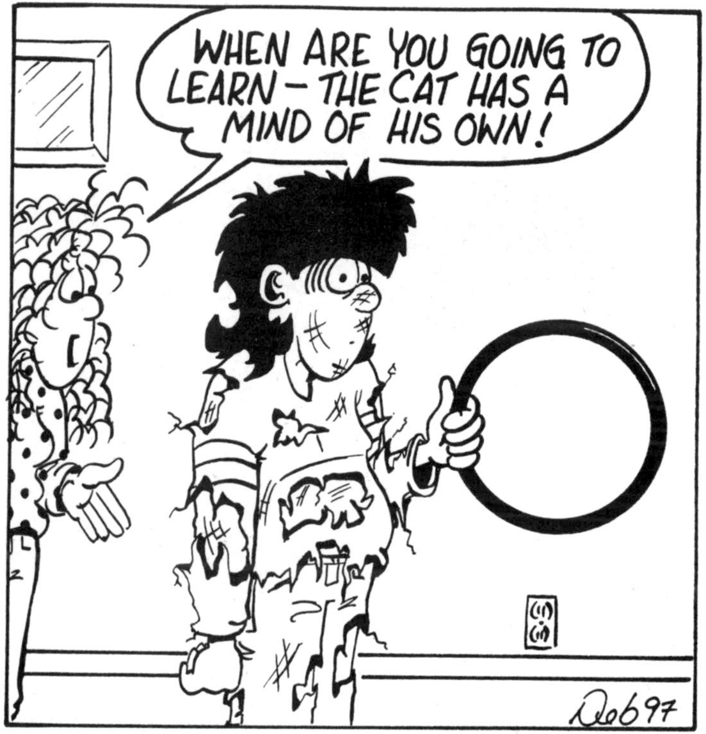
WHEN ARE YOU GOING TO LEARN – THE CAT HAS A MIND OF HIS OWN!
Deb97

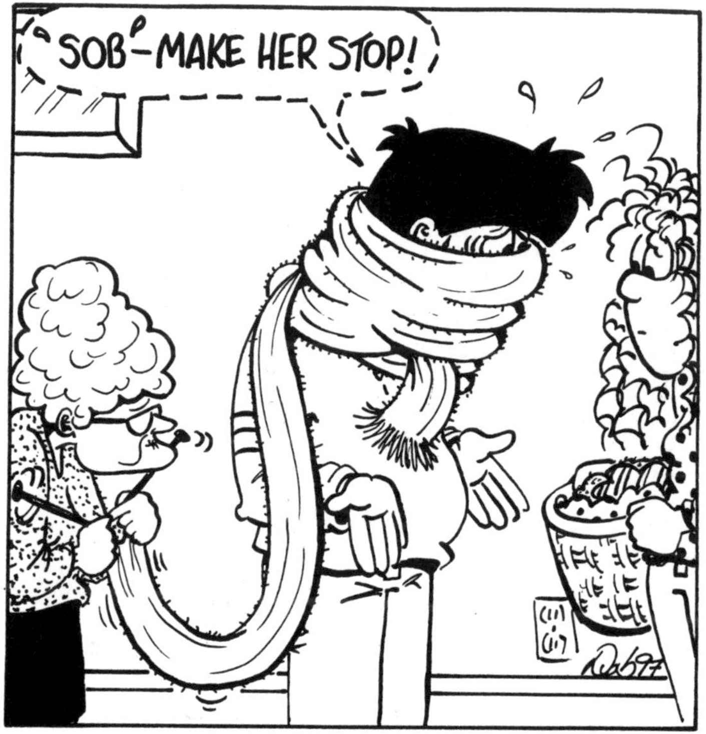
SOB – MAKE HER STOP!
Deb97

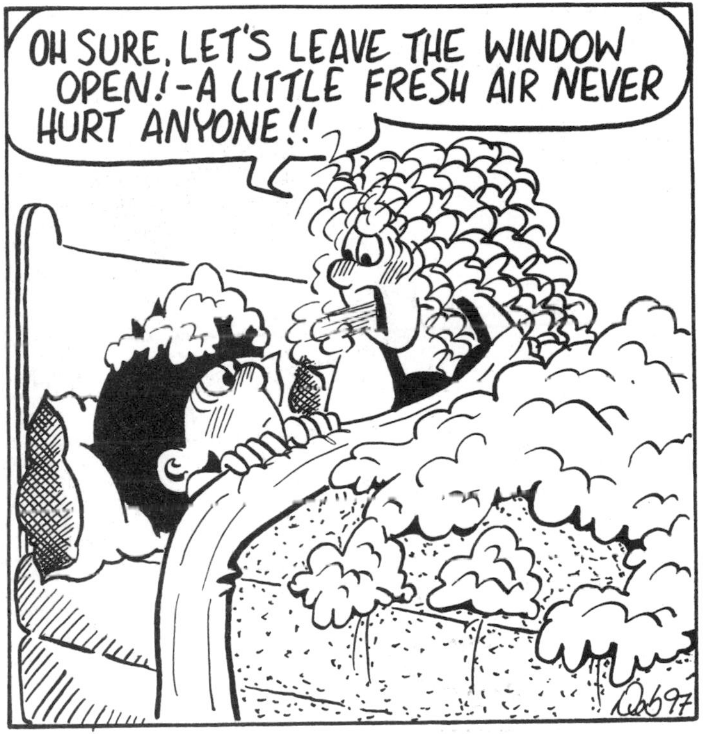
OH SURE, LET'S LEAVE THE WINDOW OPEN! - A LITTLE FRESH AIR NEVER HURT ANYONE!!

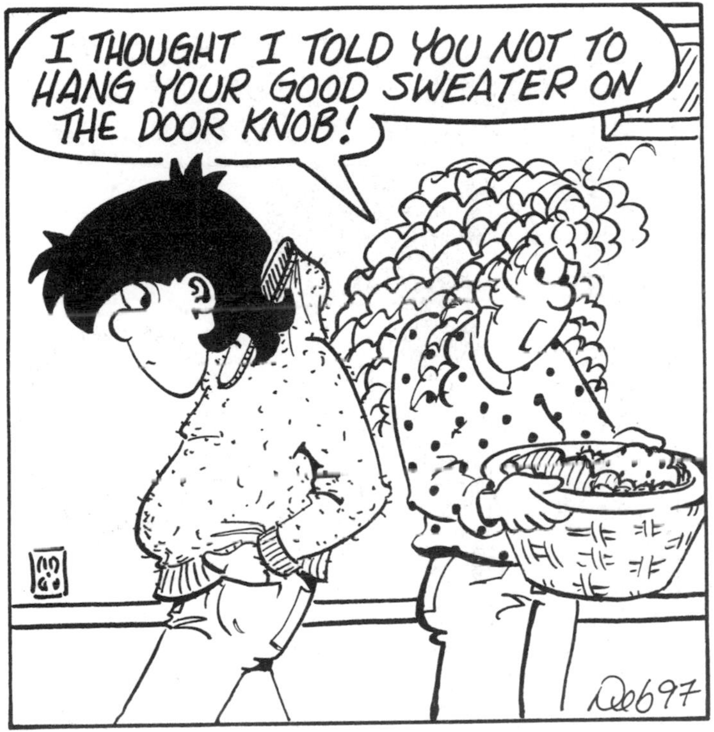
I THOUGHT I TOLD YOU NOT TO HANG YOUR GOOD SWEATER ON THE DOOR KNOB!

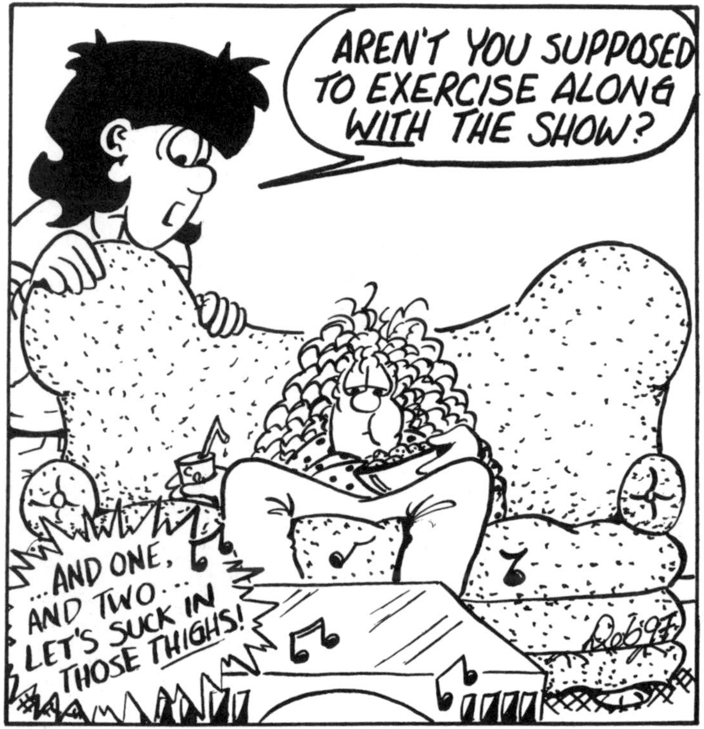
AREN'T YOU SUPPOSED TO EXERCISE ALONG WITH THE SHOW?
...AND ONE, AND TWO... LET'S SUCK IN THOSE THIGHS!

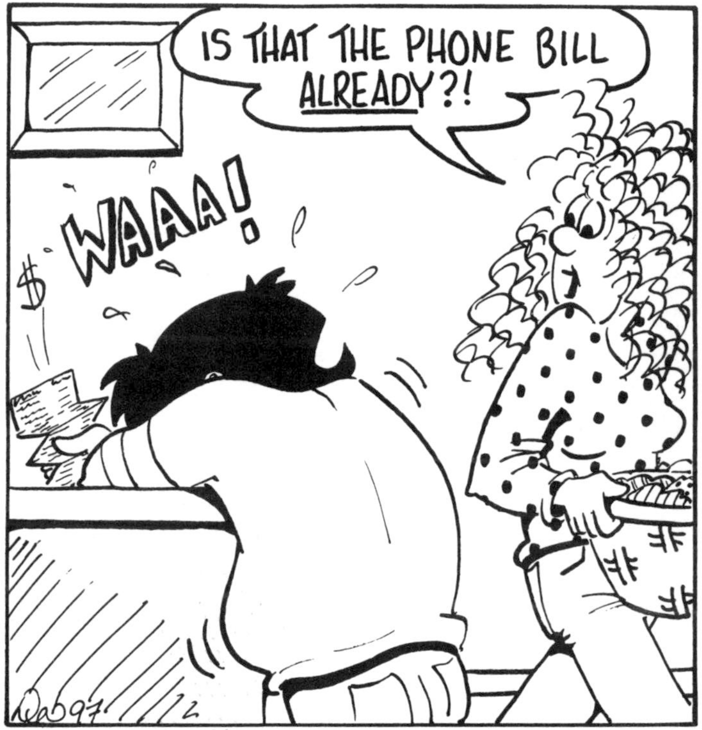
IS THAT THE PHONE BILL ALREADY?!
WAAAA!

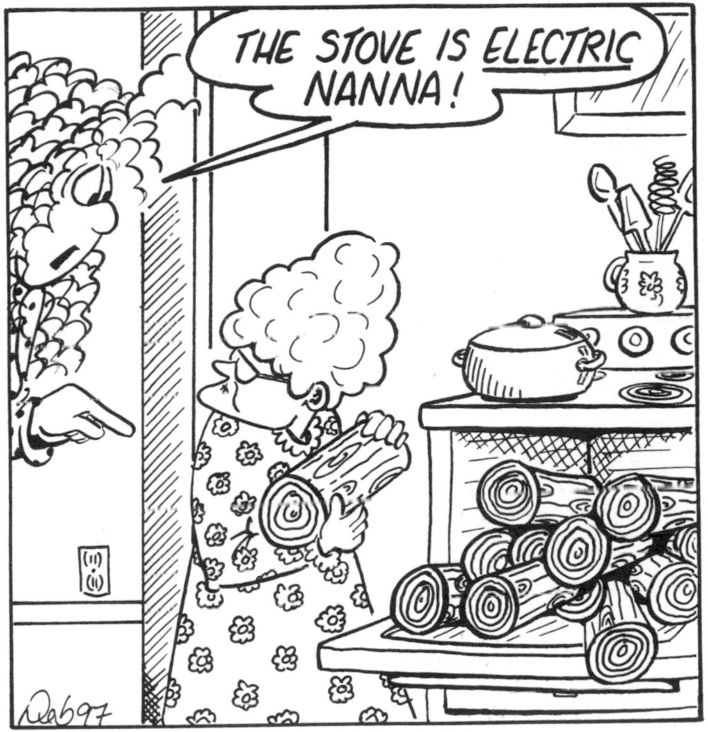
THE STOVE IS ELECTRIC NANNA!
Dab 97

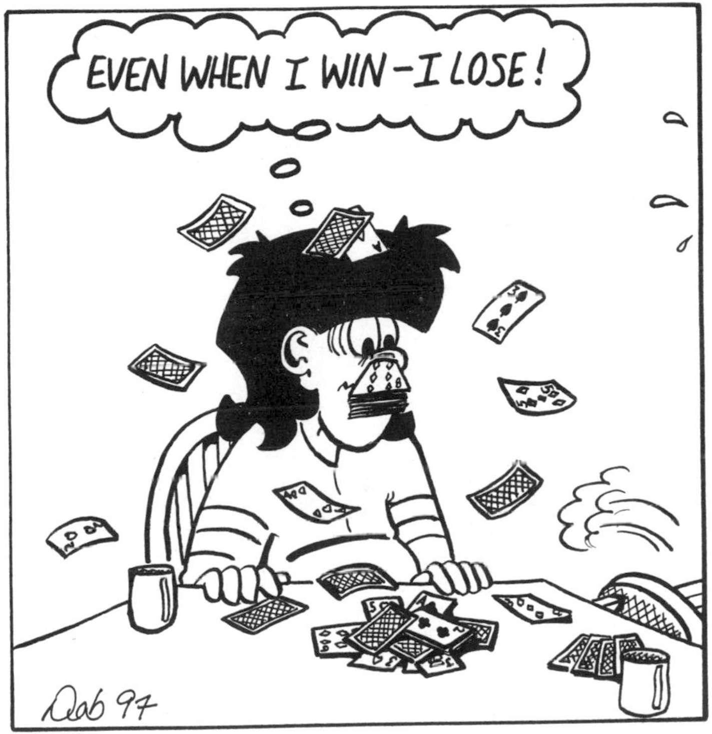
EVEN WHEN I WIN-I LOSE!
Dab 97

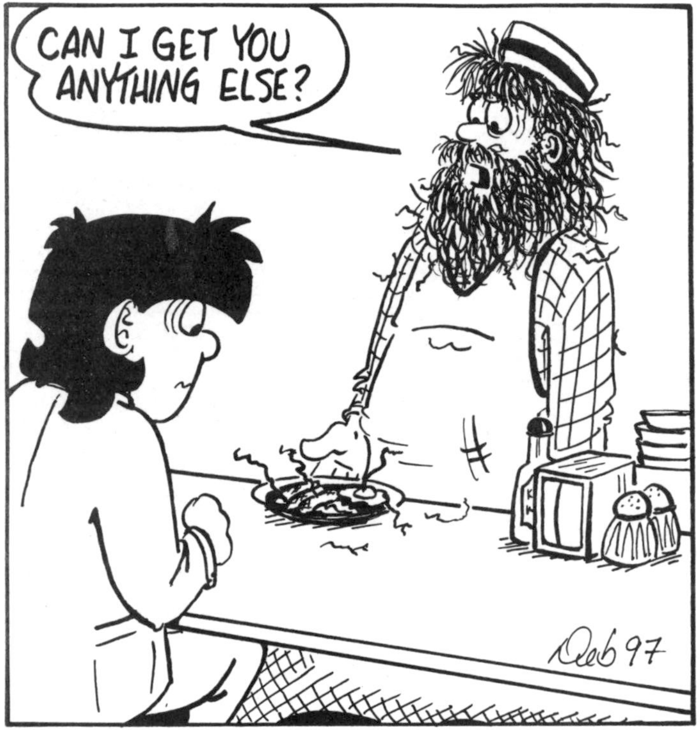
CAN I GET YOU ANYTHING ELSE?
Deb 97

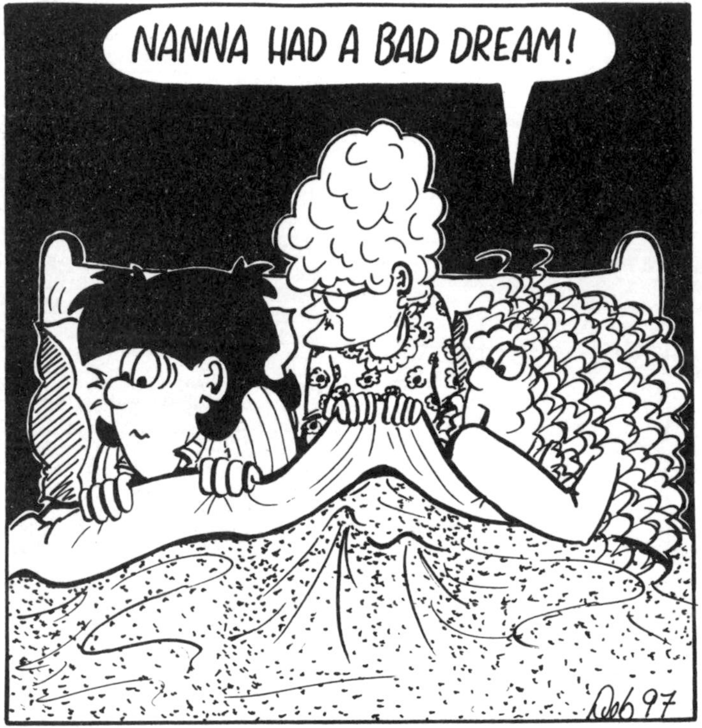
NANNA HAD A BAD DREAM!
Deb 97

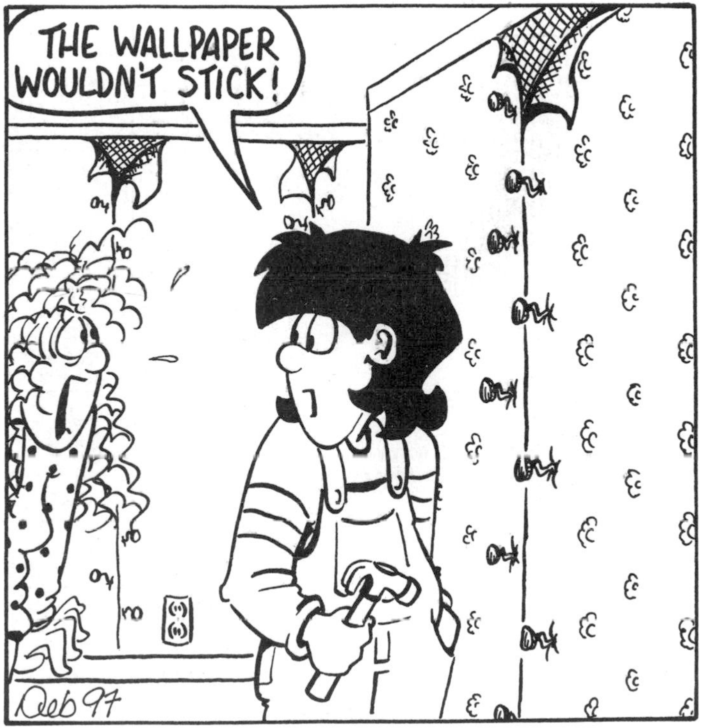
THE WALLPAPER WOULDN'T STICK!
Deb 97

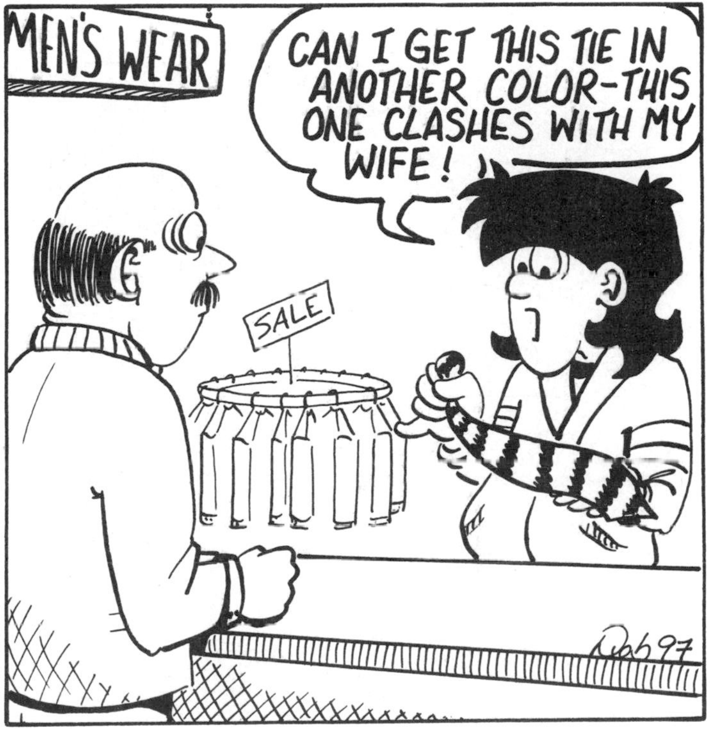
MEN'S WEAR
CAN I GET THIS TIE IN ANOTHER COLOR-THIS ONE CLASHES WITH MY WIFE!
SALE
Deb 97

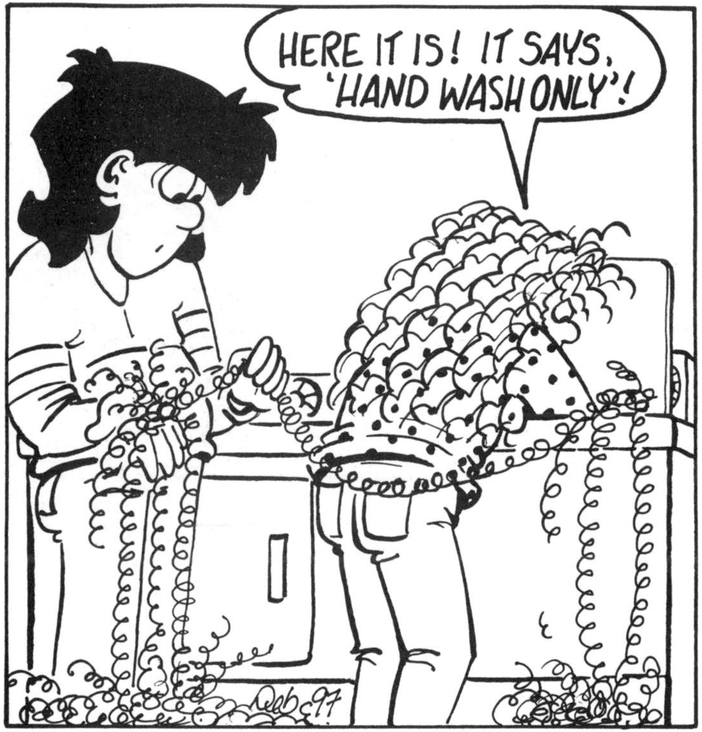
HERE IT IS! IT SAYS, 'HAND WASH ONLY'!
Dab 97

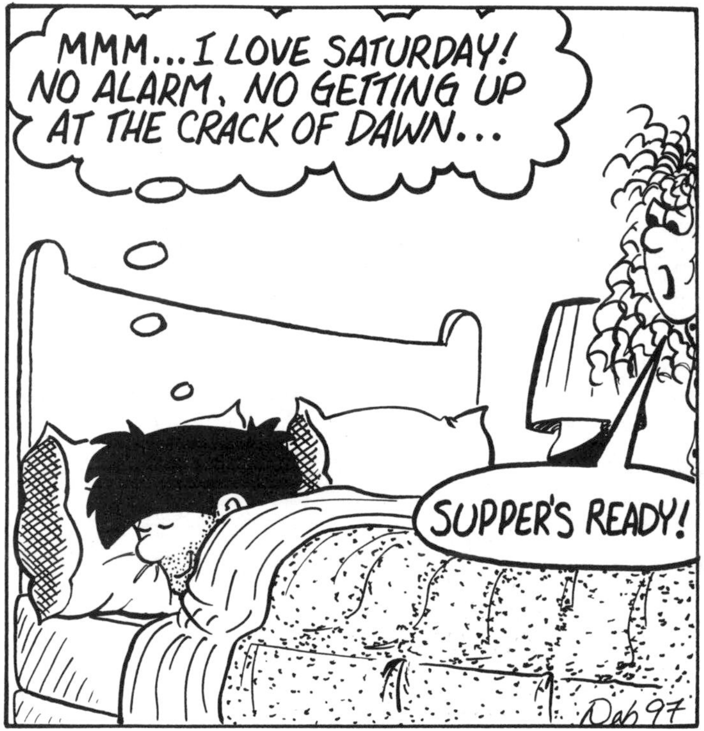
MMM...I LOVE SATURDAY! NO ALARM, NO GETTING UP AT THE CRACK OF DAWN...
SUPPER'S READY!
Dab 97

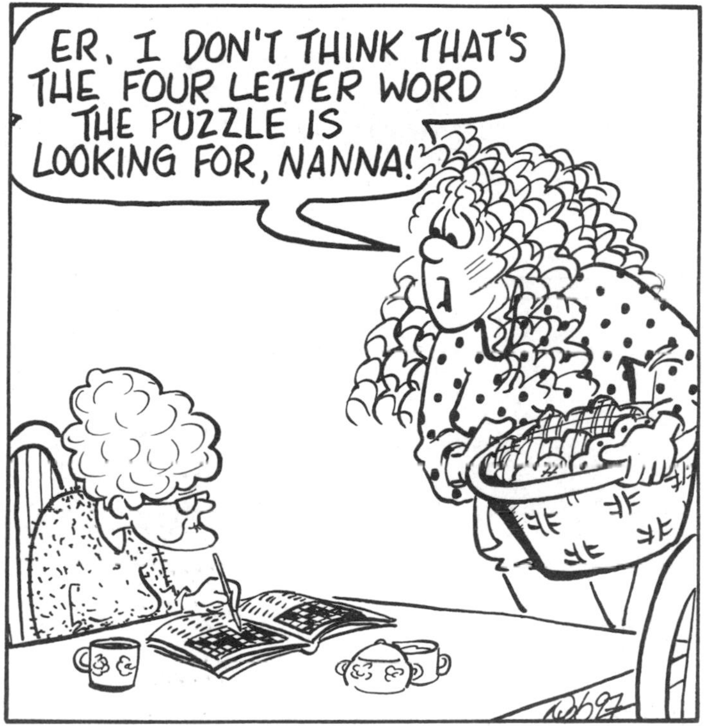
ER, I DON'T THINK THAT'S THE FOUR LETTER WORD THE PUZZLE IS LOOKING FOR, NANNA!
Deb 97

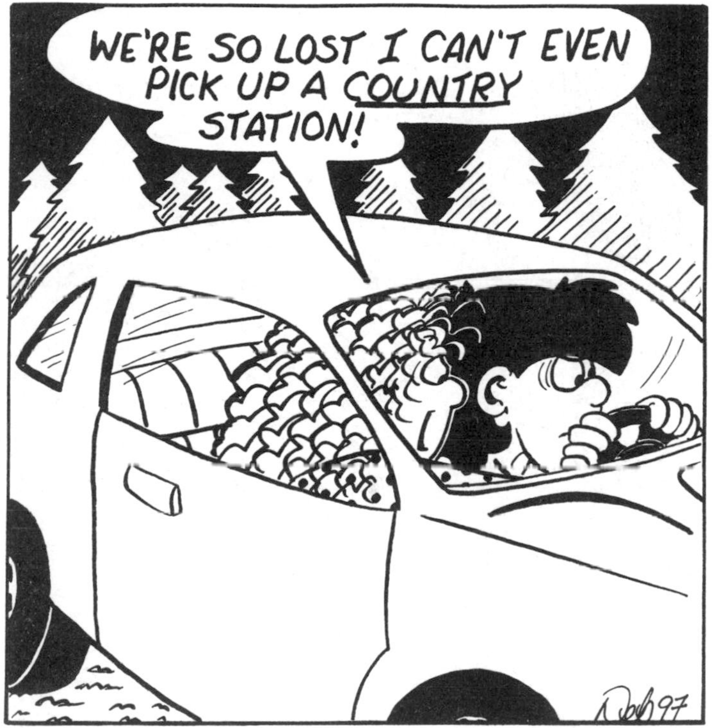
WE'RE SO LOST I CAN'T EVEN PICK UP A COUNTRY STATION!
Deb 97

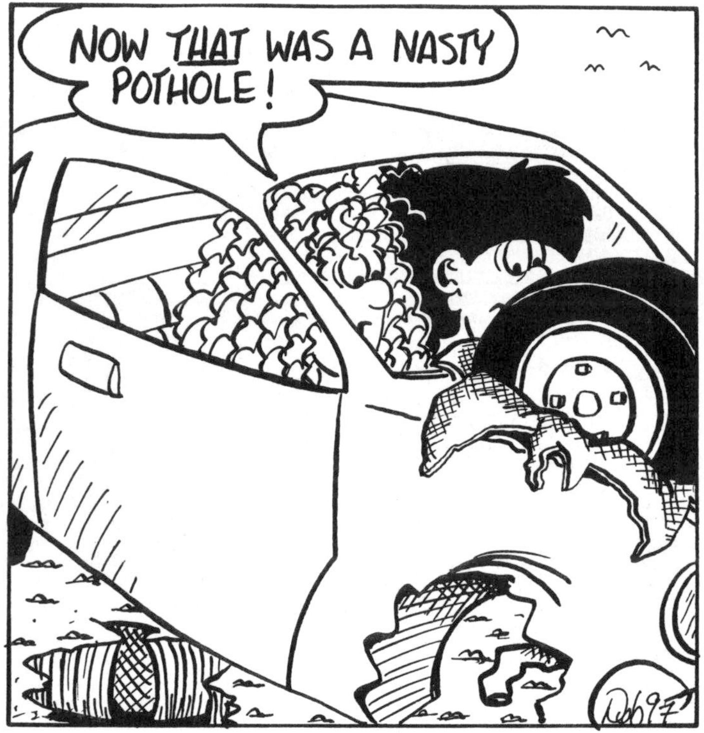
NOW THAT WAS A NASTY POTHOLE!
Deb97

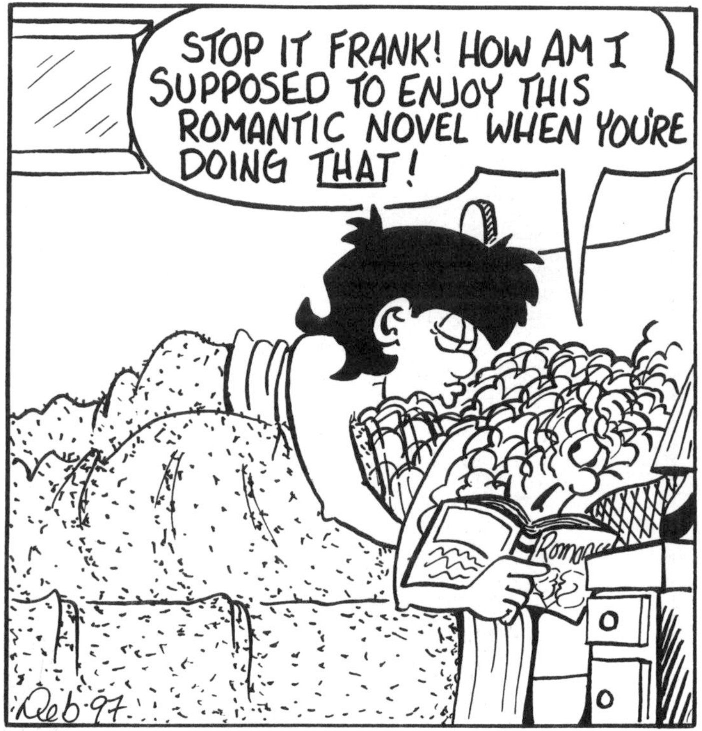
STOP IT FRANK! HOW AM I SUPPOSED TO ENJOY THIS ROMANTIC NOVEL WHEN YOU'RE DOING THAT!
Deb 97

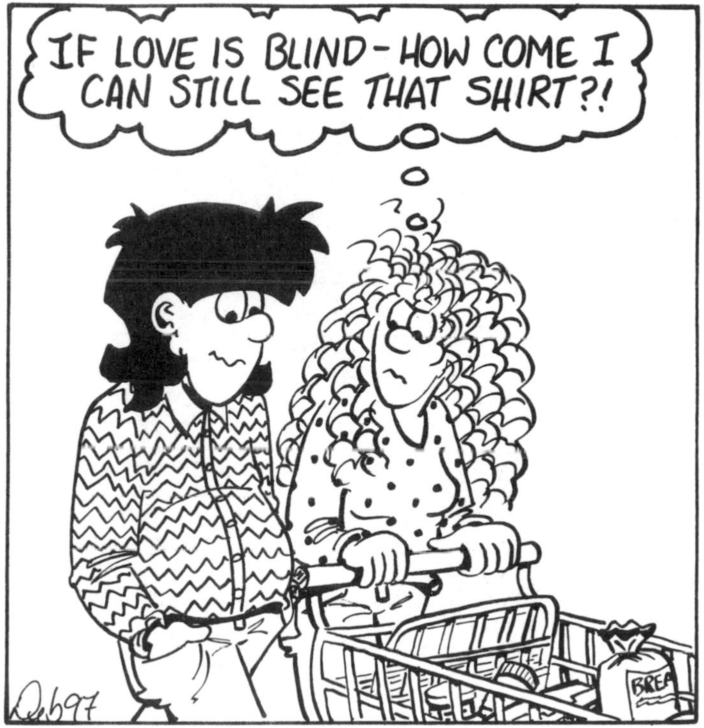
IF LOVE IS BLIND - HOW COME I CAN STILL SEE THAT SHIRT?!
BREA
Deb 97

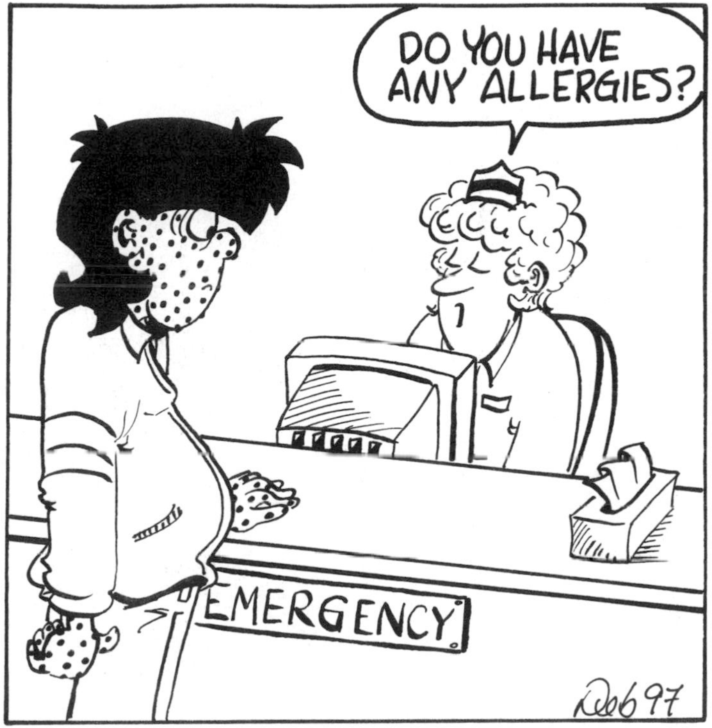
DO YOU HAVE ANY ALLERGIES?
EMERGENCY
Deb 97

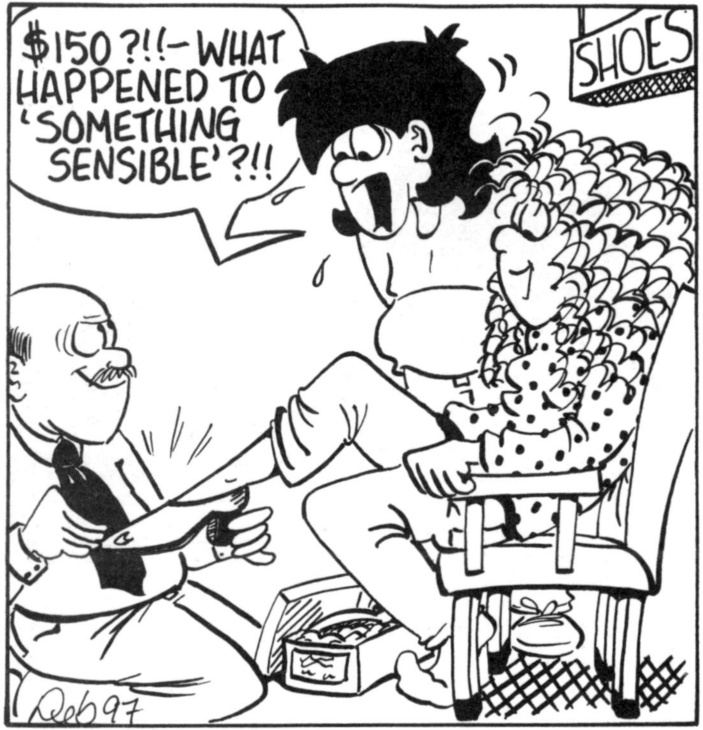
$150 ?!!-WHAT HAPPENED TO 'SOMETHING SENSIBLE'?!!
SHOES
Deb 97

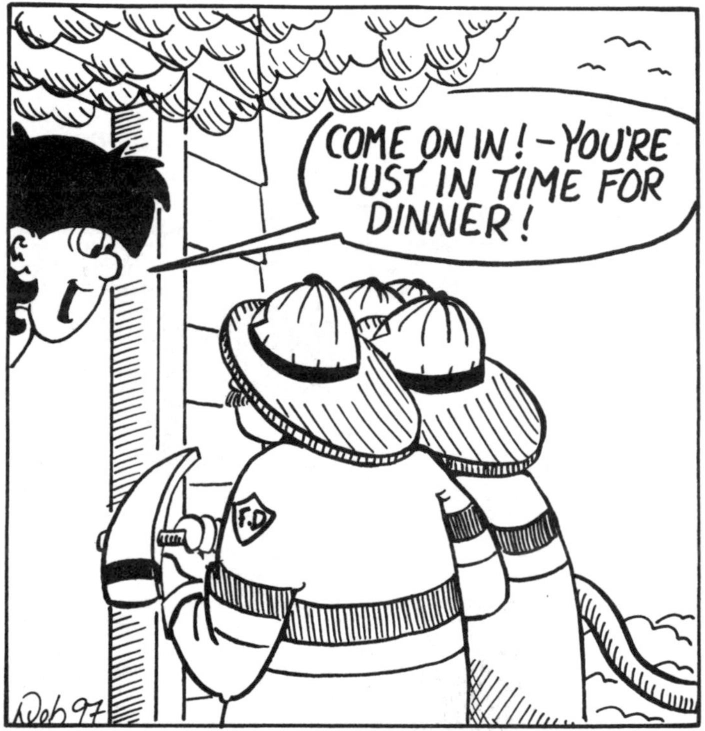
COME ON IN! - YOU'RE JUST IN TIME FOR DINNER!
F.D.
Deb 97

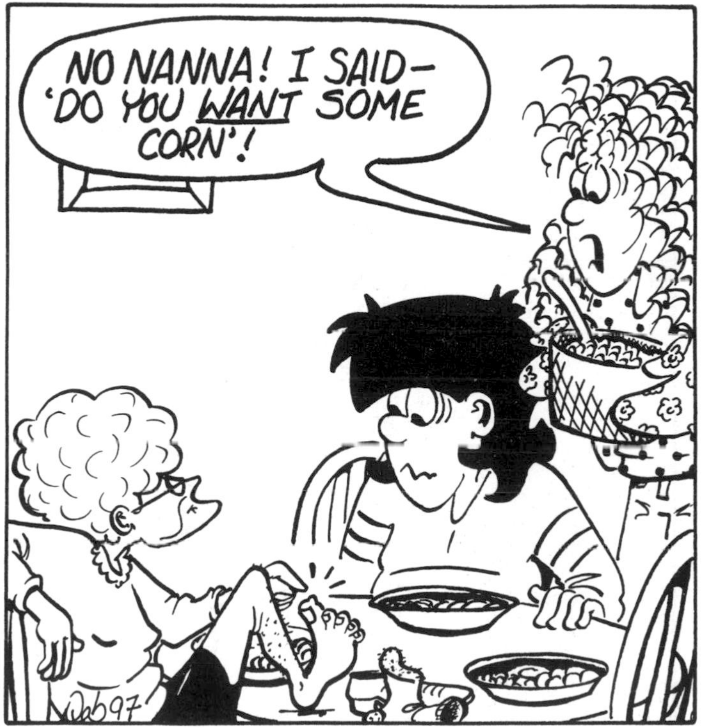
NO NANNA! I SAID—
'DO YOU WANT SOME
CORN'!
Dab97

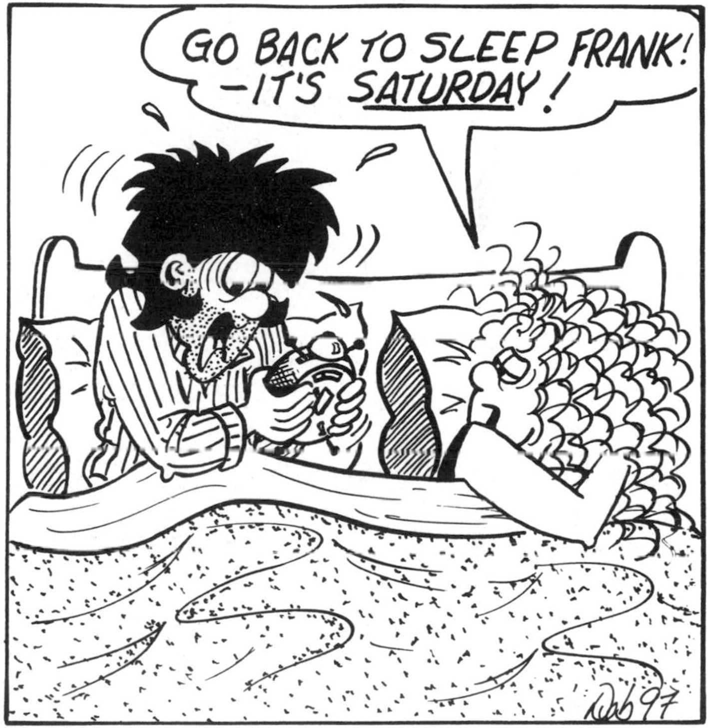
GO BACK TO SLEEP FRANK!
—IT'S SATURDAY!
Dab97

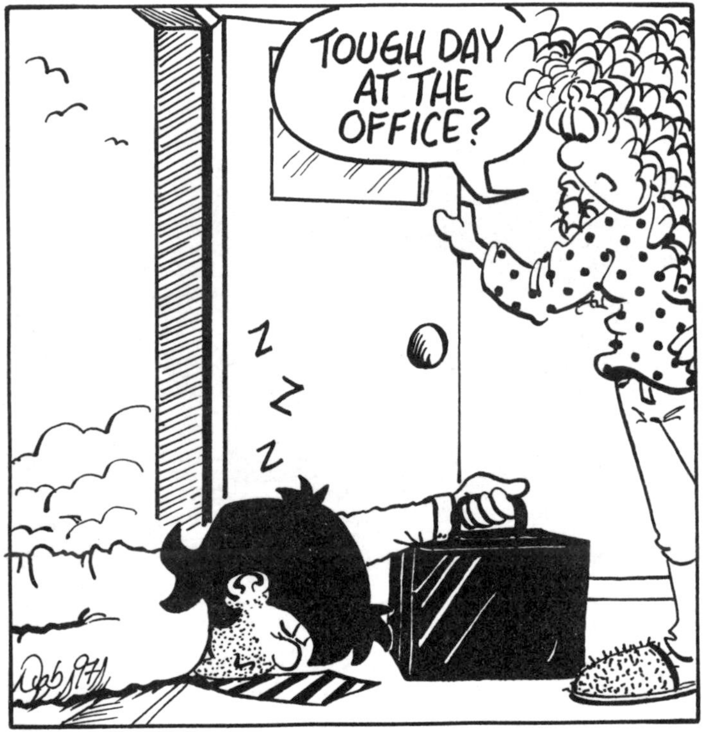
TOUGH DAY AT THE OFFICE?
Z Z Z
Deb 97

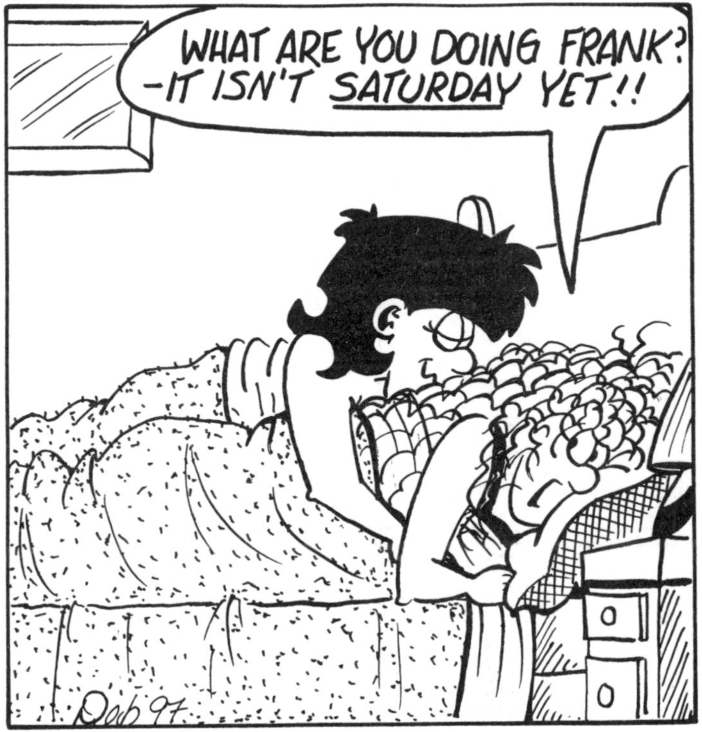
WHAT ARE YOU DOING FRANK? -IT ISN'T SATURDAY YET!!
Deb 97

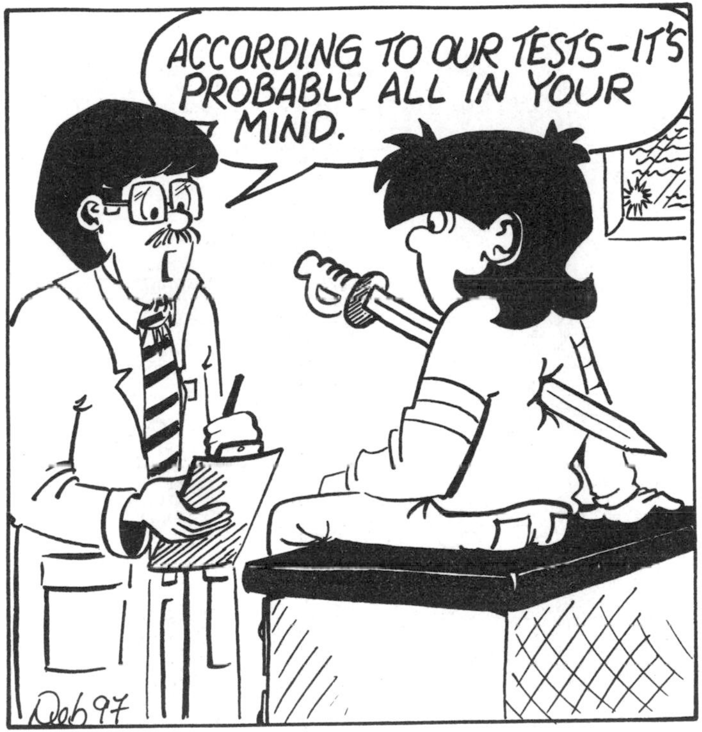
ACCORDING TO OUR TESTS-IT'S PROBABLY ALL IN YOUR MIND.
Deb 97

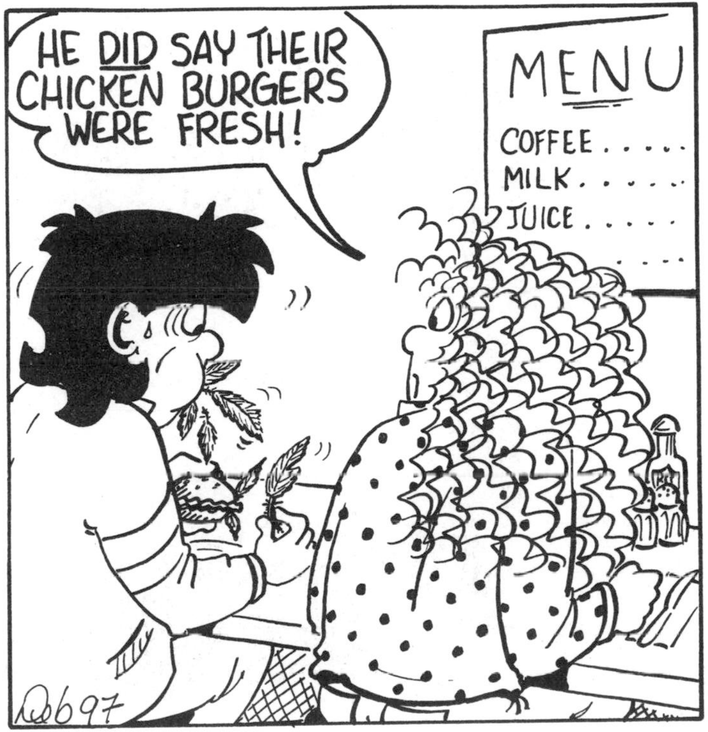
HE DID SAY THEIR CHICKEN BURGERS WERE FRESH!
MENU
COFFEE.....
MILK.......
JUICE.....
Deb 97

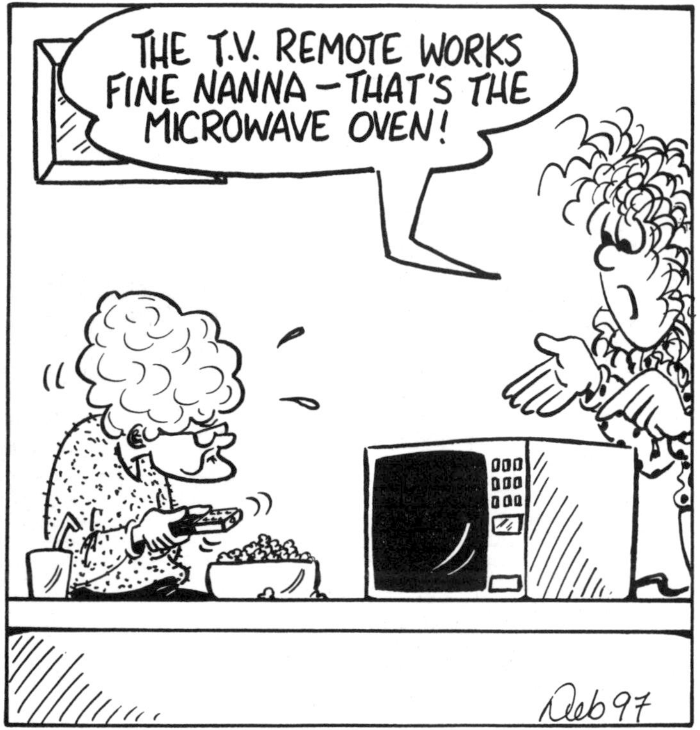
THE T.V. REMOTE WORKS FINE NANNA – THAT'S THE MICROWAVE OVEN!
Deb 97

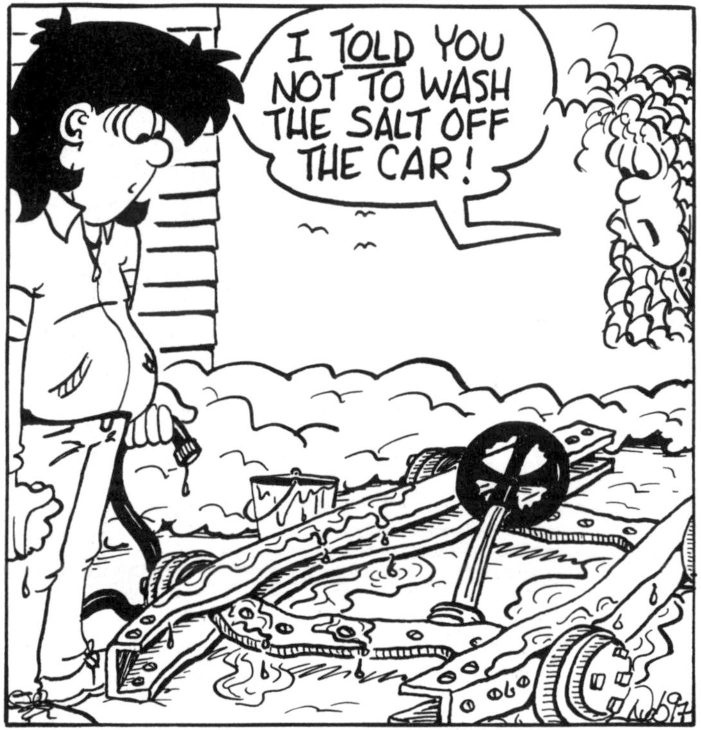
I TOLD YOU NOT TO WASH THE SALT OFF THE CAR!

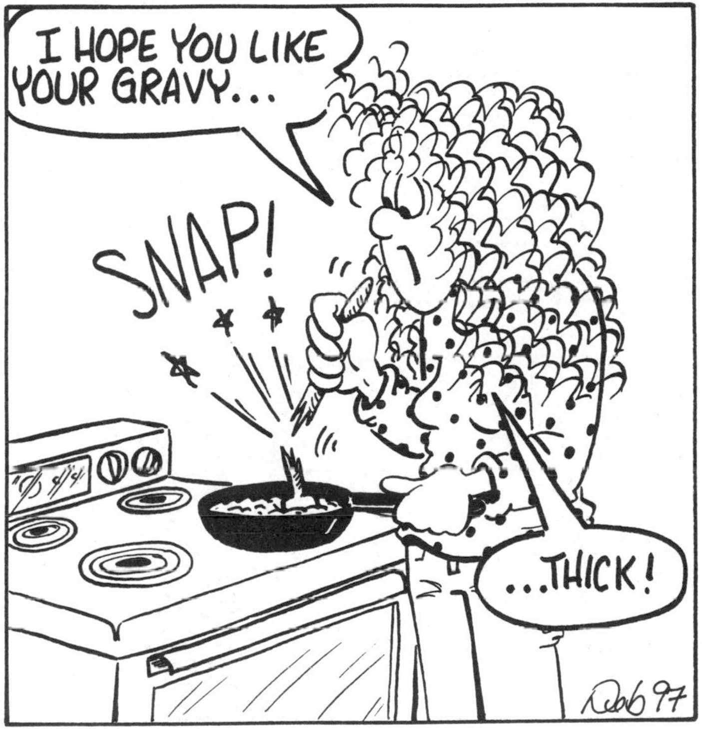
I HOPE YOU LIKE YOUR GRAVY...
SNAP!
...THICK!
Deb 97

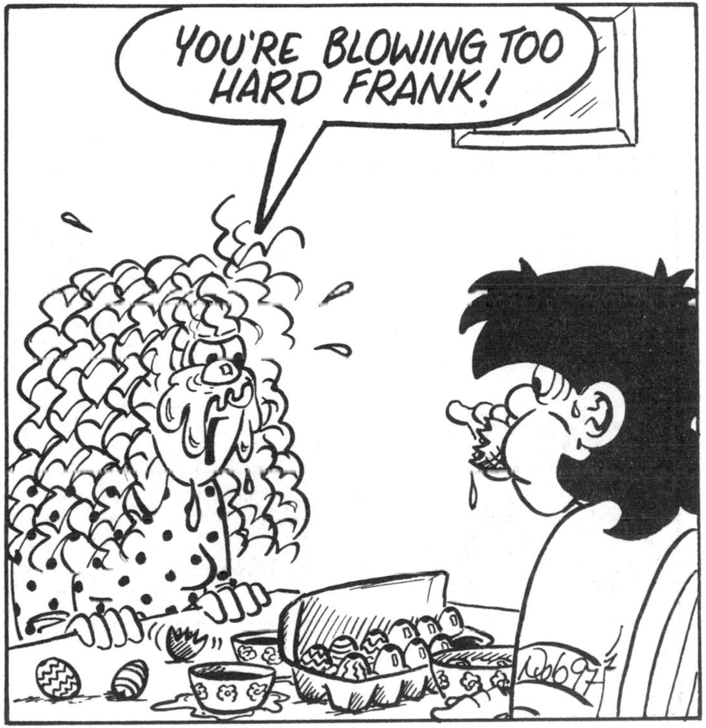
YOU'RE BLOWING TOO HARD FRANK!
Deb 97

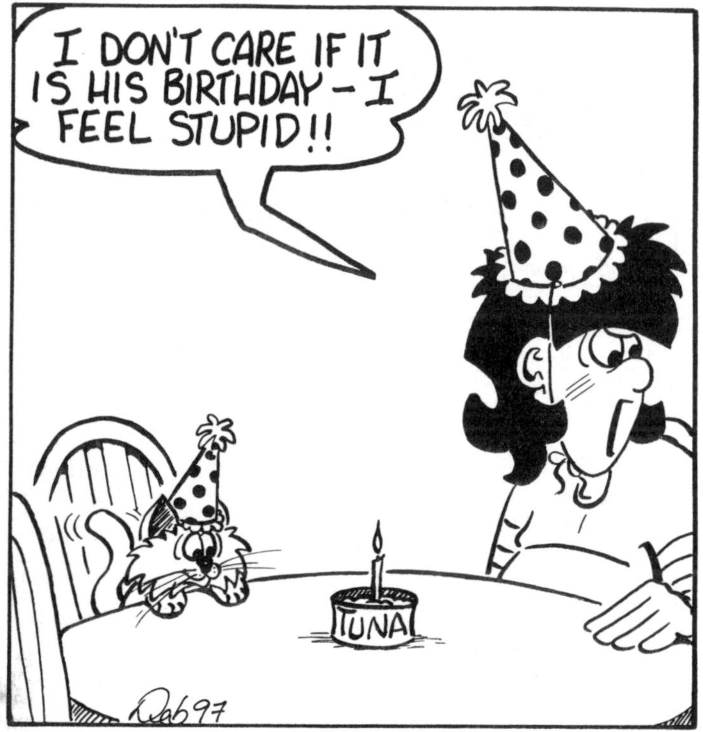
I DON'T CARE IF IT IS HIS BIRTHDAY - I FEEL STUPID!!
TUNA
Deb97

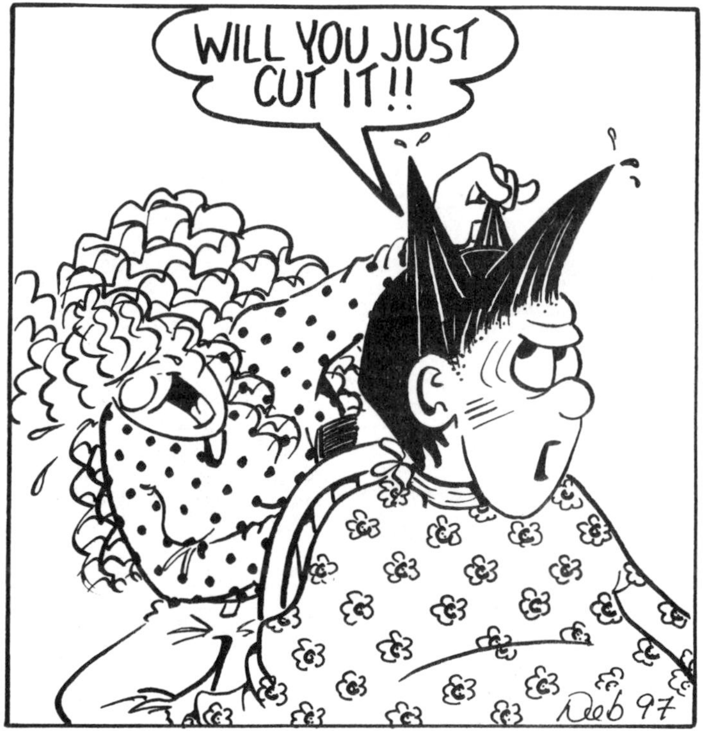
WILL YOU JUST CUT IT!!
Deb 97

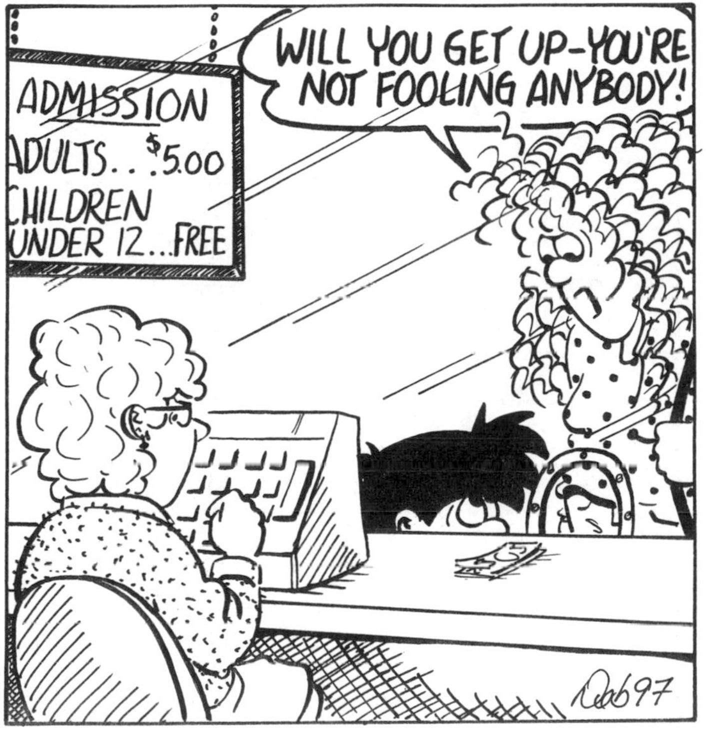
ADMISSION
ADULTS...$5.00
CHILDREN UNDER 12...FREE
WILL YOU GET UP-YOU'RE NOT FOOLING ANYBODY!
Lab97

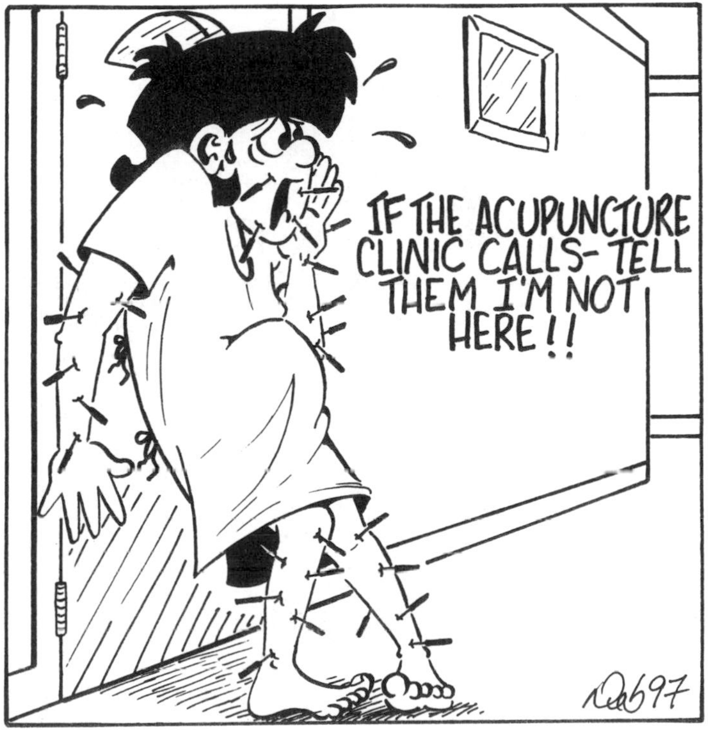
IF THE ACUPUNCTURE CLINIC CALLS- TELL THEM I'M NOT HERE!!
Lab97

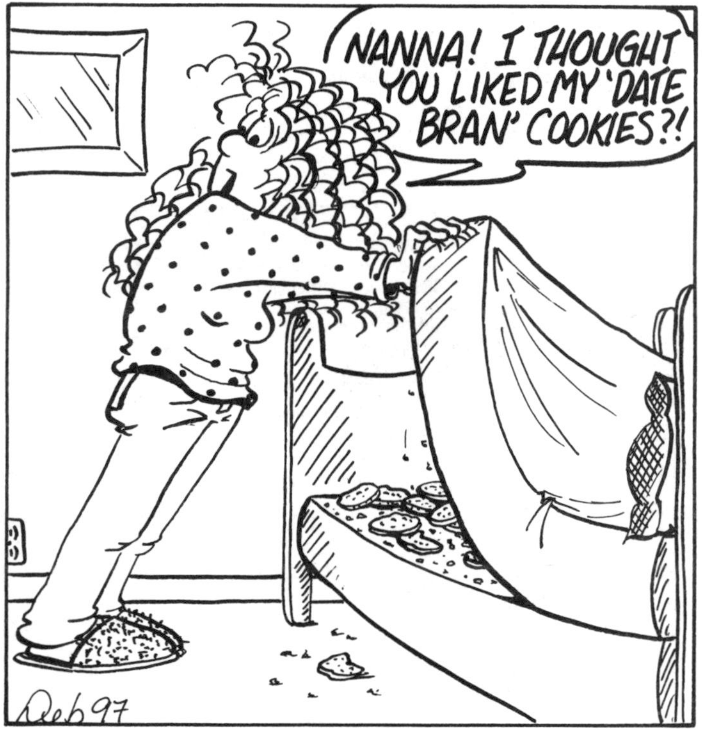
NANNA! I THOUGHT YOU LIKED MY 'DATE BRAN' COOKIES?!
Deb97

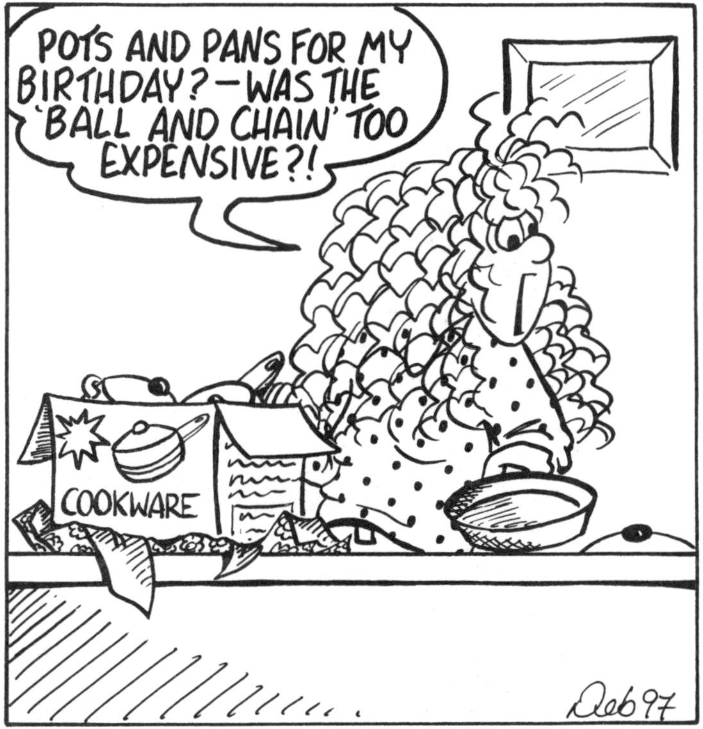
POTS AND PANS FOR MY BIRTHDAY?—WAS THE 'BALL AND CHAIN' TOO EXPENSIVE?!
COOKWARE
Deb97

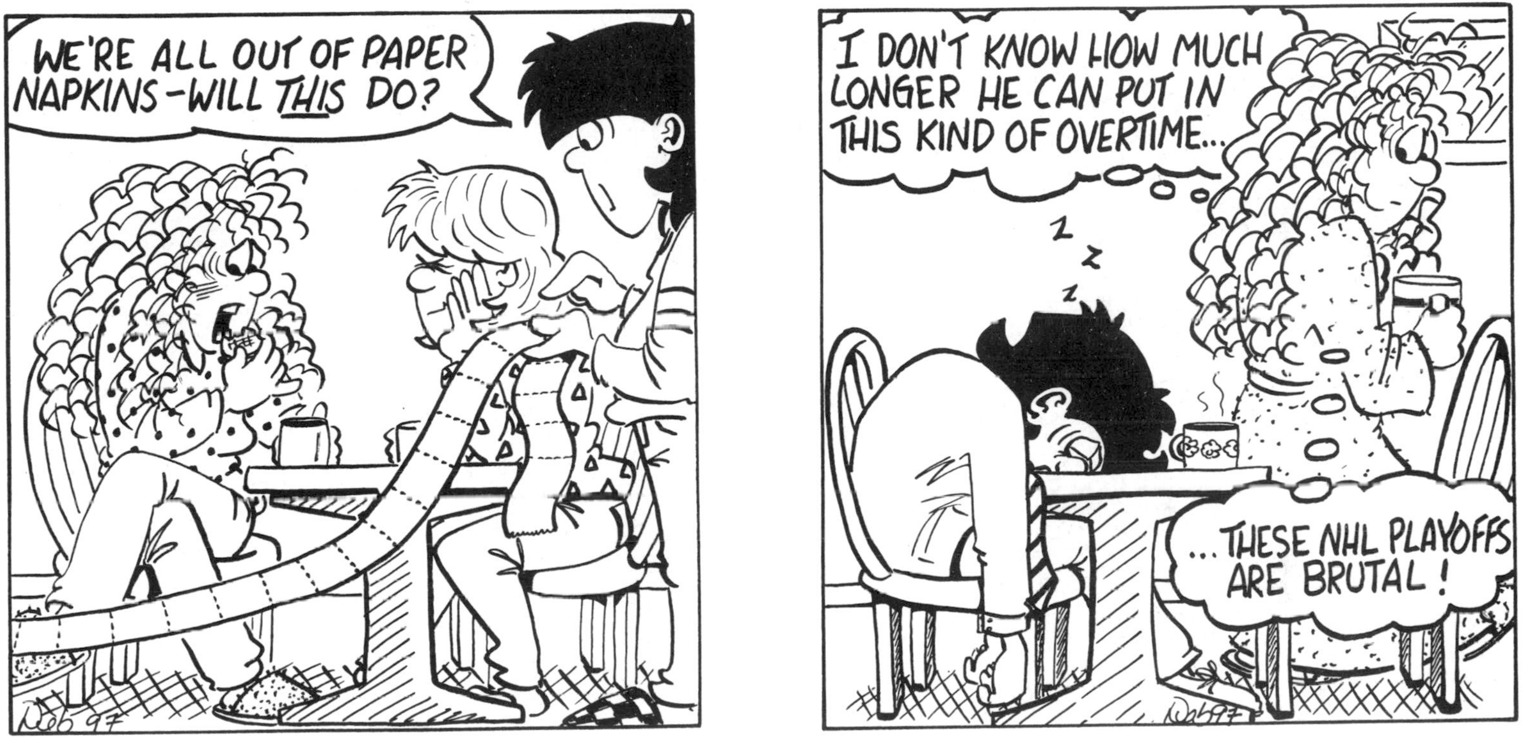
WE'RE ALL OUT OF PAPER NAPKINS-WILL THIS DO?
I DON'T KNOW HOW MUCH LONGER HE CAN PUT IN THIS KIND OF OVERTIME...
Z Z Z
...THESE NHL PLAYOFFS ARE BRUTAL!

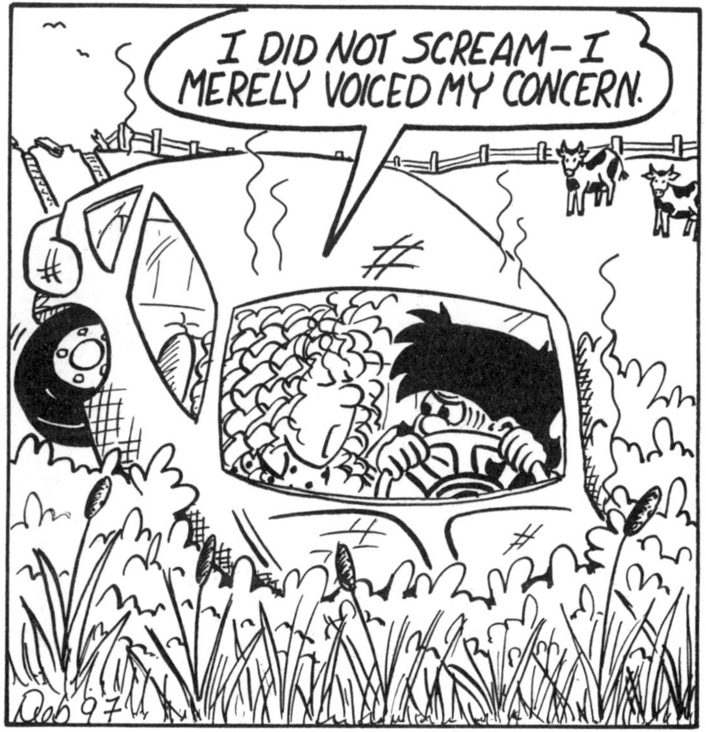
I DID NOT SCREAM- I MERELY VOICED MY CONCERN.
Deb 97

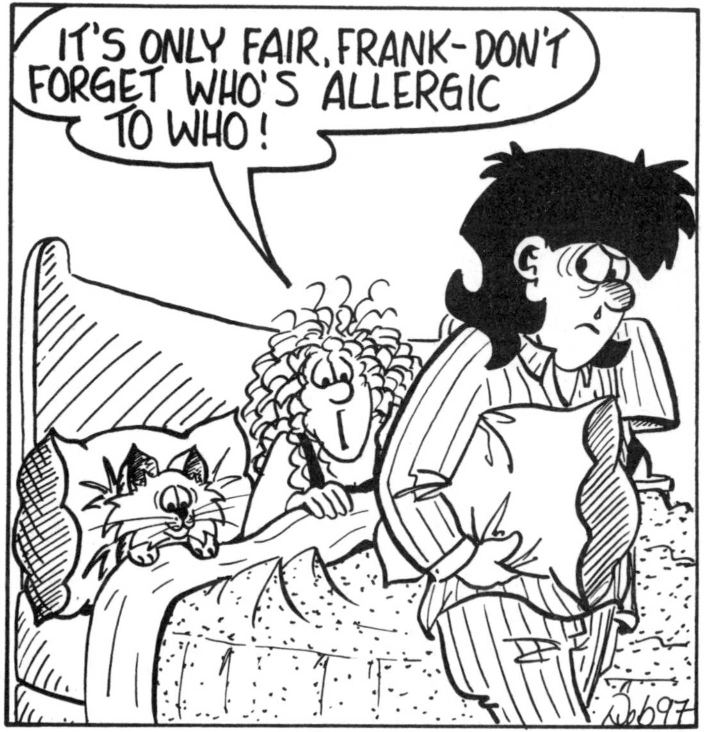
IT'S ONLY FAIR, FRANK- DON'T FORGET WHO'S ALLERGIC TO WHO!
Deb97

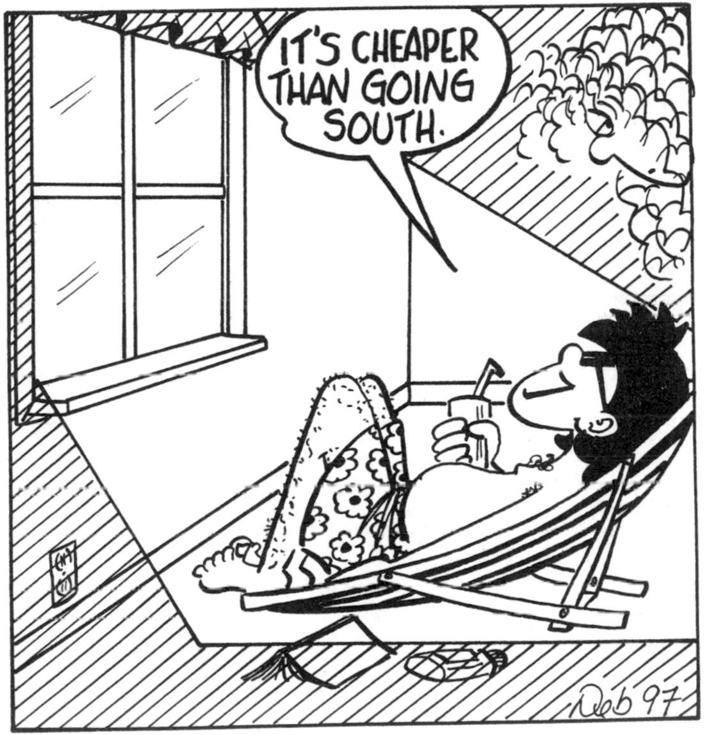
IT'S CHEAPER THAN GOING SOUTH.
Deb 97

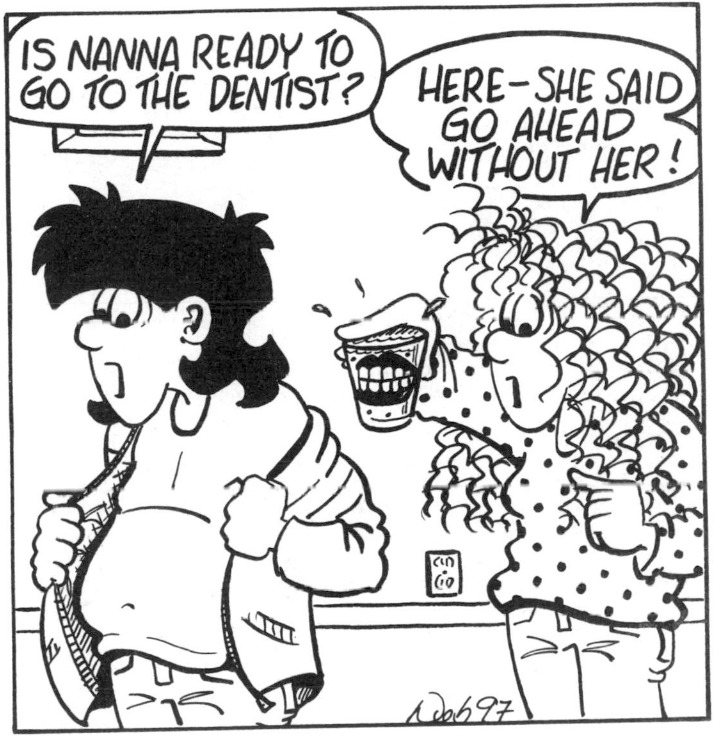
IS NANNA READY TO GO TO THE DENTIST?
HERE–SHE SAID GO AHEAD WITHOUT HER!
Deb 97

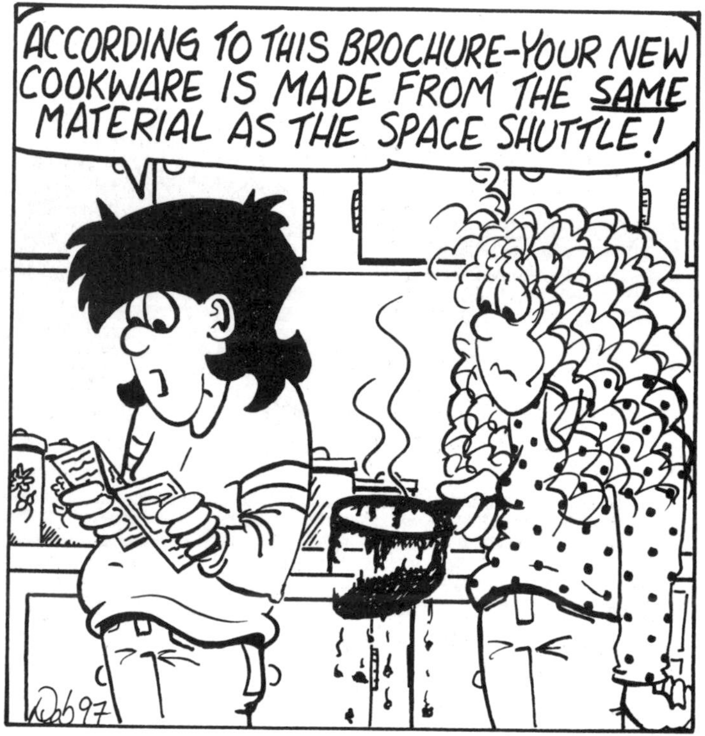
ACCORDING TO THIS BROCHURE-YOUR NEW COOKWARE IS MADE FROM THE SAME MATERIAL AS THE SPACE SHUTTLE!
Deb97

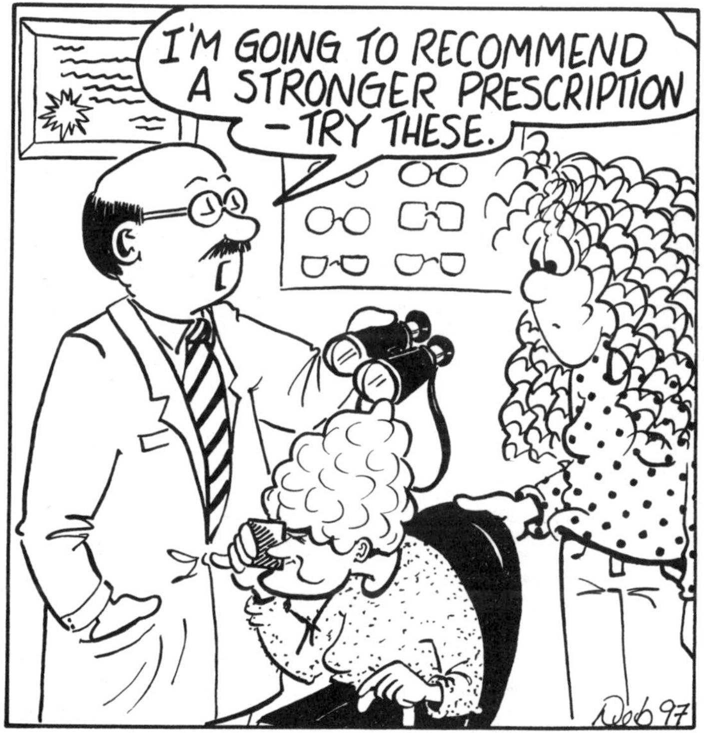
I'M GOING TO RECOMMEND A STRONGER PRESCRIPTION -TRY THESE.
Deb97

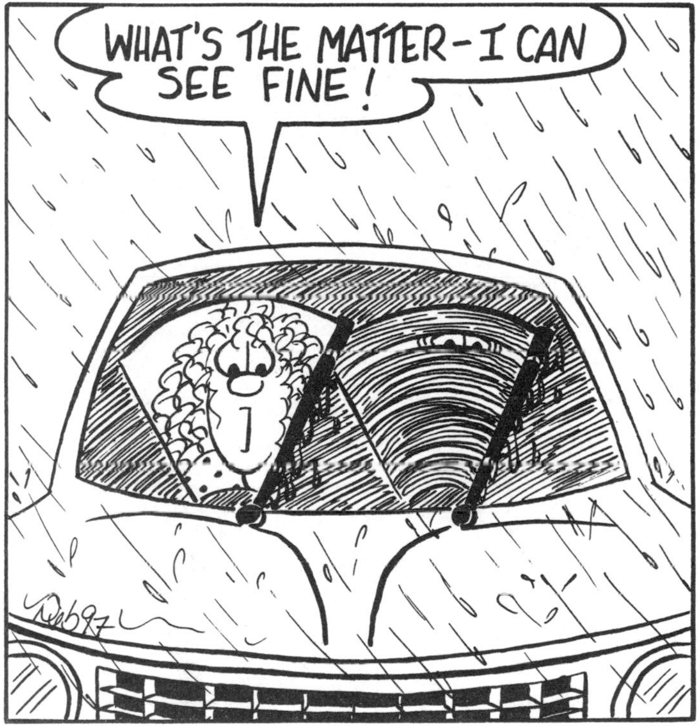
WHAT'S THE MATTER - I CAN SEE FINE!

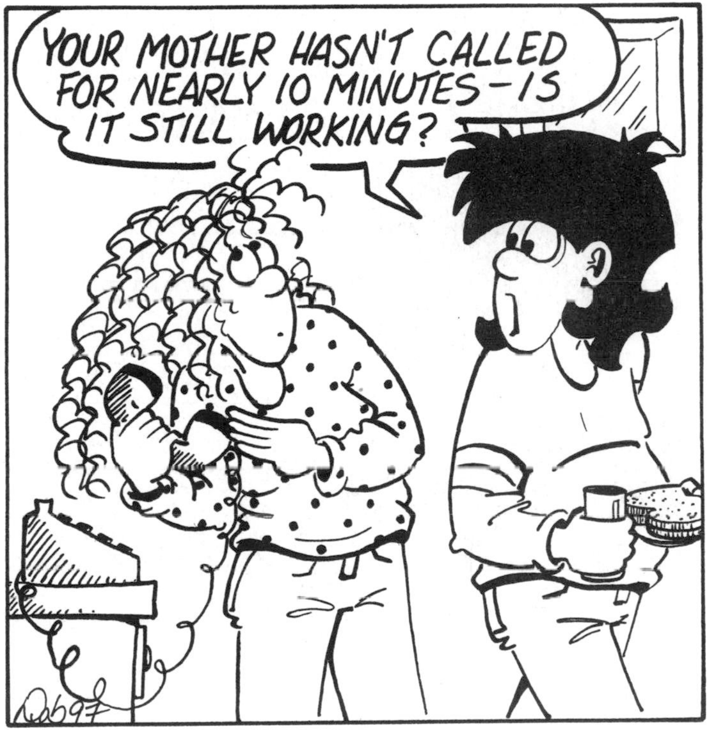
YOUR MOTHER HASN'T CALLED FOR NEARLY 10 MINUTES - IS IT STILL WORKING?

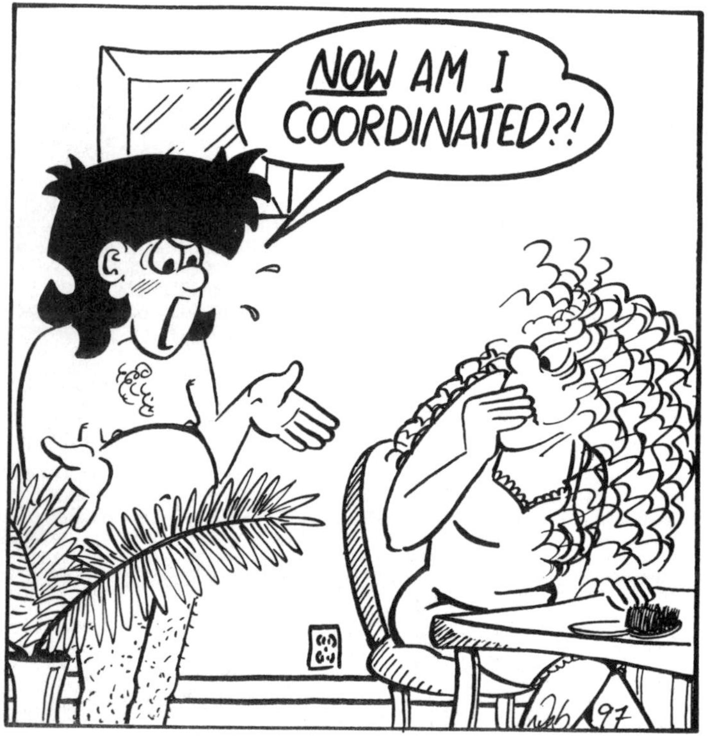
NOW AM I COORDINATED?!
Dub 97

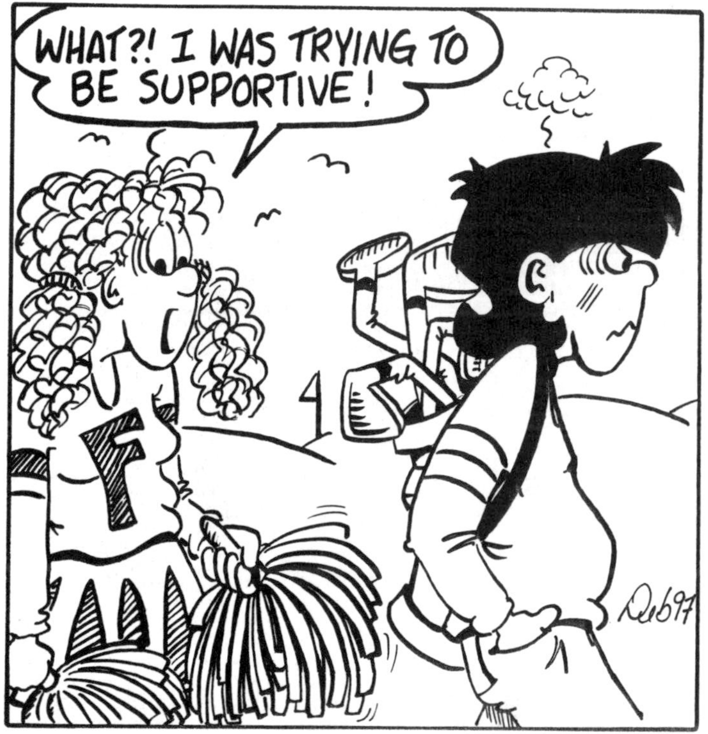
WHAT?! I WAS TRYING TO BE SUPPORTIVE!
F
Dub97

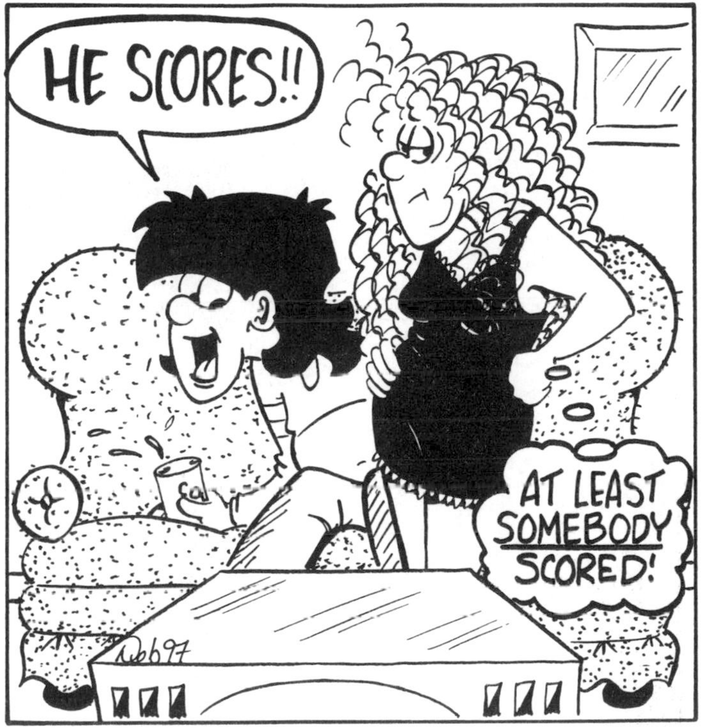
HE SCORES!!
AT LEAST SOMEBODY SCORED!
Neb97

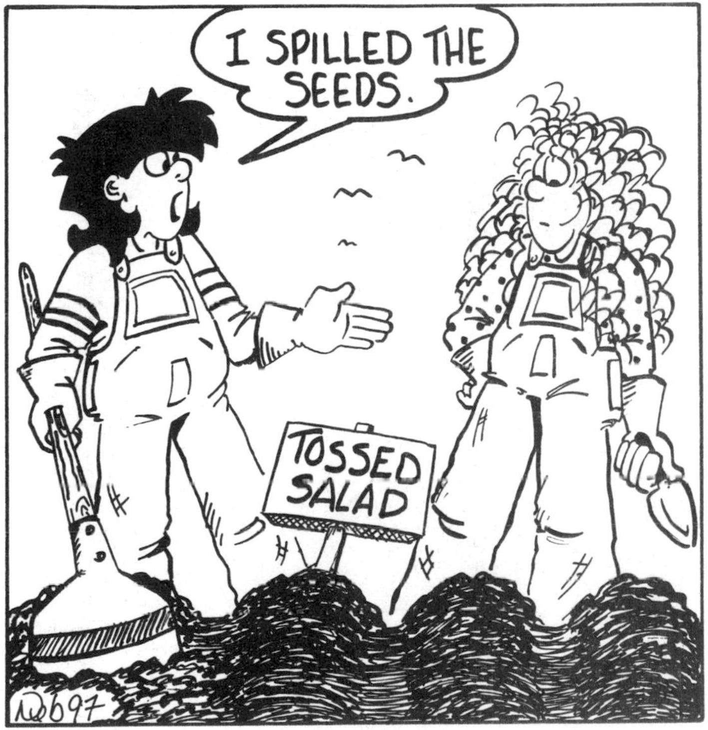
I SPILLED THE SEEDS.
TOSSED SALAD
Neb97

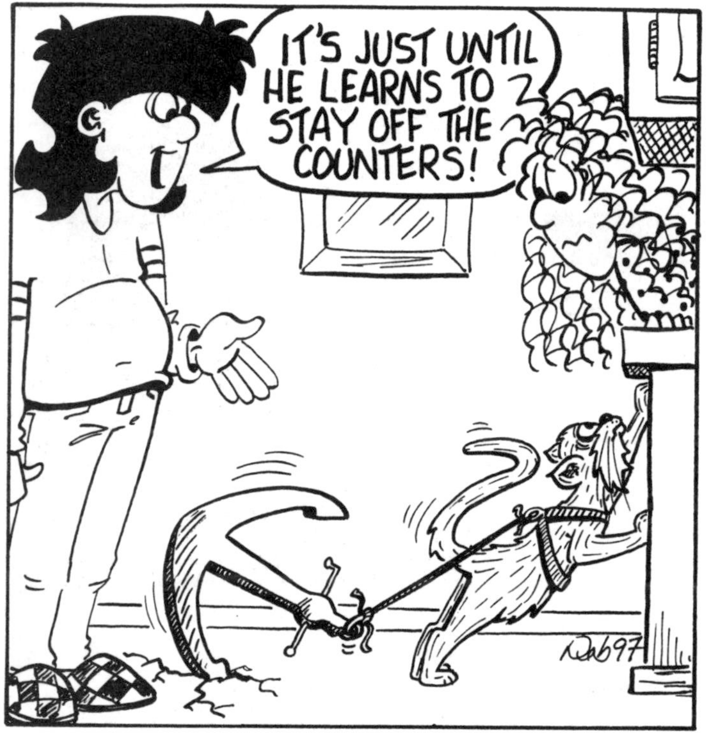
IT'S JUST UNTIL HE LEARNS TO STAY OFF THE COUNTERS!
Wab97

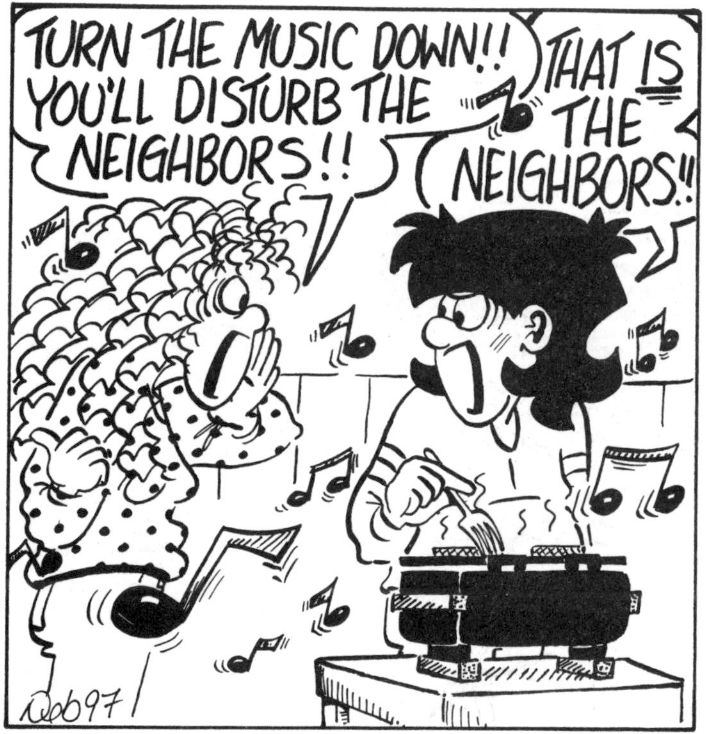
TURN THE MUSIC DOWN!! YOU'LL DISTURB THE NEIGHBORS!!
THAT IS THE NEIGHBORS!!
Wab97

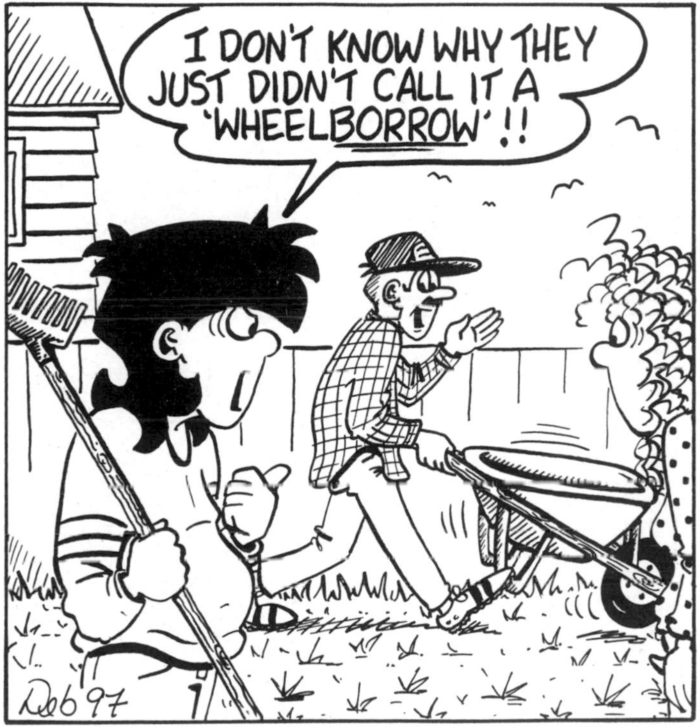
I DON'T KNOW WHY THEY JUST DIDN'T CALL IT A 'WHEELBORROW'!!
Deb 97

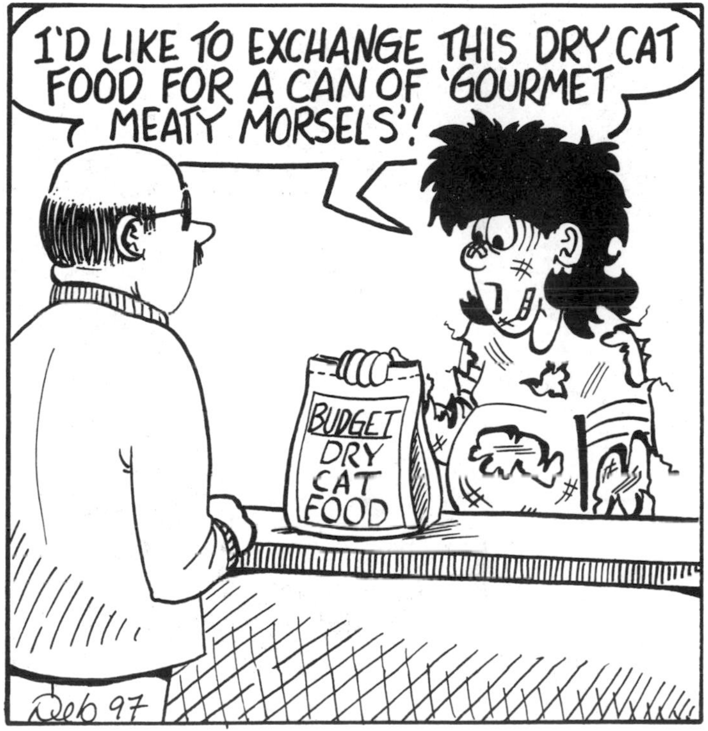
I'D LIKE TO EXCHANGE THIS DRY CAT FOOD FOR A CAN OF 'GOURMET MEATY MORSELS'!
BUDGET DRY CAT FOOD
Deb 97

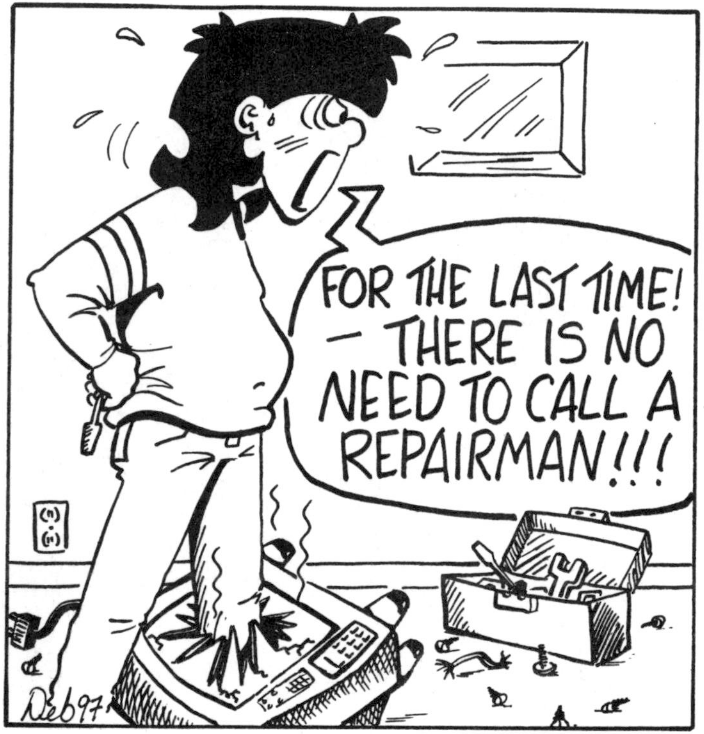
FOR THE LAST TIME! — THERE IS NO NEED TO CALL A REPAIRMAN!!!
Deb97

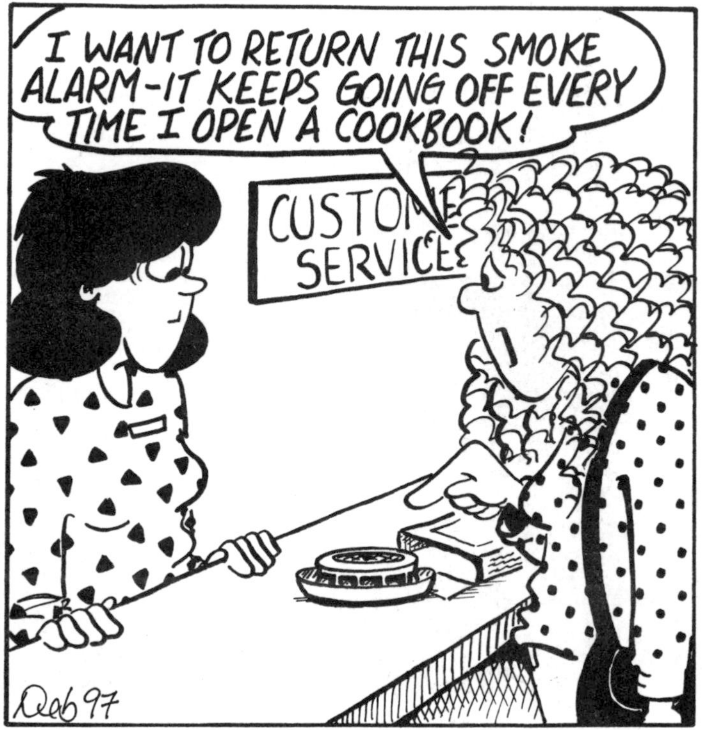
I WANT TO RETURN THIS SMOKE ALARM—IT KEEPS GOING OFF EVERY TIME I OPEN A COOKBOOK!
Deb97

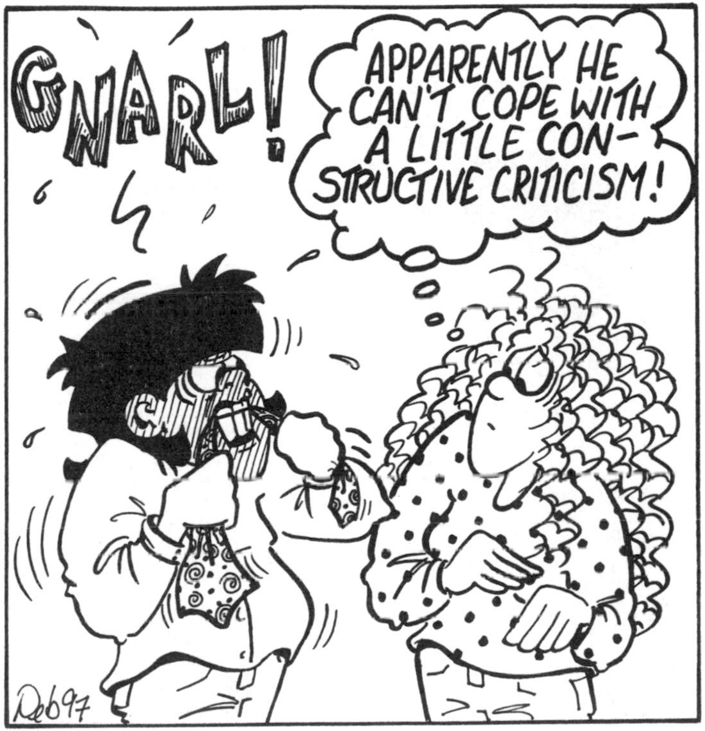
GNARL!
APPARENTLY HE CAN'T COPE WITH A LITTLE CON-STRUCTIVE CRITICISM!
Deb97

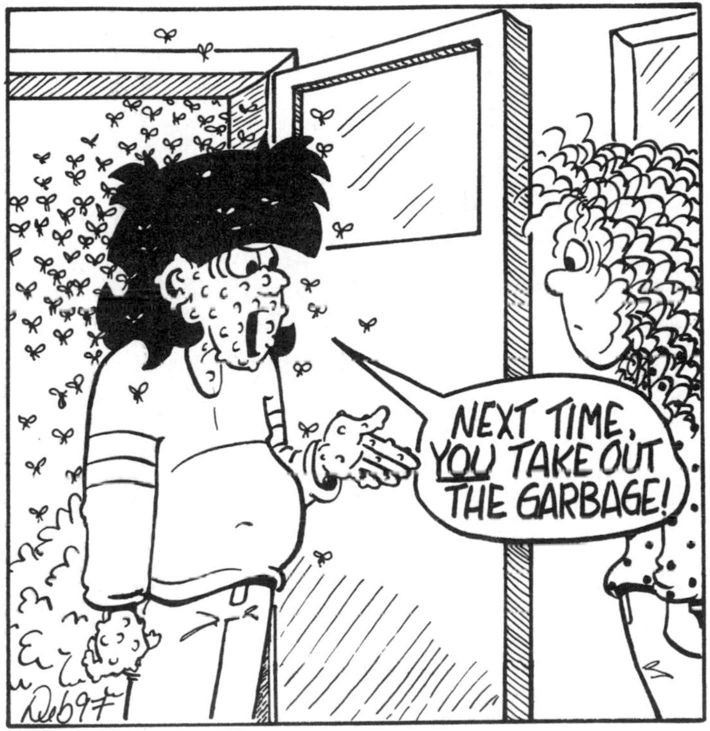
NEXT TIME, YOU TAKE OUT THE GARBAGE!
Deb97

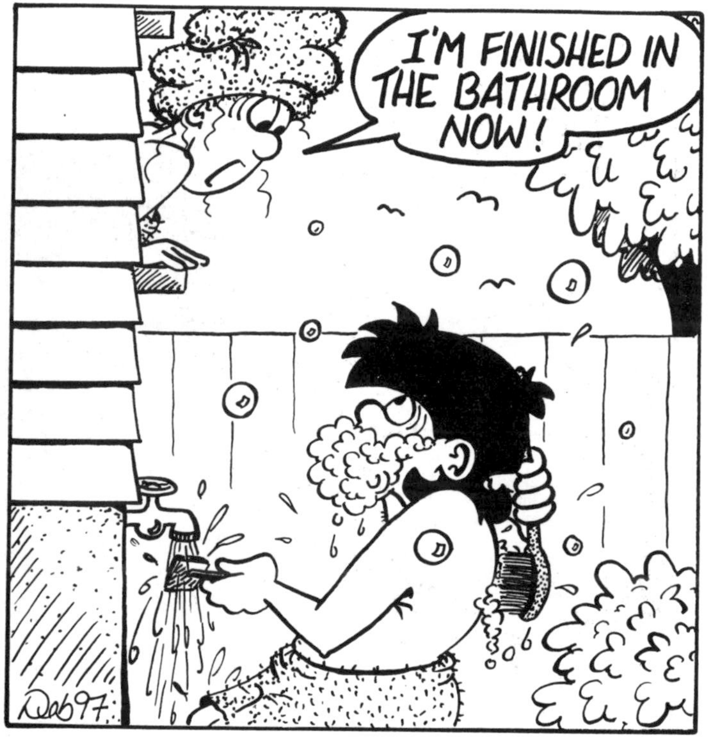
I'M FINISHED IN THE BATHROOM NOW!
Deb 97

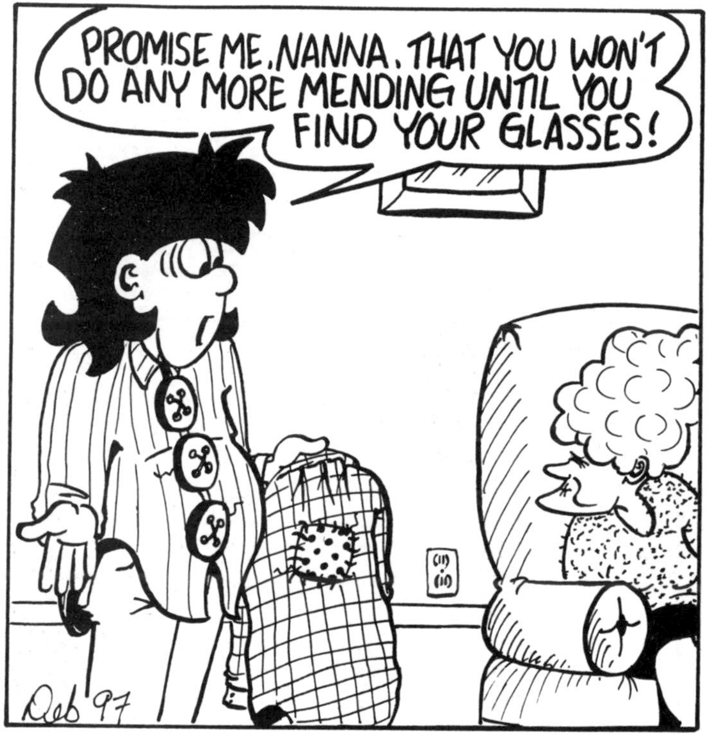
PROMISE ME, NANNA, THAT YOU WON'T DO ANY MORE MENDING UNTIL YOU FIND YOUR GLASSES!
Deb 97

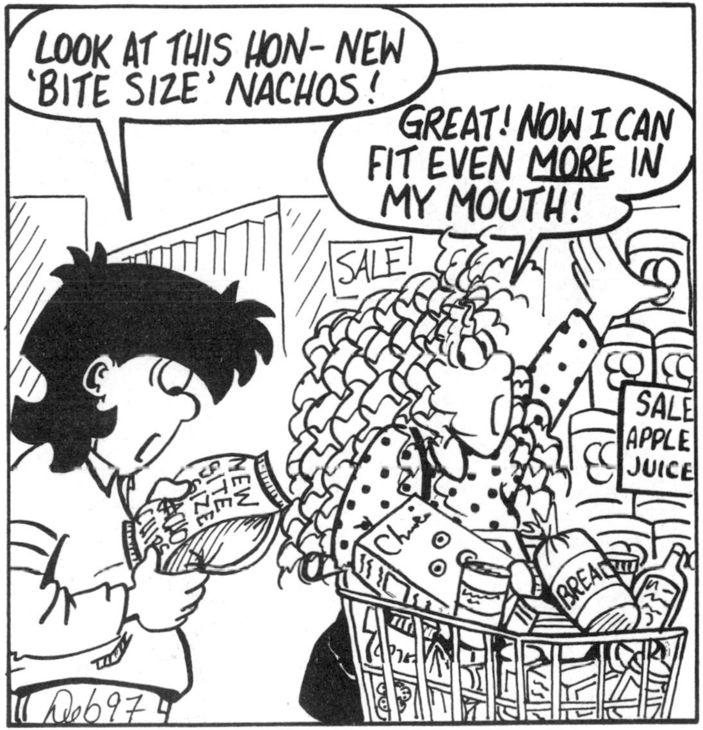
LOOK AT THIS HON- NEW 'BITE SIZE' NACHOS!
GREAT! NOW I CAN FIT EVEN MORE IN MY MOUTH!
SALE
SALE APPLE JUICE
NEW BITE SIZE
BREAD
Deb97

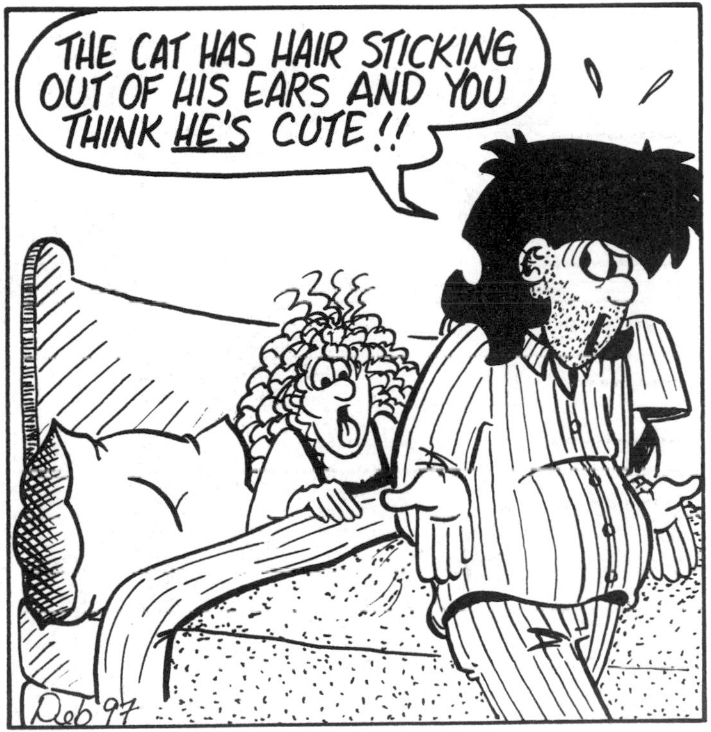
THE CAT HAS HAIR STICKING OUT OF HIS EARS AND YOU THINK HE'S CUTE!!
Deb97

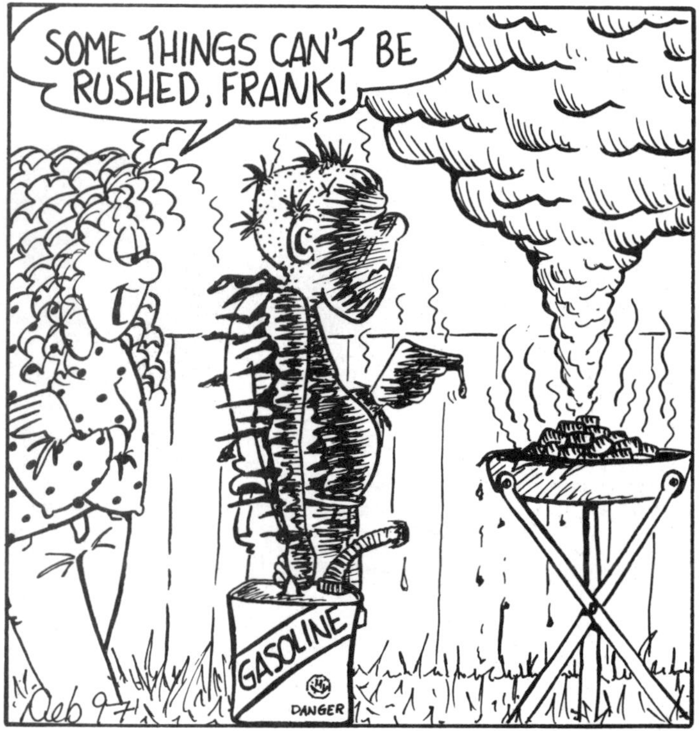
SOME THINGS CAN'T BE RUSHED, FRANK!
GASOLINE
DANGER

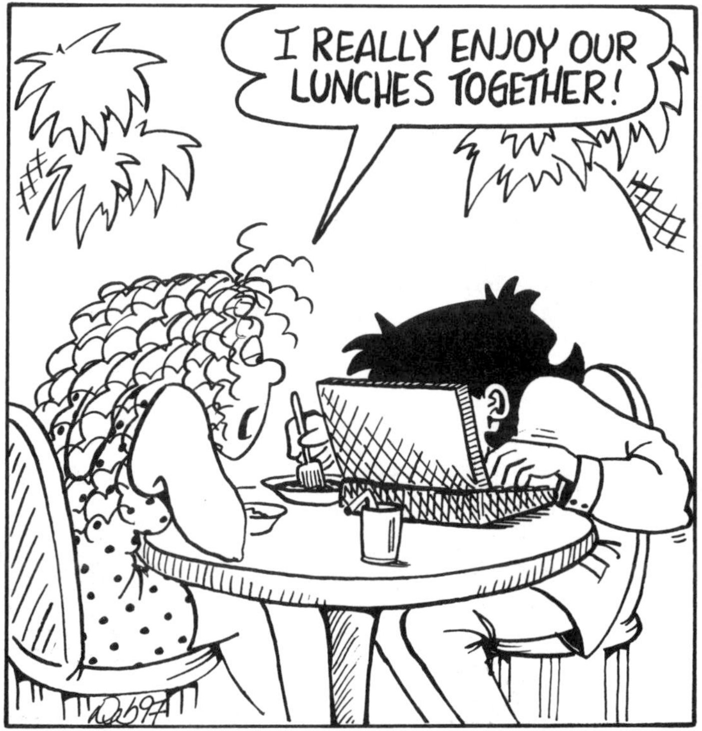
I REALLY ENJOY OUR LUNCHES TOGETHER!

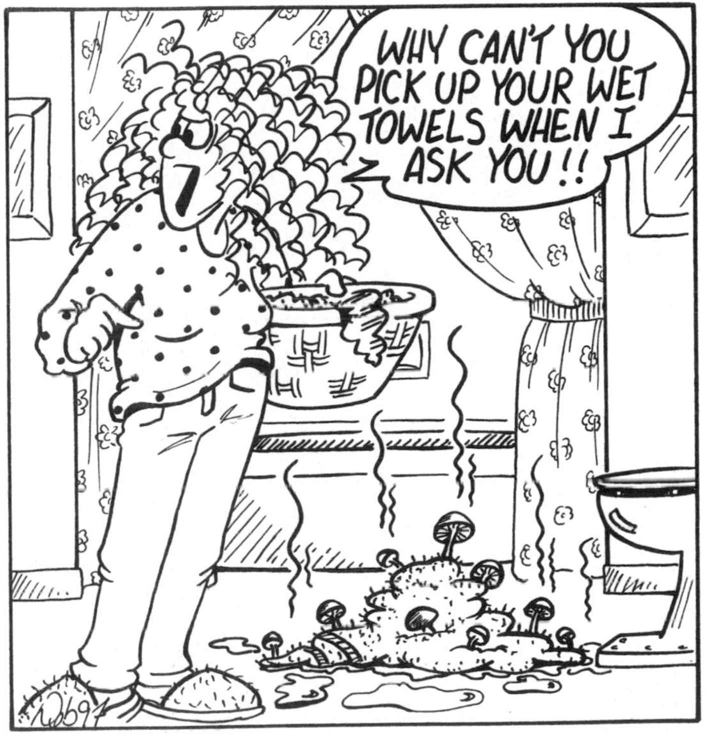
WHY CAN'T YOU PICK UP YOUR WET TOWELS WHEN I ASK YOU!!
Deb97

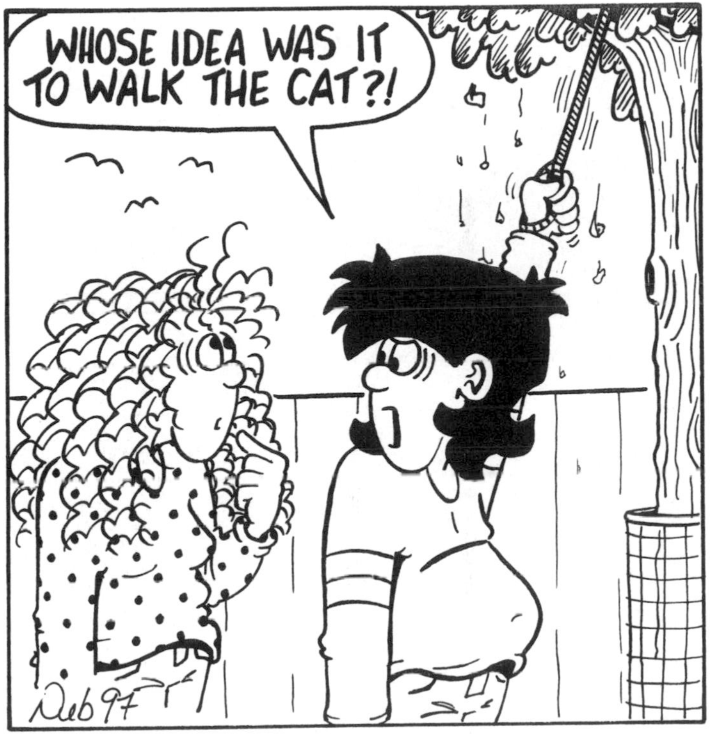
WHOSE IDEA WAS IT TO WALK THE CAT?!
Deb97

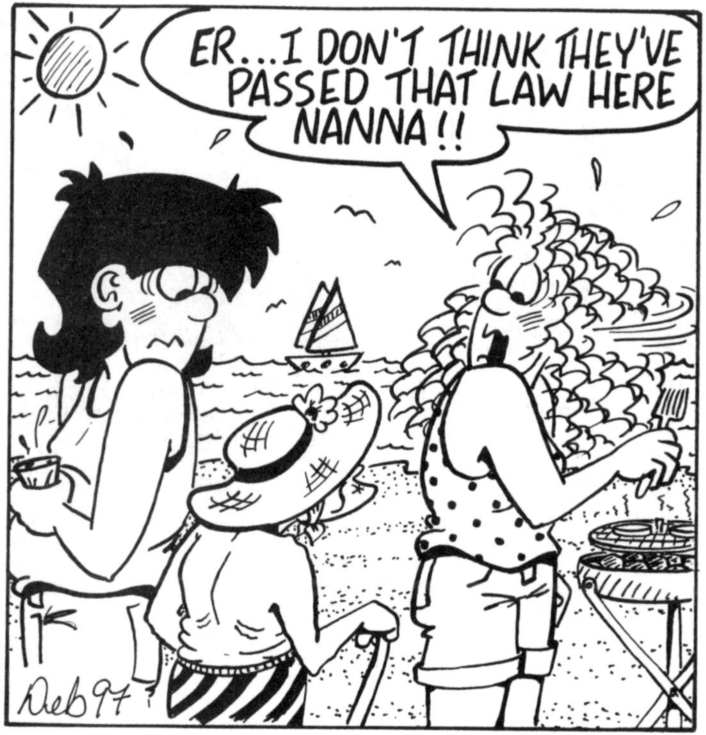
ER...I DON'T THINK THEY'VE PASSED THAT LAW HERE NANNA!!
Deb 97

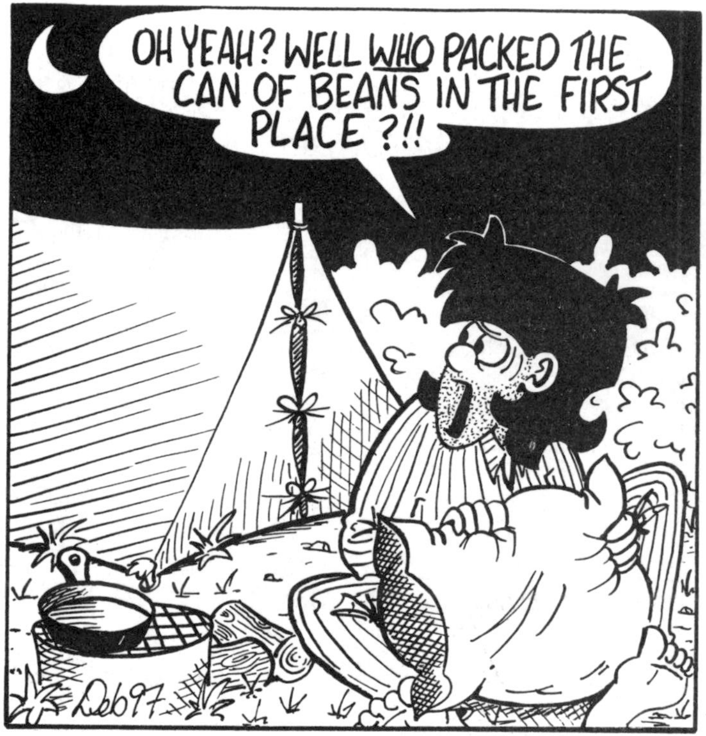
OH YEAH? WELL WHO PACKED THE CAN OF BEANS IN THE FIRST PLACE?!!
Deb 97

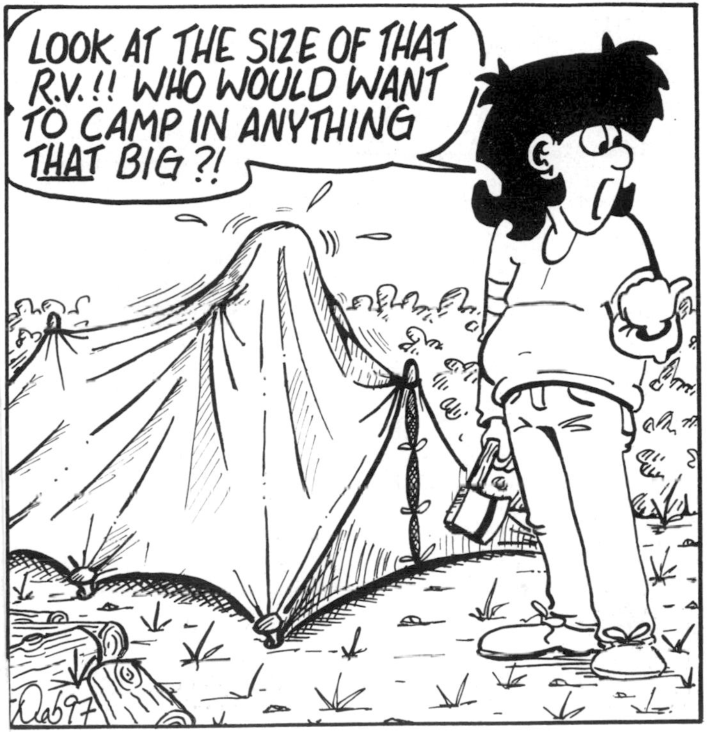
LOOK AT THE SIZE OF THAT R.V.!! WHO WOULD WANT TO CAMP IN ANYTHING THAT BIG?!

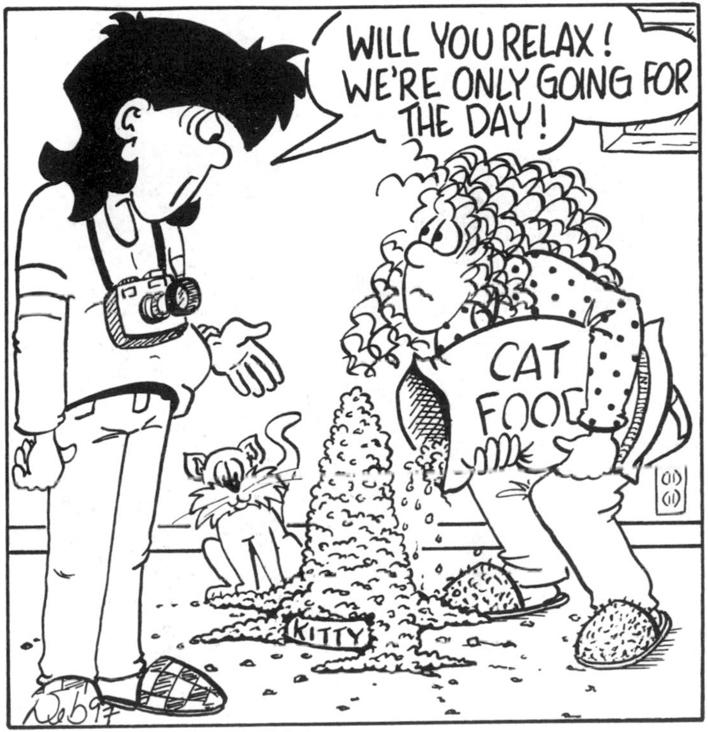
WILL YOU RELAX! WE'RE ONLY GOING FOR THE DAY!
CAT FOOD
KITTY

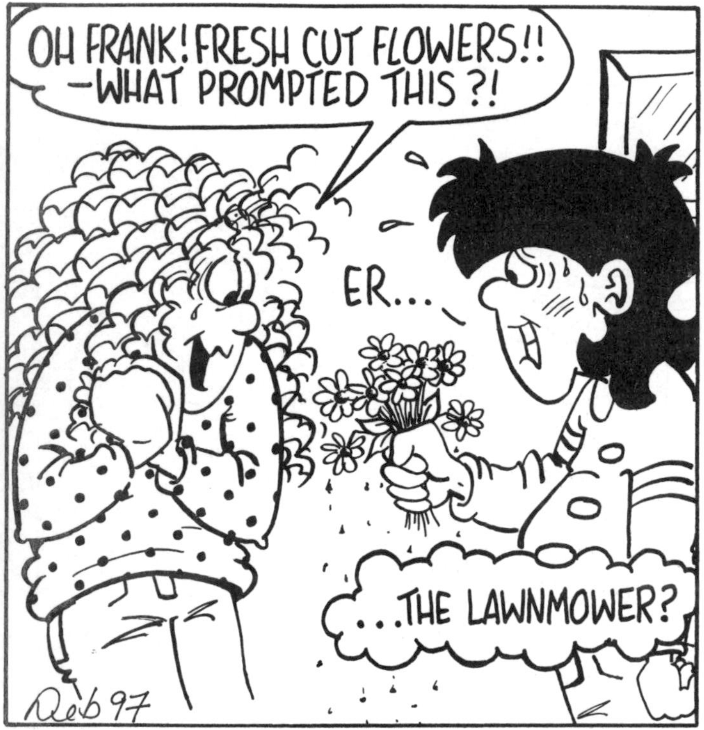
OH FRANK! FRESH CUT FLOWERS!! —WHAT PROMPTED THIS?!
ER...
...THE LAWNMOWER?
Deb 97

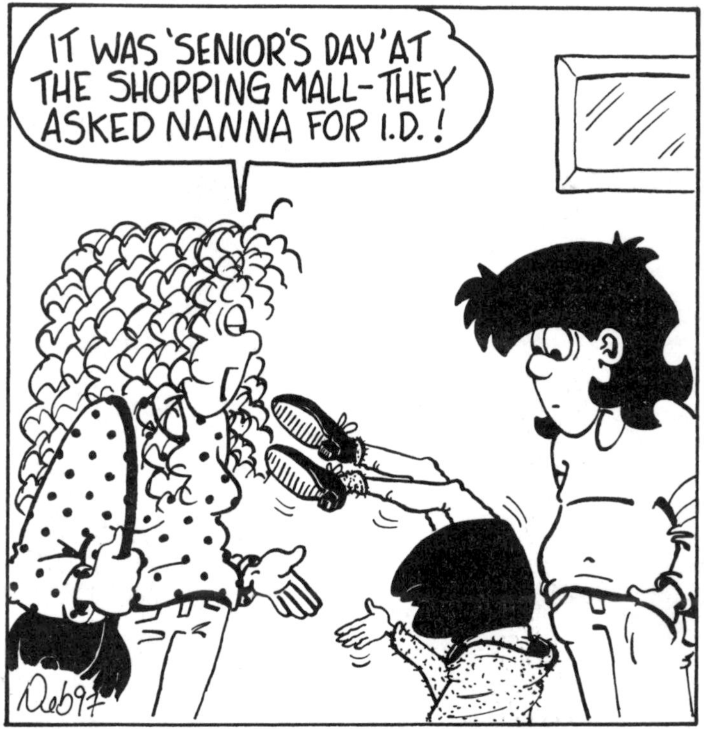
IT WAS 'SENIOR'S DAY' AT THE SHOPPING MALL—THEY ASKED NANNA FOR I.D.!
Deb97